The Which? Guide to the Internet

Richard Wentk

CONSUMERS' ASSOCIATION

Which? Books are commissioned and researched by
Consumers' Association and published by
Which? Ltd, 2 Marylebone Road, London NW1 4DF

Distributed by The Penguin Group:
Penguin Books Ltd, 27 Wrights Lane, London W8 5TZ

First edition September 1997
Reprinted November, 1997, February 1998
Revised October 1998
Revised September 1999

British Library Cataloguing-in-Publication Data
A catalogue record for this book is available from the British Library

ISBN 0 85202 774 5

For a full list of Which? books, please write to Which? Books, Castlemead,
Gascoyne Way, Hertford X. SG14 1LH, or access our web site at
www.which.net

Cover and text design by Kysen Creative Consultants
Cover photograph by Ed Horowitz/Tony Stone Images

Typeset by Business ColorPrint, Welshpool, Powys
Printed and bound in England by Clays Ltd, Bungay, Suffolk

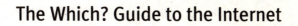

The Which? Guide to the Internet

About the author

After a decade in the software industry Richard Wentk now works mostly from his home in Wiltshire over the Internet as a writer, computer trainer and consultant. He has a particular interest in making computer technology accessible to non-technical people.

Acknowledgements

The author would like to thank Lisa Maturo, Sara Edlington, Jesa Macbeth, and everyone who contributed to the case histories.

AOL and CompuServe: a note for readers
Note that from the end of 1997 CompuServe effectively became a subsidiary of AOL. At the time of writing, the two services plan to continue independently, with the proviso that content and technology unique to one service may begin to appear on the other. Closer links between the services are expected in the longer term, but a full merger is unlikely for a variety of technical and editorial reasons. From a potential customer's point of view the two services should still be treated individually, and evaluated on their strengths and weaknesses in the usual way.

Contents

Some notes about URLs

All URLs require the letters *http://* at the beginning. However, modern browsers add these automatically, and so they have not been included in this book. If you have one of the modern browsers you may find that you do not need to type in these letters, and that the rest of the URL will be enough. For example, instead of keying in *http://www.which.net* the *www.which.net* part of the URL will be sufficient. Experiment to see if your browser can do this.

Beginners often assume that the *www* part of an URL is essential. This is not the case. Some sites (such as the BBC news site at *http://news.bbc.co.uk*) use a different combination of letters. A handful of sites get by with just two-word URLs; for example, *http://eaglenet.org* but these are rare. As usual, the rule with URLs is *type in exactly what you see, no matter how strange it looks.*

The only exception to this rule is capitalisation. Sometimes, parts of URLs are capitalised to make them easier to read, but in practice neither web browsers nor web servers distinguish between upper- and lower-case letters. As a rule, most URLs are shown entirely in lower case only by convention.

Introduction

From relative obscurity at the start of the 1990s, the Internet has rapidly become one of the most unexpected but revolutionary technical innovations of the twentieth century. In essence it is very simple: a resilient computer network that is open to everyone, and which makes it easier for people across the globe to communicate with each other. Its practical and social implications, however, have yet to be fathomed, and it is growing and evolving at such a rate that it is impossible to predict the social, political and economic effects it will have even ten years or so into the twenty-first century.

The statistics speak for themselves. According to a survey by opinion pollsters MORI, published in July 1999, more than 20 per cent of the UK population – around 10 million people – now use the Internet either at home or at work, and over a third of these use it to help with their personal finances. This is an outstanding increase on 635,000 UK Internet users in 1995. Worldwide, it is estimated that there will be 250 million people on-line by 2005.

As the numbers increase, the character of the Internet changes and its users become less exclusive. Originally designed as an experimental test-bed for academics, military researchers and computer experts, it was soon opened up to everyone. The costs involved have spiralled downwards, and are now comparable to, or even less than, the cost of using a telephone or paying for access to satellite TV. For many people it is now an essential part of their work, while for others it has become an alternative to TV, radio and the newspapers, with the added benefit of two-way instead of one-way communication. The much-announced but still tentative arrival of 'ecommerce' – Internet-based shopping for goods and services – will eventually have a huge impact on the way that consumers evaluate and buy products. The increase in the number of Internet users is speedily forcing it to grow and develop into a more accessible and less technology-oriented medium.

But even with the arrival of 'free' Internet-access promotions in many high-street stores, the Internet itself remains a mystery to many people. Despite recent technological advances it is still more complex and harder to use than it might be, and – compared to more established technologies – also less reliable. Socially, it has at times been sensationalised by the popular press as the exclusive preserve of child pornographers and other social deviants. While the Internet inevitably mirrors the seedy aspects of life, the reality of most of what goes on on-line is somewhat less sensational and a good deal more useful. For a typical home user, the advantages are obvious: near-instant communications, access to countless sources of information about almost every subject imaginable, and a chance to make contact with millions of people, some of whom are likely to become friends.

Small-business users too can benefit from the speed at which they can research products and services, conduct negotiations, and perhaps even expand their business to begin advertising or trading on the Internet itself.

This book aims to demystify the Internet, explaining in plain English what it can and cannot be used for. In the pages that follow you will find explanations of both Internet theory and practice, advice on how to get the best from the facilities it offers, and examples of how to communicate with other Internet users most effectively, including email. The guide gives details on how to assess the merits of competing commercial Internet services – and so save money; practical explanations of how to achieve basic tasks, such as searching; and instructions for more experienced users on how to avoid junk mail and create your own web pages. In addition, this new edition has information on how to shop safely and avoid on-line scams and credit-card fraud, how to get the best from Internet facilities for games and entertainment, and how to make your Net access safe and enjoyable for all the family. Whether you are planning to use the Internet for fun, for profit, for exploration or simply out of curiosity, this book will provide everything you need to get the very best from the time and money you spend on-line.

Chapter 1

What can the Internet do for me?

The Internet is the perfect tool for exchanging information and is a natural progression from the telephone and the fax machine. The telephone is a very good way of getting the sound of your voice from one place to another, and the fax machine can send an electronic copy of a printed page around the world. However, both are limited because they deal with only one kind of information.

On the Internet, the telephone handset and the fax machine are replaced by a computer. Even with a simple and relatively cheap domestic model, it now becomes possible to exchange text, documents, sounds, music, photographs, drawings, plans, video clips and even computer software. By connecting computers, and setting some up to work as automated libraries that are available 24 hours a day, the Internet can make copies of the same information available to thousands of people at once, or change the way that the information is presented, depending on who is looking at it. Or it can simply be used to send messages from one person to another.

The Internet is a library, a notice board, a messaging system, a shop-front, a debating society, a social club, an archive, a newspaper and a personal assistant, all at once. However, its potential is still being explored, and new applications – for example, on-line shopping for goods and services – are continually being developed for it.

Its uses tend to fall into two groups: communicating with like-minded people; and discovering and sharing information about almost any area of interest. On the Internet the three most widely used facilites are: electronic mail (email), the newsgroup system, and the World Wide Web. Individually, each has its merits, but the Internet's power is most obvious when they are all used together. To get a better idea of what this means it is helpful to take a closer look at each one.

Electronic mail (email)

Email is the electronic equivalent of traditional paper mail: you type a message into your computer, specify an address, then send it to the Internet. Within a few seconds, or perhaps a few minutes at most (unless the Internet is suffering from technical trouble or is very busy) the message will arrive at its destination.

Email compares favourably with the telephone, the fax and the traditional memo and letter. Unlike a telephone call, an email message does not require instant attention but remains unread until the recipient chooses to look at it. He or she can then reply to the message immediately, wait until later or simply ignore it.

This flexibility makes it an excellent medium for many kinds of business and social interactions. It is also more convenient to use than a fax, as the text is sent directly and doesn't need to be printed out and run through a fax machine. In addition, emails do not have the grainy, rough quality that makes faxed letters and memos so difficult to read.

CASE HISTORY – Juliette

Juliette Wilson is a freelance journalist who has found that email has changed the way she works, and communicates with friends.

'I work from home, and the best thing about email is that I can now send in work without using a fax, a floppy disk or a print-out. Email is quicker and cheaper, and it means I can bounce corrections back and forth to an editor if he or she doesn't like something and wants it changed. I've also found it's a good way to get information from abroad. I've even done whole email interviews with people I've never met face-to-face: instead, I've sent them a list of questions, and they've sent me the answers.

'It's great for socialising as well. A lot of my friends have email now, and recently we worked out how to set up a mailing list so that if one of us sends a message we all see it. We spend a lot of time gossiping and making stupid jokes on it, which livens up the day no end when you work from home. When we want to go out as a group we've found it's a great way to arrange the details. Trying to co-ordinate 20 people by phone for a concert or a theatre date can be a nightmare, but with email it seems to be much simpler and more relaxed.'

Email messages are cheaper to send than both faxes and letter post, and they are less likely to get lost in a busy office. While paper faxes and letters can pile up on desks and be misfiled, email messages can remain filed electronically inside a computer. This makes it possible to arrange the information in various useful ways – for example, by listing all the messages from one person, or by finding all those that mention a given word or phrase. (Of course, you need to be organised yourself to make the most of this filing facility.)

Because of these advantages, people who use email tend to do so for everything that does not require a formal letter or a personal conversation; this ranges from friendly social chatter to various business-related exchanges, such as negotiations, questions, the sending of price lists, and so on. (As an example of how widely used it is now, many schoolchildren are finding it an increasingly valuable way to swap homework tips with classmates.) Its only drawback is that home users may find it slightly unwieldy for pictures, diagrams and other information that isn't simple text. But since most messages consist only of text, this is not usually a problem.

Newsgroups

Despite its name, the newsgroup system (also known as Usenet) has nothing to do with news. Instead, it offers tens of thousands of discussion areas where people can 'chat' sociably, exchange views and information, and – in some cases – annoy each other mercilessly.

Newsgroups are like public bulletin-board systems. When you send a message – this is known as 'posting' – to a discussion group, everyone else who reads that group will see it. If someone replies, everyone will see the reply as well. In this way a conversation develops with participants all over the world.

Newsgroups are used for entertainment, debate and getting answers to questions. The list of subject areas covered is vast and includes a dazzling array of useful and not-so-useful subjects: fish-breeding, scuba diving, various computer topics, humour, discussions about different cultures, and even a support group for pizza delivery drivers. (Quirky subjects like this are not unusual on the Internet.) While some groups are inane or contain information of dubious legality, others are more serious and professional. The latter groups are useful places in which to find answers to questions about the subjects they are dedicated to.

Many newsgroups have a document called an FAQ – a Frequently Asked Questions list – which is posted regularly to it. FAQs were invented for the benefit of long-standing group members, who objected to having to answer the same questions each time anyone new joined the group. Over time many FAQs have become a summary of the wisdom of each group. At the very least they define its culture and explain what kind of messages and questions are and are not appropriate. At best they offer a surprisingly detailed summary of what is known about a particular subject. Even though these summaries are prepared by amateurs, the information they contain can be more useful than that available in bookstores and libraries.

The groups themselves are arranged either by subject matter or by geography. Some UK cities, such as London, Oxford and Birmingham, have their own newsgroups, and these are used for casual chat and discussions about local issues. The UK also has its own collection of national groups, which include professional, religious and hobbyist interests. A handful are used for job offers and job applications and non-commercial buying and selling; they work rather like the popular free classified newspapers that are widely available in the UK's larger cities.

However, most groups are international in scope, making them a truly global resource. Sometimes, though, as the readership increases, the quality of information goes down. The main problem with the newsgroup system is 'noise' – a technical term for messages that are either annoying or irrelevant. 'Spam', the newsgroup world's equivalent of junk mail, is a big part of the noise problem. Spam is advertising that is sent to as many groups as possible, irrespective of whether it is appropriate to them. It is a blatant attempt to use the newsgroup system as a mass-mailing tool, and it causes major annoyance to everyone who uses it. Fortunately, there are ways to deal with spam and other undesirable messages which can make the experience of Usenet more pleasant and useful. For more information on filtering messages and newsgroups in general, see Chapter 5.

CASE HISTORY – Paul

In the autumn of 1996 Paul Johnson, a computer consultant, was diagnosed with stomach cancer. He was already familiar with the Internet but was still surprised at how much information and support was available on-line.

'I started by looking at a newsgroup called *alt.support.cancer*, which turned out to have a lot of really useful information. You never know with newsgroups whether or not they're going to be full of rubbish, but this one certainly wasn't. It put me in touch with other people in the same boat who were asking the same kinds of questions and dealing with the same issues that I was.

'The great thing about this was that it pointed me in the direction of other resources. Some of these were on-line – such as web pages to do with self-help, diet and so on – and some were in "real life" ['real life' is the Internet term for everything that does not happen on the Internet]. There are even a couple of doctors who regularly post help and suggestions. As a result of the contacts I made on the group I found a local cancer support group, which has been amazingly helpful.

'People assume that the Internet is full of computer experts and porn merchants, and that's it. But it's just not true. Some of the things people were posting to the newsgroup were actually very personal and very moving – the kind of thing you'd find it hard to express to a friend or partner, never mind an anonymous audience. But that doesn't seem to stop people. Because of this you can get a really strong sense of community, even though you never physically meet. It is strange, and I can see it wouldn't suit everyone, but when it works it can work really well.'

The World Wide Web

The World Wide Web, often shortened to 'the Web', was invented in the early 1990s by British physicist Tim Berners-Lee. He created it to help him keep track of the various pieces of loosely related information he was keeping in his computer. Since its introduction, the World Wide Web has taken the Internet by storm. It is rather like an electronic magazine or notice board with contributions from millions of people. Articles contain 'links' – special highlighted words or phrases – which can be clicked on with a mouse and lead to related subject matter. This can contain links of its own, and so on, indefinitely.

If you are creating web articles of your own (see Appendix 5), it is possible to add links to information in someone else's articles; this is one reason why the Web is such a rich source of information on so many topics. Each article, or collection of articles, is called a 'web site' – usually shortened to 'site'. As an example, imagine someone who has created a site devoted to mountaineering. Apart from personal anecdotes and photographs, he or she can include links to information about mountaineering that has already been written by other people. These links can add more details, offer a different perspective, explain technical terms and include yet more links to various mountaineering resources such as magazines, shops and discussion groups. This web of connections makes the original article much more informative and useful than if it had been standing alone. Where a book author has to use pointers such as 'For more information on this subject see this magazine and that book', anyone using the Web can integrate these cross-references so all the information is immediately accessible.

CASE HISTORY – Elizabeth

Elizabeth Clear runs a Victorian art and poster shop in Glastonbury, Somerset. Web-based advertising transformed her business, almost overnight.

'We were approached by someone in 1996 to see if we would like to contribute to a web site for local traders that would be called The Isle of Avalon. To start with we were concerned about the price, but we compared it with the *Yellow Pages*, and it was much cheaper, which was a good start. But we decided to do a little research first.

'The first thing we asked the organiser to do was search the Web for keywords to do with our business – pre-Raphaelite, Victorian, Romantic, and so on. Apart from a few museums and university papers he found nothing. That was when we realised we were in with a chance of doing something new.

'We began by putting up a straight catalogue – just a list really, with a logo that my partner designed. Then we started adding images. Now we have a montage of our bestsellers, which gets a lot of attention.

'We had maybe a thousand email enquiries last year. Some are silly – you get people writing to you and saying things like "Burne-Jones did a painting with two people in it. Have you got it?" – but some are orders, which we ship right away. We also get a lot of phone calls from abroad. And because the business is mail order – we can put a poster in a cardboard tube and send it anywhere in no time – it works very well. We go out of our way to be very helpful, so we're starting to become known as the place to get these prints. We're dropping the *Yellow Pages* and also all our newspaper advertising. Advertising on the Web is much cheaper and better value for money. And the other advantage is that we can make changes immediately – we tell the site manager what we want, and he can do it more or less on the spot.'

The Web's great strength is that it is open to everyone, and anyone can put up information. No one has to pay a subscription or impress an editor in order to be published, and no central organisation says what is or is not appropriate. The technical skills required are modest, and people who would normally turn pale at the thought of programming a computer have created web sites with very little effort. The costs can be modest too. Private users who are not developing commercial sites can usually put up their information for free.

Because of these attributes you will find information about absolutely everything on the Web: summaries of academic research; press releases, brochures and advertising from large companies; sites created by hobbyists who want to share their enthusiasms with the world; random diary pages written and posted by ordinary people just for the sake of it, and so on. The quantity and the variety of the information available is breathtaking. Poetry, art, stockmarket quotes, DIY tips, travel details and sports facts are just a tiny selection of what is available.

Apart from entertainment and informative articles, the Web offers access to unprecedented amounts of raw information. You can find up-to-the-minute news stories and weather reports, details of cheap flights from the major travel services, and even free software.

For some businesses it is an effective way to generate new sales. Because web pages can be read by anyone anywhere in the world, the limitations of local trade no longer apply. Any business that takes credit cards can now reach an international audience for a relatively small outlay.

Is the Internet for me?

If you are an academic, a technology consultant, a teleworker or a journalist, the benefits of the Internet are obvious; the main attractions are low-cost access to unlimited quantities of information and the ability to exchange both work and comments with colleagues and employers. But the Internet is also starting to become an indispensable tool for other professionals. Doctors, lawyers and engineers can take advantage of on-line databases and other sources of information which are more convenient and accessible than those available at a large library. Information found on Internet sites is a useful complement to information available in paper form.

Small businesses can use the Web to advertise their services for a negligible amount of money. Considering that a single advertisement in a magazine can cost hundreds or perhaps thousands of pounds, a web site that can be seen by an equivalent number of people, takes about two weeks to design and costs perhaps £50 a month to maintain is obviously good value for money. Other advantages exist too: unlike an advertisement in a magazine or newspaper, a web site can maintain a record of the people who see it. This makes it easier to keep in touch with them and build a profile of potential customers.

Email also has obvious advantages for professional users. Although sending plans and diagrams can be expensive compared with a text-only email, it is still quicker, simpler and cheaper than using a courier service or a fax machine, especially if the recipient lives abroad.

In short, anyone who needs to send information from place to place quickly and cheaply or is looking for a convenient source of research material will benefit from being on the Internet. For someone who already has a computer the costs involved are very reasonable, and a trial period is well worth the time and money. Someone who does not have a computer can still try out the Internet for a small fee (see Chapter 2), and it is worth doing this to get an accurate idea of what the benefits might be.

For those who do not need these kinds of professional services, the Internet is a good way to find people who share similar interests. It is also becoming an increasingly convenient way to find local information about services and social events, such as film and concert listings, local clubs and societies, and so on. Anyone who already has an active social or professional life will most likely not find these compelling reasons for buying a computer and getting on-line. However, for those who already have a computer, and the spare time to use it, the Internet can offer a whole new world to explore for a fairly small sum.

Children will find that using the Internet is a wonderful way of doing research for homework. (Some material on the Internet is definitely not suitable for children, but there are ways to stop children from reading it, and these are discussed in more detail in Chapter 8.) As an educational resource the Web is unparalleled; newsgroups, however, are perhaps too harsh an environment for all children to feel comfortable in. Children with an inquisitive nature may find that the Web is the best toy they have ever had, although it is unlikely to make much difference to their academic achievements unless used in a structured way. Finally, they can play computer games against real opponents over the Internet.

It is important to be aware that the Internet has drawbacks, the most obvious being that it is still to some extent an experimental system. Problems occur fairly regularly – not often enough to cause most people any serious loss of money or information, but frequently enough to be irritating. To a large degree, the number of problems you encounter depends on which company you choose for your connection, although it is probably fair to say that almost all have had, or will have, some kind of technical teething trouble.

The Internet has nothing at all in common with traditional media, which present a very professional, formal front; instead, informality rules, and therefore the tone is often very different. It has a very obvious culture all of its own, and this does not appeal to everyone. Some of the more colourful newsgroups, for example, can sometimes be verbal equivalents of a pub brawl; people speak their minds without holding back. Anyone who does not have an open mind may find some of the content or the exchanges shocking or offensive, and it is important to be aware of this possibility.

CASE HISTORY – Aboodi

Aboodi Shaby is an alternative health practitioner living in Wiltshire. He was initially interested in the Internet but did not find enough to sustain his long-term interest.

'For me the appeal of the Net was about finding interesting ideas and home pages of alternative things, and it was fun for a while to surf around, look at various sites and try things out. For example, I found some interesting Islamic chants and appealing artworks that I wouldn't have been able to discover any other way. But the novelty wore off very quickly. I felt it was a bit like hanging around a big bookshop – a nice way to spend a couple of afternoons, but not the sort of thing I'd want to do permanently.

'One of the problems was that technically I didn't really know how to go about finding people with the same interests. And, besides, it seemed a bit strange trying to meet people on-line. I think I prefer to meet human beings face to face rather than through the Net. Rather like a telephone chat line, the encounter simply doesn't feel very real.

'For me it would be nice to have the opportunity to play around on someone's modem in the same way that it's nice to channel-hop on someone's cable TV system once in a while. But that doesn't mean I would want to take out a subscription. Really I'd be happiest if I could use it in a local library once in a while instead of from home – that would be the ideal for me.'

In many ways the Internet is like a foreign country. The inhabitants mostly speak English, but their customs and traditions are completely different from those most of us are used to. Almost everyone goes through a process of acclimatisation before they feel comfortable with the new environment.

At heart the Internet is simply a tool that makes communication easier with everyone else on it – without exception. Everything that people do, from the most exalted activity to the most debased, is represented on-line in an accessible way. This creates an environment that some people find very difficult, and there are those who find that email and other forms of electronic communication are simply detached and unreal.

Putting it all together

Although email, the Web and newsgroups are very useful individually, the true power of the Internet becomes clear when they are used together. Experienced Internet users are already finding that the range of tasks they can use the Internet for is steadily increasing, and for some people it has already become indispensable.

CASE HISTORY – Paul

Paul Cooper is a journalist who has been using the Internet since 1994. His experience is typical of more dedicated users.

'I think almost everyone starts off feeling baffled and bewildered. It's not just the technology. The Internet is a strange thing, and it has lots of strange people with strange ideas using it. Quite a few seem to be – how can I put this? – a few slices of bread short of a sandwich. Others are more normal, but may not be the kind of people you'd associate with in real life. So it takes a while to get used to suddenly having all these strangers in your home, all doing their best to make it a more colourful place.

'But eventually you settle down and start using the thing properly. This is where it sneaks up on you – for the first few months you think you're dabbling with it, then you wake up one day, and suddenly it's very hard to do without.

'Take my work, which is science journalism. I can look on the Net and get the latest stories before they appear *anywhere* – before anyone sees them in print or hears about them from radio and TV. And I can backtrack too – there are archives I can look through, and libraries I can raid. So I can follow a story through, put a news story into some kind of context, make connections between related stories, or even follow someone's career. Before, it used to be much harder.

'Socially – well, I've met a few people in person, even been to a couple of Internet parties, although to be honest they had too many people who talked only about computers for me to really enjoy them. Last Christmas I had cards from Cornwall, the States, Australia and even Brazil, all from people I exchange email with but have never met. This summer I've arranged a flat-swap with someone from New Zealand. She gets to see London, we get to see Wellington. No hotel bills for either of us. Obviously email has saved me a lot in international calls, too.

'But it's useful in all kinds of unexpected ways. I've arranged CD swaps with people in other countries (they can get CDs I can't and *vice versa*), found cheap flights for a weekend in Barcelona, bought software, magazines and books from the States, checked rail timetables and ordered flowers for my girlfriend. Really, the only thing stopping everyone from using it is that it's still too complicated – I had to get a friend to help me set it up – and too expensive. Not everyone can afford £1,000 or so for a decent computer. I think once the price comes down it will be just like the phone and the TV and the radio – everyone will use it without thinking twice. Although I do sometimes waste time on it – it's frighteningly easy to do that – I wouldn't give it up for anything now.'

Chapter 2

Getting a connection

To access the Internet, home and small-business users need five things: a modern telephone connection with a socket, a computer, an optional extra for the computer called a modem, a subscription to an Internet service and suitable software. (At the time of writing, other alternatives are starting to become available, but these are still not in wide use. For more information see page 33.)

Alternative ways of getting on-line are through educational establishments and workplaces. All universities have an Internet connection, as do an increasing number of schools. Access for students is usually free, although it may be restricted in some ways: for example, some newsgroups may not be available.

A similar situation often applies in the workplace. Many companies and institutions now offer Internet access to their employees, although again the service may be limited. Some companies ban newsgroups altogether, because they feel they are a possible source of distraction. Sometimes only an email service is provided.

Of course, universities and companies do not make their connections available for public use, so in some ways home users are in a better position, because they can pick and choose between the different service providers. If they find that one is not good enough they can try another.

Counting the cost

While 'professional' connections are usually free for employees and students (although the companies and universities involved still pay for them), the situation is more complex for home users. The two possible costs are a subscription to an Internet service, and the telephone charges required for an Internet connection. Originally the most common system was for Internet subscriptions to be paid for by a flat fee, either monthly or annually, and for phone charges to accumulate in the usual way. But now a number of other options have become available.

Internet access charges	Telephone charges	Example service
By the minute	Local rate, by the minute	CompuServe
Flat fee	Local rate, by the minute	AOL, Which? Online, Direct Connection (Dircon)
Free	Local rate, by the minute	Freeserve, Tesconet, Barclaynet
Flat fee	Reduced, or partially free	BT Internet, claranet
Free	Partially free*	screaming.net, X-stream

*Partially free services typically offer free calls at evenings and weekends. Outside of these periods, the usual local rate telephone charges apply.

At first glance, it may seem pointless paying for a service that is available free elsewhere. It may also seem strange that some companies can offer their services free at all. To make sense of what the different options are, it can be helpful to divide the various services into three groups:

1. **Companies that provide specialised information not available elsewhere on the Internet** (for example CompuServe, AOL, Which? Online) Although it is often assumed that 'the Internet' is a single service, this is not quite true. Some service companies charge more in return for a wider, or easier to use, set of services.

2. **Companies that attempt to compete by offering a high quality, reliable service** (for example Demon and Dircon) These are often older Internet companies that see no commercial need to stop charging their customers for the service they provide.

3. **Companies that attempt to compete on price** (for example Freeserve, screaming.net and X-stream) These are newer companies that are attempting to find completely new customers, as well as attempting to steal some of the existing customers from the companies in group 2. Many are associated with household names such as banks, building societies, supermarkets, other high-street

stores, and even football clubs and night clubs, and are attempting to add to their profits by 'converting' customers who already know and trust them to Internet use.

AOL and CompuServe in the first group are sometimes known as on-line services, and are considered in more detail below. These are popular with beginners, and with users who are looking for new friends. They tend to emphasise communities of interest (see page 25). Which? Online is an example of a combined service (see page 30).

The second and third groups are both known as internet service providers (ISPs). Costs aside, they provide a very similar service, which is essentially just a simple connection to the Internet with no frills. Ideally, the line between these two groups would be clear cut, and it would be possible to choose between them according to whether quality of service was more important than cost. In practice, this is not true at all. A 'free' ISP may – perhaps – provide a better service than a paid-for one. Fortunately there are ways to assess the quality of a service, and these make deciding which ISP to choose less complicated (see below).

Before going any further it is helpful to understand the difference between an on-line service and an ISP, and what these two kinds of services offer their customers.

Internet service providers (ISPs)

ISPs offer two things: a connection to the Internet and a package of suitable software which lets you use the facilities the connection offers. These facilities typically include one or more personal email addresses, access to the newsgroup network (Usenet), and access to the World Wide Web. (As part of the deal many providers also include 'space on the Web' at no extra cost; this is used to publish your own web pages, see Appendix 5.)

It is important to note that these facilities can be extended with extra software. A raw Internet connection can be used in many different ways, and the software that an ISP supplies is really just a starting point. Many people find they use this software for a while, and when they are more experienced they change to other software which suits their needs more closely. This can be bought commercially or

How your connection to an Internet service provider (ISP) works

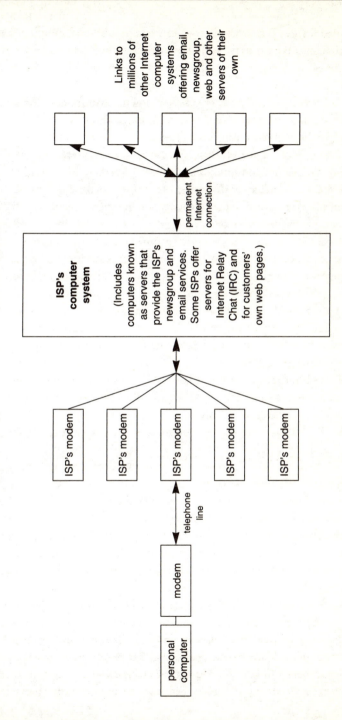

personal computer

modem

telephone line

ISP's modem

ISP's modem

ISP's modem

ISP's modem

ISP's modem

ISP's computer system

(Includes computers known as servers that provide the ISP's newsgroup and email services. Some ISPs offer servers for Internet Relay Chat (IRC) and for customers' own web pages.)

permanent Internet connection

Links to millions of other Internet computer systems offering email, newsgroup, web and other servers of their own copied for free from the Internet itself. Some ISPs skimp on software, which means you may be denied certain more advanced Internet facilities (such as those mentioned in Chapter 3) or forced to use email and newsgroups in an expensive and inefficient way. The easiest way to tell if this is the case is to check if you are being offered anything more than a 'web browser'. If not, you will almost certainly not be getting the best from your connection.

The cost of using an ISP's services varies from nothing at all to a flat fee of perhaps £12 a month. Free services, which, as mentioned above, are often associated with household names, make their money by charging for technical support, and by making an arrangement with BT, which allows them to collect a percentage of their subscribers' telephone charges. Some also charge for advertising on their web pages. Their software is set up so that customers see these pages (which are sometimes known as 'portals') every time they use the service. ISPs run by supermarkets and banks typically advertise their own products instead.

Free ISPs that also offer partially free phone charges make this possible by working with a telephone company. Tempo's screaming.net, for example, works with LocalTel. Subscribers are asked to switch their telephone line from BT to LocalTel, which then charges for non-Internet calls in the usual way. (At the time of writing LocalTel is offering a 10 per cent discount on BT's phone charges.) From a customer's point of view, this works exactly the same way as switching from BT to any other competing service, such as Cable and Wireless (formerly Mercury).

Paid-for ISPs simply collect a subscription from their customers, and in return offer Internet access. Some also charge a one-off 'set-up' fee for new customers. In theory these ISPs have an incentive to offer a better service, because customers can switch to a free ISP with relatively little inconvenience. In practice a certain amount of inertia among paying customers means that their customer base is relatively stable, while service quality – a problem among all ISPs, to a greater or less extent – remains uncertain. Because of this their future is uncertain. It is unlikely that by about 2005 any paid-for ISPs will still be doing business in the same way as now. One possible exception to this are local ISPs which serve a small geographical area. (Most ISPs attempt to serve the whole of the UK, but make special arrangements so that users are only charged for calls to the ISP at the local rate, no matter where they call from.) Local ISPs can run with much lower overheads, and because they are relatively unknown, they can sometimes – but by no means always – offer a good local service.

On-line services

The best-known – America Online (AOL) and CompuServe – offer a very different experience to that available from an Internet access provider. They are more like electronic magazines, which offer a connection to the Internet as a sideline.

If you subscribe to an on-line service, you effectively get two services in one. The first gives you access to magazine- and TV-style features on a wide range of subjects, the ability to exchange messages and chat electronically with other subscribers, and a chance to read and contribute to various discussion areas. These facilities are available only to members of the same service, and are hidden from the rest of the Internet. The other part of the service is a link to the Internet, which offers the usual newsgroup, web and email facilities. On an on-line service this connection is no more important than any of the other features and facilities – it appears as one option among many others.

Which is best for me?

For beginners, on-line services offer a number of advantages. The first is that they smooth the way to an introductory experience of on-line life by supplying software that is very easy to install and use. This software is proprietary, and you do not have the option of changing it for something better; other Internet software will not work with an on-line service except in a few special cases (see page 236).

The second benefit is that on-line services provide immediate starting points for exploration; newcomers do not feel lost and unsure as to what their options are. Connecting to the Internet via an ISP for the first time can be daunting, because there is no obvious way to find interesting information. Connecting to an on-line service is usually much more straightforward, because an index appears on your computer's screen, listing all the different options.

The third advantage is that these on-line services attempt to make information easier to find by leading you to it and gathering details about similar subjects together. Having these prepared for you saves you from having to search for them for yourself. However, it can limit less adventurous users, who may be less likely to explore the other information on the rest of the Internet as a result.

The main disadvantage of on-line services is their cost. They typically charge slightly more than even a paid-for ISP; for example, AOL charges just under £10 a month for unlimited access. A cheaper scheme is available for light users, who pay a much lower monthly fee which includes a set amount of 'free' time. When the free time runs out, charges start to accumulate by the minute. This means that you are paying for Internet access by the minute *in addition to* any telephone charges which are also accumulating by the minute. CompuServe also charges by the minute for certain specialised features. Per-minute Internet access can easily become very expensive indeed. It is also worth noting that some of the information that CompuServe charges extra for is available elsewhere on the Internet for free.

Other, subtle, disadvantages of on-line services are obvious to more experienced users. Although the software offered by on-line services is simple to use, it is sometimes not quite compatible with the rest of

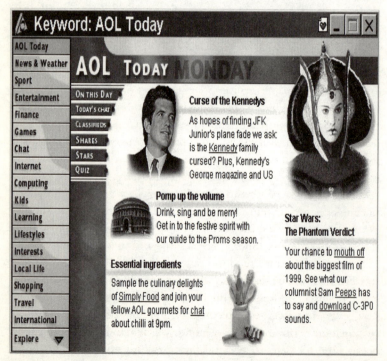

The software used by many on-line services, such as AOL, is very straightforward for beginners.

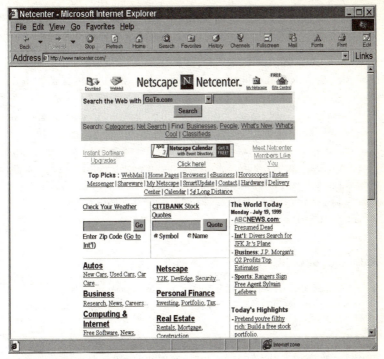

Netscape's web site offers plenty of starting points for web exploration, as well as free copies of the Communicator web browser.

the Internet. This means that some information, particularly on the Web, will not appear as it should. In extreme cases it will not be possible to read it at all. Although certain on-line services are moving towards allowing their subscribers the option of using other software – in effect, offering the same kind of general-purpose connection offered by an ISP – getting it to work can be an awkward process. All the on-line services are working to remedy this, but in the meantime the access they offer to the Internet can be slightly flawed compared with that available from an ISP.

Spam and junk mail tend to be more of a problem on the on-line services, because the shady characters who send this material can easily 'harvest' email addresses from the on-line services. Although the services provide facilities to block unwanted messages, these are not as comprehensive or powerful as the ones available to ISP users. This can be an issue for parents, because there may be no way to filter out messages advertising adult information.

Another point to consider is a cultural one. There is the common perception among established Internet users that some on-line services are more respectable than others (see page 103). If you attempt to join in a discussion in a newsgroup while using one of these less popular on-line services you will have to contend with prejudice, making it difficult to persuade others to take your views seriously.

Finally, the community offered by on-line services may not suit everyone. 'Live chat' – where groups of people type messages that immediately appear on each other's screens – is a popular feature of on-line services, but in practice much of it can be trite and uninteresting. Although the same can be said of some parts of the Internet, the latter offers a much wider variety of choices – some of still lower but others of much higher quality.

A practical comparison

For a better idea of what the differences are between ISPs and on-line services, it is useful to look at one particular example – how news is presented by both.

All the on-line services offer news features that are very similar to those in electronic newspapers, with headlines and background stories. They are always easy to find and concentrate on the same subject matter you might expect from a national daily newspaper, although because of the international nature of the Internet, foreign coverage is usually better. But the stories are much shorter than their equivalents in a daily newspaper, and you will not find the editorial depth you may be used to.

Searching for news on the Internet is a completely different experience. If you want news, you have to search the Web to find it for yourself. This can take a fair amount of time initially, because you will need to do some exploring to find the sources of news that interest you. But once you have done this, you can return to these sources very quickly.

This approach gives you much more control over which news you read, when you read it and the amount of background and other detail you want. It also gives you a much broader selection of possible sources. On the Web you can find electronic versions of UK and foreign newspapers, direct connections to various press agencies and newswire services, various technical journals and publications, electronic versions of popular magazines, electronic magazines that have never been in print, and so on. The level of editorial comment varies from none at all to the same as that in a traditional newspaper. One advantage of the Internet is that the web versions of some magazines and newspapers publish readers' comments as soon as they are received. This gives the medium an immediacy that cannot be matched anywhere else.

It is the difference in depth, effort and detail that most obviously separates on-line services from the Internet as a whole. With an on-line service you will get easy access to information that is known to be interesting and useful, but your ability to explore it in detail is relatively limited. On the Internet the volume and diversity of information can be overwhelming initially, but with a little practice you can find almost anything you want. You can then start to create a personalised library of high-quality news and information services to suit your individual needs.

In short, if you have an enquiring and open mind, and can appreciate the attraction of getting information that is hard to find elsewhere, then a direct connection to the Internet via an ISP is ideal for you. It is also a better choice if you plan to spend a large amount of time on-line.

However, if you prefer to get information with the minimum of effort, if you are interested in socialising and making new friends or if you do not intend to use the Internet a great deal, then you will almost certainly find that an on-line service will suit you better.

CASE HISTORY – Michael

Michael Jeffries is in his final year at a sixth-form college. He is studying sciences and is a keen amateur astronomer. When looking for information on his hobby he found that the depth of material available on the Internet was far greater than that offered by an on-line service.

'College has its own Internet link, and at home my Dad has an AOL account, so I've had time to look at both. The good thing about the astronomy areas on-line is that AOL has links to the astronomy information available on the Internet. The different AOL-specific discussion areas are actually pretty interesting too. There's a lot to get you started, and it's very easy to use.

'But once you start looking around the Internet for real you realise just how much more there is. There are hundreds of web pages, including ones put up by NASA with details of all its latest missions, the latest pictures from the Hubble Space Telescope, and so on. And the astronomy and science newsgroups have a much wider range of readers than AOL has, and professional astronomers contribute too, which is really good.

'If I was just dabbling or looking for people to chat to, then AOL would be fine. But I think people who are more serious about a subject or keen on something obscure or unusual will need to spend a lot of time on the Internet to get what they want.'

Other options

Not all services fall neatly into these two categories. Some attempt to use the Web to simulate an on-line service, but without the need for special software (you access it like you would any other web site). Others offer more obscure Internet-related services which use Internet technology in an unusual way. These are discussed below.

Combined services

Which? Online and the Microsoft Network (MSN) are examples of combined services. Although they offer all the usual Internet facilities and use Internet technology, they also maintain a private web site with information that is available only to paying customers. Although slightly more expensive than the services of most ISPs, they can be good value if you find the information they offer unusually interesting or useful.

Bulletin boards

Socially, bulletin board services (BBSs) are the Internet's immediate ancestor. Although they use much simpler and cruder technology, they were the source of the first public experiments with facilities similar to email and Usenet. Unlike the Internet, which was designed by and for computer professionals, academics and military users, BBSs have always been the preserve of the amateur and open to the general public.

The various BBS networks communicate with each other over telephone lines; they do not have access to the high-speed links that are the backbone of the Internet. Information is passed from computer to computer during the night. It can often take days to get a reply to an email even if the recipient writes a response as soon as it arrives.

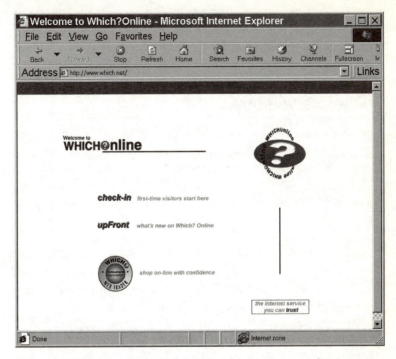

The Which? web site offers a chance to try out Which? Online's consumer-oriented Internet service.

The attraction of BBSs is that they are small and local, the users can be quite sociable, and access is usually free. Some even offer a kind of email link to the Internet, although again it is not as instantaneous as that offered by an ISP or on–line service.

With the growth of interest in the Internet, BBSs have become marginalised as a specialised hobby, rather like amateur radio or CB. Although they continue to attract younger users who do not have access to a true Internet connection, and anyone else who likes the idea of socialising with others locally, these limitations mean that they cannot be recommended except perhaps out of curiosity.

Intranets and extranets

These are private networks, usually used by businesses, which use Internet facilities, such as the Web and email, to exchange information within a company. The information may be linked to other company resources, such as databases. Intranets tend to be in a single building or site, while extranets work across the Internet, but the communications are hidden and private, so that no one else can read them. These are strictly business-only tools and are not available to the general public.

Try before you buy?

The easiest way to discover what the Internet can do for you is to try it for yourself. Fortunately, a number of low-cost trial options are open to everyone. Some of these do not even require a home computer.

Many large county-libraries offer Internet access on a pay-as-you-go basis. You simply pay a few pounds an hour for the time you are on-line. This fee sometimes includes a single email address and perhaps even space for your own web site.

Similar services are available at cybercafés – futuristic teashops with a collection of Internet-ready computers – as well as a small number of restaurants and pubs. If you live in or near one of the UK's major cities you should be able to find one locally.

Although these facilities provide a good insight into the Internet, it is important to be aware of their drawbacks. The first is that they assume everyone has a basic level of computer literacy. If you have never used a computer before, it is wise to learn the basics – including mouse control and how to use the windowing system used on modern computers – somewhere else. Ideally, this should be a place where you can experiment at your own pace, for example at a friend's house. Otherwise, you can waste a frustrating initial couple of hours working out how to use the computer while the seconds tick away, instead of exploring the on-line world. Even if you are already computer-literate, make sure someone is on-hand to answer questions and help you learn the basic techniques, so that your time is used as effectively as possible.

Another disadvantage of these facilities is that you will be forced to use one particular brand of software. Since some software that works well for the Web may not be quite so convenient for email, you may be left with a false impression about the ease of use – or otherwise – of the Internet as a whole. It is also worth remembering that the software you use in one of these places has already been set up for you. You should allow for the fact that setting up an equivalent connection at home will not be as straightforward as sitting down at the computer and turning it on in a cybercafé.

However, it will soon be possible to use the Internet from within a phone-booth, or a photo kiosk. Both BT and PhotoMe have announced schemes which make it possible to send email (the latter with recent photos included) from a limited number of public access booths, concentrated in the centres of larger cities. The supermarket chain Safeway has also made Internet access available in its larger stores. The charges for these services so far appear to be high, and in no way representative of how much it costs to use the Internet from home. The facilities they offer are also very limited. But, for anyone who needs to send a message in a hurry, they can be worth looking out for.

CASE HISTORY – Felicity

Felicity Green is a graphic designer who is suspicious of computers. However, she found that using the Internet connection at her local library was a good way of keeping in touch with her friends overseas and exploring.

'I'm really not keen on computers – I think they're incredibly badly designed and much harder to use than they should be, and I usually get totally frustrated with them. But a lot of my friends were starting to get on-line, and one in particular moved out of the UK to America. She was moving around a lot so there wasn't any other practical way to keep in touch.

'To be honest, even though it was all set up for me, I didn't find it easy to use to start with. I was learning the basics and aware that time was ticking away and my bill was running up. It's not expensive here at £3 an hour, but it's still nerve-wracking when I'm paying for the time spent on-line.

'Eventually I got the hang of it. And actually I found the Web delightful – there are hundreds of art and design resources on there that I would never have heard of otherwise. Email wasn't quite so straightforward, but that's because the library here doesn't supply proper software – just a web browser, which is fine for the Web but very clumsy for email. Still, I've managed to keep in touch with my friend and have even found some new people with similar interests to "talk" to. It can be strange having a conversation with someone on the other side of the world who I've never even met, but it does seem to work.

'The best thing is that this library offers people web space of their own. So I learned how to use that, put up a kind of electronic CV with a list of my work, some samples, and something about me. Apart from getting occasional passing comments from people who have seen the site and liked it, it's even got me some new work.'

Trying out on-line services

Almost all the on-line services publicise their products by offering free trials. These are made available on the front cover of computer and Internet magazines. On-line services will often supply free trials if you contact them directly. To take advantage of a free trial offer you need a recent computer and a modem. If you already have these, then experimenting with free trials is an excellent way to explore the different on-line services. If you do not have your own equipment, the only way to try an on-line service is to ask a friend who is already using one to let you try it for a few hours.

A typical free trial takes the form of a CD-ROM (offers on floppy disk no longer seem to be available), which supplies the special software needed to use the service. You will also be credited with a certain amount of 'free time' on-line. This amount varies enormously – some companies have offered hundreds of free hours.

Once you have installed the software and made a connection you will be asked to give your credit-card details. Although you may think you are running a trial account, once you give these details to all intents and purposes you have joined the service. When your free time has run out, money will be debited from your account unless you give notice that you no longer wish to stay on-line. In some cases this can be given only in writing. So it is important to keep track of the time you use and to remember to cancel if you decide the service is not what you are looking for. All of them include some kind of on-line accounting system which shows you how much time and money you have spent, and it is a good idea to locate this first so you can keep track of your expenditure and not run up a huge bill.

Be very wary of the details of your free trial. Some on-line services appear to assume that you will not use the trial much, and sign you up for their 'pay as you go' tariff. When the trial period is over you can find yourself paying by the minute and running up a huge bill, even though a flat-rate scheme is available for the asking. Always check what payment schemes are available, and never assume that the one offered during the trial will be the most cost-effective.

Trying out combined services

Combined services also tend to offer free-trial accounts. These can be a good way of learning about the Internet at home without paying by the hour for it – although of course this is only possible if you already have a PC and a modem. This type of trial gives you a taste of the Internet proper, although with some services it can be less than clear where the Internet ends and the private subscription–only information starts. In general, however, what you will see is the Internet as it is in real life and not the simplified, modified or stylised version that the main on–line services tend to present.

Some combined services have less aggressive marketing policies than the on–line ones, and will assume that you do not want to continue with your subscription after a free trial unless you tell them otherwise. They are ideal for testing the water, especially since the main Internet providers do not – as a rule – offer free trials themselves.

Trying out ISPs

Although most ISPs do not offer a free trial, experimenting with them is not necessarily an expensive experience. If you already have a computer at home it can sometimes be worth trying out one or two

---

ISPs provide:
- raw connection to the Internet
- email address or addresses (can be accessed from a different ISP, even in a different country – for example, a cybercafé abroad)
- access to the ISP's newsgroup computer
- (sometimes) free personal web space
- 'free' software. Other software can be used instead quite easily.

On-line services provide:
- access to magazine-style features with related articles, user contributions, live chat, and links to the Web
- email address or addresses (can be accessed from abroad if the on-line service has a suitable telephone number – cannot be accessed from a cybercafé or via an ISP)
- access to Internet features (newsgroups, the Web) but sometimes with technical limitations
- (sometimes) free personal web space
- 'free' software, proprietary to the service. Other software can be used only with difficulty, if at all.

ISPs to see how well they perform. Note, however, that some ISPs not only charge a set-up fee, but also expect you to agree to a minimum contract period.

One problem with attempting this, is that it can be very difficult to set up certain computers (especially those which use the Windows 95/98 system) to work with more than one ISP at the same time. Even if you delete one ISP's software, it may still leave traces, which can prevent software from another ISP from working properly. This can cause problems if you try two trials one after the other or at the same time, or if you use one ISP and want to try a different one to see if its service is better. These are not the kinds of difficulties that can be solved by a beginner – if you have these problems, your ISP should be able to sort them out for you. For more details about choosing an ISP see Appendix 1.

Chapter 3

Communicating with others

The Internet is highly successful at bringing people together. While the traditional letter post is popular and still very widely used, compared with the Internet's ability to transfer messages almost instantly at negligible cost, it is slow and old-fashioned.

Email is the most popular tool for keeping in touch on the Internet, but other facilities are also available: Internet Relay Chat (IRC), on-line chat, mailing lists, Talk and Instant Messages, WebPhones and video links. Some of these are still at an experimental stage, but all enable the user to communicate with other Internet users around the world at relatively low cost.

Email

For many people, email is the main reason why they use the Internet. The ability to send messages around the world almost instantly has obvious attractions for both business and private use.

A large number of companies now have internal email systems which make it easy for employees to send information from any computer to any other within the organisation. In a business setting, email is ideal for arranging meetings, sending memos, agreeing agendas, and even sending presentations and reports. Although many offices still like to use printed documents, email can minimise much of the administration required to keep information flowing smoothly.

For example, a memo sent by email is quicker and more convenient than a paper memo which needs to be either written or typed and then photocopied and delivered by hand. Email memos can also be sent between buildings on the same site, or even between different sites, much more quickly.

Some companies have found that email facilities can help deal with internal political problems and morale. Senior managers have found that they are suddenly more accessible, and an exchange of ideas and views in both directions, which is facilitated by email, can benefit the company enormously. Future Publishing, one of the UK's largest publishers of computer and other magazines, uses its internal email system to create a 'forum'. Each month an employee is asked to host the forum. Staff send him or her email questions; he or she then edits them to make them anonymous and passes them to the Managing Director, who posts public replies through email.

CASE HISTORY – Anne

Anne Simpson is a lawyer who has been experimenting with email. Although she finds it more immediate and useful than some other forms of communication, she also finds it something of a distraction.

'There are two partners and four solicitors here, and we do a moderate amount of work with clients overseas. Email has been very useful for that – we've been able to do things like send over draft contracts to our South African office. It was much cheaper than faxing them, and they had no problems with reading them at the other end, which isn't always true of faxes.

'One drawback is the way that email arrives straight on my desk – or rather, in my computer. There's no secretary to field emails in the way that my secretary fields telephone calls and some of the post. This can be a distraction at times. I do admit, though, that it is much harder to filter email through someone else, as most of it really is for my attention, and some of it really is urgent.

'It's also not as immediate as a fax. We use a dial-up connection to the Internet, which means incoming mail stays on our ISP's computer until our computer dials in automatically – at the moment it does this three times a day. A permanent Internet connection would cost thousands, and we just couldn't justify that at the moment. So I've tended to use email for messages that are important but not absolutely crucial. If something has to go through quickly, I'll still send a fax or call the person.

'But, despite that, it's been useful. We also use it internally. If I have a question for someone here I can email them, and it doesn't interrupt the flow of my work the way making a call would. It wasn't hugely expensive to set up, so on the whole I'd say it's been a good thing.'

Home users can use email to keep in touch with friends and family, both in the UK and abroad, make new friends and join some of the Internet's equivalents of various clubs and organisations.

Email in practice

Email is very easy to use. The hardest part is setting up your connection to the Internet. Less good ISPs expect you to type in a series of technical details before you can make a connection. (The ISP will send you an information sheet listing them; they include the Internet addresses of the computers the ISP uses for email and all the others on its network which are needed to create and maintain any kind of Internet connection.) But the better ones provide software which does it all for you; in fact this part of the setting-up process is hidden from you completely. To avoid the difficulties beginners can get into in the

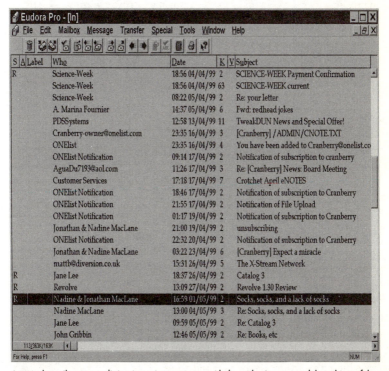

A typical email program, listing incoming messages with the author's name and the subject of the message. An 'R' indicates that a reply has been sent.

former case it is a good idea to ask just how much help you can expect to get when you attempt to install the software for the first time.

Email can be used in two ways. 'On-line' email is written and sent while you are connected to the Internet. 'Off-line' email is written before you make a connection, then all the messages you have prepared are sent in bulk when you connect. At the same time, any messages that are waiting for you are quickly copied to your computer. You should use the off-line option wherever possible as it saves you money and allows you to write and read email at a much more leisurely pace. Whether or not you have the option to do this depends on the software supplied by your ISP. Almost all software includes off-line facilities, although sometimes it is not obvious how to use them.

Once everything is installed, the only information you need in order to send someone an email is his or her address. This appears as a collection of words separated by dots, with an '@' (at) sign – for example, *someone@which.co.uk* You must write the address exactly as shown; include all the punctuation and do not put in any extra spaces, otherwise the address will not work. When giving this address verbally it is pronounced 'someone at which dot co dot uk'. Once you have typed in the address in the area marked 'To:' in your software, and added a subject to the subject line, you can add as much or as little text as you like. This text is known as the 'body' of the message.

If you are replying to someone else's message his or her address will appear in the 'To:' area automatically, so you do not have to type it in again. The subject the sender specified will also appear in the 'Subject:' area, usually with a 'Re:' in front of it – for example, 'Re: My cheque'. When replying it is usual for software to include a copy of the sender's text preceded by quote marks – which are typically '>'s. This saves you having to re-type the parts of the message that you want to respond to, and also makes it clear which parts are written by you and which by the original sender. To make email more conversational, it is common practice to edit some of the quoted text and reply to each paragraph in turn, leaving a gap to make it clearer and easier to read.

For example:

```
From: ras@angel.i-way.co.uk
To: jw@skydancer.com
Subject: An email example
>Here is an example of quoted text.
>
>There can be lots of quoted paragraphs. Each is marked
>with the quote mark to show that it was written by
>someone else.

And here is the reply section. It doesn't have quote
marks.

>Here is some more quoted text in a different
>paragraph.

And here is another reply to it. It's usual to break up
conversations like this.
```

Paragraphs can be quoted more than once. If someone replies and quotes your quote the results can look like this:

```
>>Something I said originally, with two quotes because it
>>has been through the quoting process twice - once when
>>the other person replied and again when I quoted their
>>reply.

>The other person's reply to my message

My reply to their reply doesn't have any quote marks,
because this is a fresh reply.
```

Limit the number of quoted quotes, otherwise a message can become hard to read. Often there is enough context in the most recent reply to make it clear what the conversation is about.

Email on the Internet and on on-line services

There are small but significant differences between the email facilities that on-line services offer their members and those available on the rest of the Internet. On the Internet, email is a text–only system. In other words, an email is simply a list of words. All the other attributes that appear in a printed letter – the size and style of the lettering, the page layout, and so on – are not included. Although this seems limiting, it guarantees that a message will be readable on any computer system no matter which software it uses. Text is the 'lowest common denominator', and a text-only message will always get through.

Because on-line services supply their own software, they can be slightly more creative. Most offer email which can include extras such as **BOLD**, *italic* or <u>underlined</u> text, or letters that appear in different sizes or colours. It is also easier to add non-text information such as diagrams and charts to an email and be sure that it will be readable at the other end. (This process, known as sending an attachment, is described in more detail on page 44.)

Perhaps the most significant difference between ISPs and on-line services is that emails sent between members of the same on-line service are more secure. While the information is passing over the Internet it can be tapped, because it is effectively available for public scrutiny. As a result, Internet email is not at all secure and can in theory be read by any third party (see Chapter 8). Fortunately the skills and equipment needed to read email without the sender's knowledge are well beyond those available to home users. Although millions of messages are sent every day, the number of proven cases where email has been deliberately intercepted remains tiny. But in theory, if you use Internet email to order something with a credit card, a third party might be able to intercept your order, copy your card details and then use the card without you knowing.

On-line services offer a much higher level of security. According to the staff of AOL, nobody can read anyone's mail – not even the system's administrators, who usually have the ability to monitor anything that happens within their computer networks. This security gives on-line services a commercial advantage over the Internet. Many companies use one of these services simply because it is a secure way to do business with their customers. However, this extra security only applies as long as the email is being sent to someone else using the same service. If it is sent to an Internet address it is just as vulnerable as any other message. However, there are ways to improve the security of Internet email (see Chapter 8).

The other difference between on-line services and ISPs is that some on-line services allow you to unsend email (if you have changed your mind about posting it) and also check whether or not the recipient has read your message. Although the Internet has an optional 'receipt' scheme, which sends a message back to you telling you that someone has read your message, it is quite cumbersome. Receipts appear as long lines of computer gibberish which are hard to make sense of and if you use the receipt option you will get one of these messages for every email you send; you are unlikely to find this useful in practice. Receipts can also wreak havoc if you send the same email to a group of people. Instead of one receipt you will receive a large number, and again this is more of an annoyance than a useful option. On-line services offer a simpler facility which shows you much more clearly when a message has been read.

Address books

Most email software includes an address book facility. This lists people you email frequently and makes it possible to create a new message for them without having to type in their full address each time. The facilities on offer vary depending on which software you use. Sometimes you can use personal nicknames for people as a kind of shorthand – for example, you may be able to type in a friend's name, and the address book will find his or her email address and enter it into the appropriate part of an email message for you. Or the software will automatically compile a list of correspondents, allowing you to pick someone from the list, instead of having to remember the relevant address.

While useful, address books are not essential. In practice most people keep copies of their old emails and use the 'reply' option whenever they want to write back to someone. This option copies the address into the appropriate part of the message automatically.

More advanced software can link postal addresses, telephone numbers and contact details with email addresses. One example of this is Microsoft's Outlook Express which integrates email with other contact management and time-management facilities, such as diaries and to-do lists. A disadvantage of this approach is that the email facilities on offer are rarely as comprehensive as those from a dedicated email package, although for some people the convenience of having all the information in one place outweighs any disadvantages.

Another valuable facility offered by some software is the ability to filter and sort messages according to author, or perhaps other criteria such as posting address. Messages can be automatically directed into separate mailboxes. This helps keep correspondence organised, so that email from certain individuals or from a mailing list (see page 49) can be kept distinct from messages of more general interest.

Attachments

The word 'attachment' is used to describe any information that cannot be sent as text. This includes photographs, diagrams, illustrations, and so on. With modern software, attachments are easy to use; you simply create an email message, tell the package which information you want 'attached' to it and then send it in the usual way. Messages with attachments are much longer than standard text messages, so it can take a while for them to be sent.

At the other end, the attached information can be 'detached' and saved for later, viewed, listened to or whatever is appropriate (an attachment may contain software). This is also a straightforward process – often the information appears 'inside' the email, and the email software understands what to do with it automatically.

Originally, Internet users had to add attachments by hand. This involved running the information through software that converted it into a special format, cutting and pasting the resulting gibberish into an email, and then sending it. The process was reversed at the other end. This was time-consuming and laborious, so a system called MIME (Multipurpose Internet Mail Extensions) was developed. MIME is now a standard feature of most email software and is used to hide the conversion process. Any software that uses the MIME system makes it possible for the user to send attachments with very little effort.

However, attachments do still have problems. The first of these is a size restriction. Some of the older computers on the Internet can work only with small email messages – larger messages are mangled or marked undeliverable and sent back ('bounced'). Because of this, very large attachments sometimes have to be split into smaller chunks. Each of these is sent in a separate message.

Unfortunately, it is not possible to know whether or not a message needs to be split before you send it. In fact, it is usually easier to try to send it all at once and resort to splitting it only if it does not get through.

Recent software can deal with split messages quite easily. When sending a large attachment, it usually asks if you want to split it into multiple parts. When receiving one, the different parts are glued together automatically, and a single big message appears in your in-tray.

As some older software cannot do this, it is useful to know how attachments work, and also how to send them in parts and glue them back together. This process is described in more detail in Chapter 7.

The final problem with attachments is caused by a common misunderstanding: beginners sometimes forget that information in one form on their computer may not work on a different kind of computer. For example, many programs that work with Windows 95/98 and Microsoft's Office do not produce information that can be read on an Apple Macintosh, and *vice versa*.

Windows 95/98 and Microsoft's Office software are particular culprits in this respect. They have email features that hide away the attachment process completely, making it seem as if you can send any kind of document to anyone. In fact you can only use these features to send information to someone else who is using Windows 95/98. These systems work very well in an office where everyone has the same software, but on the Internet, where people use thousands of different computer systems, they do not work at all and can lead to unreadable messages which appear as long streams of computer-generated gibberish. For Internet use it is better to use email software that handles attachments in the usual way.

A related problem can occur when using a web browser instead of email software to work with email. Because web browsers allow 'styled text' (i.e. bold, italics and other special text effects) it is possible to send a message that makes use of these. But, as with attachments, the message will only appear with these refinements if the recipient is using compatible software. Anyone else will see the text scattered among pages of gibberish. A patient recipient can still make sense of such an email, but unless you know for sure that your email can be read successfully at the other end, it is prudent to avoid sending emails styled in this way.

Beginners are sometimes confused by the relationship between the size of an attachment and the speed at which it travels across the Internet. There is no connection between the two. An email with a large attachment will arrive just as quickly (or slowly) as one with only a few lines of text. It will of course take longer to be copied from the sender's computer to the Internet, and then at the other end from the Internet to the recipient's computer. But this depends solely on the speed at which the two computers can connect to the Internet itself. When travelling across the Internet, the size of a message is irrelevant.

CASE HISTORY – Martin

Martin Brown composes music for television and video productions. He has experimented with sending in sketches and short demo pieces by attachment, and is looking forward to the day when it will be possible to send in a complete piece of music.

'I was recently talking to someone at one of the satellite TV companies who wanted me to write some demos for them for their next season. This music is the kind that is played in the background when the station logo appears. It never needs to be more than about a minute long.

'Normally we supply music on special tapes called DATs, which are about half the size of ordinary cassettes but have CD recording quality. The problem with DATs is getting them to your client. Since I live in a village in the middle of nowhere, this is a problem. Usually I don't have time to fight my way through the traffic in London to drop off a tape. Instead I use a courier service, which gets the tape there the next day before midday. If someone is in a real hurry I'll send it to arrive the same day, although this costs a small fortune.

'I'd been using my Internet connection for a while, when one day it occurred to me – I could send the music as an attachment. For fun I sent the producer some demos via email so he could listen to them on his PC.

'The idea almost worked. A minute of mono sound at reasonable quality is rather huge – over 5Mb – and this takes over an hour to send. I could have lowered the quality but I wanted to try out the real thing to see how well it worked.

'In spite of the size they got through easily, although it took most of the morning to send them. It was much cheaper than using a same-day courier, but I still wouldn't do it again until I get a faster connection. There are other ways to compress the information, although some of the sound quality may be lost. The next step is to experiment with those, and they may be fine for TV sound.

'But, anyway, it's reassuring to know that I'll be able to send in work this way within the next few years. It will make a big difference to what I do – although I doubt the courier company will be quite so happy.'

Automated email services

One of the more novel differences between email and conventional mail is that you can send email to a computer as well as to a person. Certain kinds of computers have been programmed to respond to email in a useful way. These fall into three main categories – autoresponders, email/fax gateways, and mailing list maintainers.

Autoresponders

An autoresponder sends a 'canned' reply to a request for information. For example, *Wired* magazine has an autoresponder that sends out submission guidelines for prospective authors. To use it, an author sends an email message to a special address at *Wired*, and the guidelines are sent back automatically. This is the simplest form of autoresponder. When it receives a message, it looks for a return address and throws away everything else in the message.

More advanced autoresponders look for certain words in the subject line of an email, and compose their response accordingly. For example, Demon Internet offers pre-written help articles on a number of subjects. Whenever someone sends an email request for help to Demon, he or she receives a list of these articles, together with 'request words' for each one. Sending an email with a given request word tells the autoresponder to reply with a copy of the relevant article.

As with other computers that respond to email automatically, autoresponders are very literal-minded. They do not understand English at all, and will respond only to certain words or phrases. When using any of these automated systems it is important to follow the instructions exactly – otherwise the computer will not respond as it should, and you will get an error message instead of the information you want.

Email/fax messages

It is now possible to send a fax to someone by sending an email to a special kind of address (given below). The email is directed to a computer which is connected to a telephone line and a fax modem that uses special software. When it receives your email, the computer converts the text into pages of fax information, dials out using the number you specify in the email address and sends the fax in the usual way.

This service is free, although it is still experimental. The only drawback is that sometimes the recipient gets a cover sheet which advertises the services of your ISP – but this can be a small price to pay for a fax that is sent abroad almost instantly at minimal cost.

These services are very easy to use. Demon Internet is one company that provides an email/fax gateway for its customers. To use it you send a message to an address of the form:

remote-printer.<any_name>@<faxnumber>.iddd.tpc.int (The details within the angle brackets change, depending on where you would like the fax to be sent – the others should be typed exactly as shown.) The fax number must be an international number, including the standard international prefix for a country (for example, 1 for the USA, 44 for the UK, and so on) but does not include the special codes used to call abroad, for example, '00' which is used to dial any international number from the UK.

Within the UK, the usual '0' at the front of the number is replaced by '44'. For example, to send a fax to Fred Someone on 0171-123 4567 you would send an email to:

remote-printer.Fred_Someone@441711234567.iddd.tpc.int

Note that the first and second parts of the name are separated by an underscore ('_') character rather than a dash ('-'). It is possible to include attachments of certain kinds with the faxes, and these will be printed in the usual way. Other kinds of attachments will be ignored. For more information about this service see page 258.

Free email?

A number of facilities on the Internet offer a free email service. These hide email behind the World Wide Web. Email is read and written on special web pages which are created for you automatically when you sign on to the service. These services are password-based and so can be used from libraries and cybercafés all over the world. You do not need a permanent account with an ISP or on-line service.

While these services are free, they have their drawbacks. The email facilities on offer are very basic – there are no address books, and email cannot be sorted by sender. Advertising appears with the email and cannot be turned off. Also some of these services are known as sources of junk mail, and messages from them are blocked out automatically by other Internet users. For all that, they are an excellent choice for anyone who needs email only occasionally and does not want to pay a regular monthly fee to an ISP or on-line service.

One of the most famous and most popular of these services is Hotmail at *www.hotmail.com*, which has tens of millions of users and is now a subsidiary of Microsoft. Similar facilities are being offered by many of the popular web search engines and also by BT, which plans to give everyone in the UK a free email address to mark the start of the next millennium.

Mailing lists

Mailing lists are used for exchanging email with a group of people instead of with a single person. Most email software includes 'cc' (carbon copy) and 'bcc' (blind carbon copy) options which make it possible to send the same message to more than one person at once. Mailing lists automate this process and remove any need to keep track of everyone's email address by hand.

A computer – which can be anywhere on the Internet, and will probably be owned and operated by a third party – serves as a 'post office'. A message sent to this address is copied to everyone in the group automatically. A computer program on this computer also administers the list and adds and removes people from it when they request it to. This is done without any human intervention, although all lists have a manager – called a moderator – who makes sure the computer does its job properly and steps in if problems occur.

Busy lists can attract a flood of messages, so most have a 'digest' option, which turns a collection of messages into a single long one. This is compiled and sent at a fixed time every day, or whenever the volume of contributions reaches a certain level. Most people prefer the convenience offered by the digest option, even though it makes a list less spontaneous. List members have to wait until they receive the digest and then wait again until their replies appear in the next one. Even though all the messages arrive at once, it is still standard practice to treat each one individually, and to send any replies in separate messages. This is less confusing for the list's readers, and also makes the comments and conversations shorter and more manageable.

It is possible to find mailing lists devoted to almost any subject. They are usually much more pleasant and informative than newsgroups (see Chapter 5), and the people who frequent lists seem to be more mature and less argumentative. Every list has stages when someone on it is provocative or controversial, but these usually pass fairly quickly. List managers can generally be relied upon to step in to urge people back towards the main subject of the list, or occasionally to defuse arguments and restore order. Most moderators are fairly polite and some even supply guidelines for what is and is not acceptable to the list – for example, it is usually acceptable to disagree with someone's point of view, but not to indulge in name calling. As a result, lists offer some of the most tightly knit and supportive communities available on-line. They are usually open to everyone, and are almost always free.

Finding a list

Compared with other Internet resources, mailing lists can be hard to find. They are not widely advertised, so you will usually need to take an indirect approach when looking for them. Unfortunately, there is no one central directory that lists them all, although attempts are being made to remedy this.

You can find them by using web search engines (see Chapter 4), by reading newsgroups or by word of mouth. If all else fails and you cannot find something suitable, it is relatively easy to start a mailing list yourself. Most ISPs can provide the facilities to do this. For more information see page 249.

When you find a list, you should make a note of three things: the name and address of the moderator, the subscription address for the list; and any special instructions about how to join. The special instructions specify the information to send to the computer that administers the list, so that it knows who you are and which list you want to join.

CASE HISTORY – Kyle

Kyle Hamilton is a Californian member of the Amarok mailing list, which is run by and for fans of the musician Mike Oldfield. Apart from finding the list a very sociable place, he also gets other benefits from it.

'Amarok has subscribers from everywhere. Maurice Lafleur, the moderator, is Canadian, and the regular posters include people from Spain, England, Germany, Portugal, Denmark, Poland, and a few other countries. Only about ten per cent of the people on the list post messages. Most seem happy just lurking – reading the list but not contributing to it.

'It is quite friendly, especially compared with newsgroups. People tend not to give each other a hard time, although we have had a few disagreements. We talk about all sorts of things. Even within the list you can tell there are different groups – people who are more into Mike's guitar playing, or his folk or rock connections.

'I've found I can get friends on the list to send me CDs. Payment is a problem, because it can cost more than the CD is worth to wire the money over. Instead we usually arrange CD swaps. They'll send me Mike's latest, and I'll find something for them they can't get over there. It is strange doing this with people I've never met, and maybe never will. But some of these people have become real friends. And it's always good to find someone who shares an interest – even if they do all live on different continents from each other.'

Joining a list

To join a list, you have to send an email to the list's 'post-office' address. The form and content of this message vary from list to list, but you should have found some instructions with its other details. At the very least you should know the email address of the moderator, who can explain what you need to do.

It is important to follow these instructions carefully, as mailing lists are administered automatically, and the software – the two most common programs are called Majordomo and ListServ – works literally. Adding extra words, questions or comments to a subscription message is pointless, because these programs do not understand English. They can understand only messages that appear in a certain form. A typical example of a subscription message might be: *subscribe whatever-the-name-of-the-list-is*.

Possible variations include adding your email address before or after the name of the list, and adding an option such as 'digest' at the end. Sometimes you need to include the required text in the subject header of the message, and sometimes in the body. Occasionally you will need to add punctuation marks at various points, or send a confirmation message within a certain time period.

Whatever the details are, as long as you follow them *to the letter* you should have no problems. If what you are doing does not seem to work, you can ask the moderator for help. As a last resort he or she can also subscribe you by hand.

Once you have subscribed, you will immediately receive an email message welcoming you to the list and explaining how to cancel your subscription – a process known as unsubscribing. Keep a copy of this message somewhere safe. If you decide the list is not for you, it is a lot quicker, and also a lot less embarrassing, to be able to follow these instructions without having to send an email to the moderator asking how to do it.

List etiquette

It is a good idea to unsubscribe from any lists when you go on holiday. Otherwise you might find hundreds or even thousands of unread messages waiting for you when you get back. You should also unsubscribe from any lists when you change your ISP or email address. This is common courtesy, but also avoids the situation where email that should have reached you is returned to the list with an error message. The email will then be sent back to you, and everyone else, again, then returned to the list again, and so on indefinitely, until the moderator steps in to clear up the mess.

Moderators' opinions carry a lot of weight on mailing lists, but fortunately very few take advantage of this in a negative way. Apart from personal contributions, most content themselves with occasional comments that steer the conversation away from obscure topics of no interest to most members back towards the subject of the list. This is known as staying 'on topic'. Drifting off topic is not a heinous crime, and some drift is often essential to maintain interest, but too much is a bad thing.

Unless you have a very good reason for doing so, and know for certain that it will not cause any problems, you should never try to send an attachment to a mailing list. You should also avoid advertising goods and services, preaching – religious, political, or otherwise – and sending extremely long replies. Advertising and preaching will irritate list members, and long messages will usually be ignored because most people will not take the time to read them.

You should also be tactful and polite with other list members. Although moderators do not often remove people from a list for bad behaviour, they will do so if sorely provoked. Vigorous debate is acceptable, but being rude about other list members is not – no matter how justified it may be.

One problem with lists is that if you save all the messages for posterity, they will take up a great deal of your computer's filing space. You should get into the habit of deleting messages that are not particularly interesting and saving only those which you feel you may want to refer to again. Some lists are archived on the Web, so there is no reason to keep personal copies of messages from these. You can search the archive for a specific piece of information whenever you want. It is a good idea to find out if a list is archived on the Web before you start posting messages to it. Information on the Web can be read by anyone, and you may find your comments have inadvertently reached a much wider audience than you originally intended.

Instant communications

For those who prefer a more immediate form of contact, the Internet offers a selection of 'live' options – Internet Relay Chat (IRC), on-line chat, Instant Messages and Talk. These all link your keyboard and screen with those of one or more people. When you type a message, it appears immediately on the recipient's screen, and *vice versa*. Unlike email messages, in which the text is carefully composed, these 'conversations' are instant and spontaneous, and similar to a chat-line or telephone call.

IRC

IRC is an Internet facility that works internationally, so you can chat to anyone anywhere in the world. Chats are organised into 'channels', for example '#uk', which is used by UK residents and those around the world who enjoy chatting to them. There are thousands of channels covering a huge range of interests.

To use IRC you need special software, because the software supplied by most ISPs does not include this feature. You also need to be connected to an IRC server (a special computer that provides a local link to the IRC system). Some software includes a list of servers you can choose from, although it can sometimes be out of date or include private or academic servers that do not allow public access. Often the easiest way to find one is to work through the list by trial and error.

Once you find a server, you will be asked to choose a nickname. Most people on IRC use silly nicknames, so you might want to do the same to make sure you fit in with the IRC culture. Names that alternate upper- and lower-case letters are popular, as is anything that sounds colourful and informal: 'Skoob', 'Iwetec' and 'wEbGgRl' are all typical examples.

When you have decided on a nickname, you can join a conversation by selecting a channel with an interesting name. Most software shows a list of people using the channel, so everyone else will know you are listening even if you do not type anything. This is known as 'lurking'. If you cannot find a suitable channel you can create one of your own by typing in a name that does not exist and setting a subject. If the name is interesting enough, someone will eventually come across it and start a conversation with you.

Conversations appear as a list of messages on your screen. Each person's words are preceded by his or her name. As new messages appear the old ones disappear. Some software keeps a record of an entire IRC session so you can look at the conversation later in full. With older software, messages simply disappear altogether. If the software (and you) can cope, you can have as many simultaneous conversations as you like. Virtuoso IRC users can be in as many as ten channels at the same time, although attempting to keep track of everything that everyone said while doing this is something of a challenge.

IRC messages do not have to be public. If you want to have a private conversation with someone, you can either create a channel of your own and 'hide' it so it does not appear on any lists, and then invite the person into the channel, or you can use a feature of IRC which allows you to type messages to another person directly. All these features are explained in the help facility supplied with the IRC software.

Even at its best, IRC is quite badly flawed. One problem is the length of time it takes for messages to make their way around the world. At peak times it can take up to a minute for a message to appear, making conversation very difficult. It can sometimes take a few minutes just for someone to say 'Hello' to everyone when he or she joins a channel. The world of IRC can also be very strange for anyone who is not used to it. The chat is largely trivial, and some people are happy to talk just for the sake of it.

Another drawback is that conversations can be hopelessly disjointed because people arrive, leave and interrupt each other continuously. Compared with the relatively lucid flow of a conversation on a mailing list, the result is chaotic. It is impossible to create a situation in which one person talks while everyone else listens. As soon as someone attempts this, someone else will arrive and change the mood with a trivial question such as 'Hi – so what's happening tonight?'.

IRC has its own social code:

- The creator of a channel, known as the operator, has special privileges, such as being able to throw people off the channel if he or she does not like them.

- One way to welcome someone on to a channel is to make them an operator too, so they have the same privileges. Operators typically have '@' signs in front of their names. (These are not to be confused with the '@' sign that appears in an email address. Although it is the same character, its meaning and usage are completely different.)
- Confusingly, some 'people' are not people at all – they are actually computer programs, which add their own comments according to how they have been programmed. These are known as 'bots'. Only the foolish or the naive ever mistake a bot for a real person. (This does happen sometimes – it is not unheard of for bots with female names to be asked out for the evening. Or worse.)

IRC can be marred by 'bot wars'. These occur when bots are set loose on the other users of a channel, swamping the conversation or throwing people off. (Fortunately bot wars break out fairly infrequently. However, nothing can be done about them when they do.)

Apart from chat, IRC also includes a facility that can be used to find out more about somebody. 'Who' and 'Whois' list the details of other participants – such as their location and their email address – either for individuals or for everyone using the channel at the time. This is useful if you decide you want to email someone after a chat to continue the conversation.

IRC seems to be the preserve of younger Internet users, or at least those with a younger attitude. Conversations do not generally become serious or profound, so if you are looking for more intellectual stimulation and satisfying debates, then mailing lists, or even newsgroups, will have more to offer you.

However, some people do find IRC compulsive. It is a part of the Internet that everyone should try at least once. And it can be an excellent way to make new friends.

CASE HISTORY – Sylvia

Sylvia Engle is an IRC enthusiast and uses it nearly every evening to keep in touch with a selection of friends from around the world.

'I know I'm wasting time really. But I'm lucky because I get free after-hours calls from my cable company, instead of paying money to BT. So I can spend as much time on-line as I like and it doesn't cost me a penny. I wouldn't use it so much otherwise – all that time on-line would soon get very expensive.

'I started out of curiosity. There were a lot of channels that seemed to be full of dubious activities, and I avoided those because I'm not into that sort of thing. Although, from what I've seen, there are a lot of people who are.

'I mostly enjoy straight gossip. It's just like talking to friends on the phone, except that you're typing instead. If you always use the same channels you soon get recognised and people say "Hi" when you sign on.

'To be honest it's quite studenty. A lot of 18-year-olds sit in university computer rooms around the world typing to each other. So I wouldn't say it's a good place for deep conversations about the meaning of life. There's a lot of flirting, a lot of sparring and sometimes a lot of put-downs. But if someone annoys you, you can try another channel.

'One strange thing is, you can use any nickname you like. I sometimes use "Skoob" because it looks male. If you try an instant sex change people treat you differently. It's really weird – it's something that a lot of people do. On IRC, you never know who you're talking to really – but that's all part of the fun.'

On-line chat

On-line services have their own version of IRC. This is built into the special software provided by the service and does not require any further setting up. It is also likely to be much easier to use than 'true' IRC – the options are much less confusing, and a lot of the features that might confuse newcomers are either absent or very well disguised.

On-line services offer chat in 'rooms'. These are similar to channels, except that they are usually linked to other information on the same subject, such as message areas, lists of web pages, short magazine-style articles, and so on. At the very least, the chat rooms are organised into categories. (This system is less confusing than that of IRC, where list of channels arranged in alphabetical order can seem endless.) Apart from the 'official' rooms, which are created by the on-line service itself, members can create 'private' rooms of their own. As with IRC, they can be hidden so that conversations in them are by invitation only.

Other advantages of on-line chat include much shorter delays (most messages appear instantly, even when they have come from across the

Atlantic), and the list of messages on-screen is generally much clearer and neater. The main attraction is that chat makes it easy for people to find others with similar interests. People do occasionally make good friends through chat, and will sometimes use it to ask for practical or emotional support. But this can be difficult in the more public rooms, which are used by anyone and everyone.

Finally, chat makes it possible for people to talk to experts and celebrities in special staged events – rather like a press conference with participants from all over the world, except that everyone is equipped with a keyboard and screen.

Unfortunately, many of the criticisms of IRC also apply to chat rooms. In reality, chat is a way to kill time, and it is certainly difficult to have an interesting debate.

CASE HISTORY – Chris

Chris Binns tried out the chat rooms on AOL but was not too impressed with what he found.

'Originally, I used CompuServe but it was starting to cost too much, so I thought I'd try AOL through one of its free trials. Chat on CompuServe isn't too bad – not world-class maybe, but a lot of the people seem quite grown-up. AOL can be rather different.

'I have an interest in alternative philosophies and ways of looking at the world, and eventually I found a room devoted to metaphysics. The chat there seemed typical of a lot of chat. A large number of people would come in announcing themselves, sometimes just saying "So what's happening?", others would make a big dramatic entrance just so everyone knew they'd arrived. It was really wearing after a while. It really breaks up the flow of the conversation and makes it hard to follow.

'But even when it did flow, I wasn't very impressed. Many people would say "So what's metaphysics, then?". I know it's not exactly a common interest, but answering the question for the hundredth time wasn't a good way to keep the conversation interesting. People would also cause trouble and disrupt the room by typing rubbish or being argumentative just to get attention. They'd come in and say "This room is really stupid" or something like that. Then everyone would be lured into being rude back to them, even though there's an "ignore" feature that kills annoying people's messages so you never see them.

'I eventually decided not to bother with the public chat rooms. It's so easy to waste time and money on them. I did find some slightly better chat rooms that were off the beaten track. The most interesting ones are not so easily found. But I still don't use them very often.'

Talk and Instant Messages

Talk is similar to IRC except that it is a one-to-one Internet service where the conversation is private and limited to two people. It is quite rare and is most widely available on academic and business computers that use the Unix system. Talk software for home computers is hard to find, as it is not included as a standard feature in any of the popular Internet software packages. In addition, both people need to have the software before it is possible to have a conversation, and this limits its usefulness.

Although IRC is usually used by groups, its one-to-one facility is often used instead. The main difference between Talk and IRC is that Talk can be used to interrupt someone at work, but IRC cannot. Talk is more spontaneous, whereas IRC requires two people to make an appointment with each other when they want a chat.

On-line services offer a similar system, called Instant Message (IM) or some equivalent. To send an IM you specify the person you want to talk to and type a message. A window appears instantly on his or her screen with your text in it. That person can type underneath it and send a reply to you. It is an effective, if slightly slow, way to have a long-distance conversation with someone. Of course, if the recipient does not want to chat, he or she can ignore you or block your messages completely.

Although these systems are usually used for gossip and idle chatter, they do have their uses. Even though they are slow, they are still much cheaper than an international telephone call. While no one would use them to have a business discussion, they can be ideal for talking about holiday arrangements and making plans with friends and relatives in another country.

IMs are ideal for introducing yourself to someone on-line. If you are in a chat room and like what someone has said, sending them an instant message is an ideal way to strike up a more private conversation. IM names are the same as chat names, so it is obvious who to send the message to.

Now that AOL has merged with Netscape (which makes web browsing software), IM software is included free with the Netscape browser. This makes the facilities that IM offers available to anyone, whether they use AOL or not.

CASE HISTORY – Sean

Although IRC and IMs are generally used for entertainment, they also have more serious uses. In April 1997 Sean Redden, a 12-year-old from Texas, was using IRC when he saw a message that said 'Hello – help me!'.

Most people on the channel thought someone was play-acting, but Sean took the message seriously. He discovered they were being sent by Tarija Latinen, a 20-year-old business student in Finland who was suffering from a serious asthma attack after being locked into the computer room by accident. Sean called in his mother who immediately rang the Texan emergency services. Guided by messages from Sean, they in turn contacted the Finnish emergency services. Eventually they were able to track down the student and send an ambulance.

At this point Tarija's sign-on disappeared, and everyone – including Sean – was worried that it had been a hoax after all. In fact she had been taken to hospital, and Sean's intervention had saved her life.

Chat and beyond

Users of certain Microsoft products have access to NetMeeting, Microsoft's attempt to create a live chat system. NetMeeting users can chat in the usual way, and can also swap computer files (such as pictures, or even software) and draw on a shared 'white board' – doodles and diagrams appear on the screens of all the participants in a 'meeting'. NetMeeting is business-oriented and not particularly slick, but for those who have the software it can work well for more serious chat sessions.

ICQ, a system created by Mirabilis (*www.mirabilis.com*), is an attempt to create a more sophisticated Internet chat system. ICQ offers Internet users many of the chat features of on-line services, including instant messages, user directories, chat rooms and information about whether or not friends are using the system. The software and the service are currently free, albeit in a time-limited beta form. (In other words, the software isn't finished yet, and may have some rough edges.)

ICQ is a vast and sprawling conglomeration of chat and chat-related facilities. It is much more sophisticated than IRC, but lacks the simplicity and clarity of the systems offered by the on-line services. For example, users are identified by a long number instead of a name. Beginners may find its huge array of options and settings rather bewildering, although there is plenty of on-line documentation to help new users through their faltering first steps. It has become extremely popular in a very short time (it now has more than 5 million users), and for this reason alone it is well worth experimenting with.

Versions of ICQ are available for less common computer systems, including 'pocket' computers such as various Windows CE machines, and 3Com the Palm Pilot. The system is also available for older computers, such as those which use the now-obsolete Windows 3.1 instead of Windows 95/98, and older models of the Macintosh.

WebPhones

Because the Internet can be used to send any sort of information, it can be coaxed into behaving like a telephone connection. To do this you need special software and a computer that has a microphone and speakers or headphones. The computer must have a two-way – known as a 'full-duplex' – sound facility, so that it can make sound while recording the sound of your voice through the microphone. Most computers now have soundcards with this facility. Models bought before 1996 most probably will not, although in most cases this can be remedied by adding a cheap modern soundcard at moderate costs. Dedicated users can now buy true WebPhones that look and work like a telephone handset and plug into the computer.

WebPhone software takes the sound from the microphone and converts it into a form that can be sent over the Internet. If the person at the other end has a similar system, and if he or she is expecting you to call, it is possible to have a normal telephone conversation in this way.

The big advantage of this system is that it is possible to talk to anyone in the world for the price of a local call. One disadvantage is that the speech quality depends on the speed of your connection to the Internet, and also to some extent on the amount of Internet traffic between you and the person at the other end. The kind of slow connections available to home users tend to result in low-quality speech which has a lot of gaps.

The other drawback is that, unless you happen to be connected to the Internet when a call comes in, there is no indication to show that the WebPhone is 'ringing'. So conversations have to be arranged beforehand. This is less of a problem in the USA, where local calls are free (or very cheap), and Internet users can leave their machines connected permanently. But in the UK, where this is not an option for home users, the lack of spontaneity is irritating.

Once this is solved and the connection speed improved, WebPhones are likely to become very popular indeed. They are already being used by some businesses which can afford a permanent connection. As speeds increase, it is likely that the present long-distance telephone rates will become obsolete, as more and more people use the Internet instead of the telephone network to make long-distance and international calls. An experimental system called IPVoice is now being tested on-line. This makes the WebPhone system easier to use, as it is possible to make someone's phone ring and initiate a conversation by clicking on a web link.

Video links

The idea of a video phone that shows an image of someone while they talk has been in existence since at least the 1950s. But it has now become a real possibility on the Internet – although, as with WebPhones, this facility is best thought of as experimental until connection speeds improve.

A number of companies offer video facilities over the Internet. The cheapest use a small camera, which perches on top of your computer's screen, and special software which compresses the video information so that it can be sent over the Internet as quickly as possible. The image from the camera is small and not very detailed, but good enough to make it possible to see who is talking. More expensive systems can use ordinary camcorders for live video.

One of the most popular systems is known as CU-SeeMe. CU-SeeMe software can be tried for free, and even if you do not have a camera you can watch people who do. At the moment the system is rather crude when used over a slow link – instead of smooth video, the images are jerky and tend to break up completely. But businesses with faster links can use it quite successfully.

Chapter 4

Finding information

THE MOST popular medium for electronic publishing is the World Wide Web, and although the technology that drives it was finalised only in the early 1990s, it has already taken the world by storm. As far as most people are concerned, the World Wide Web *is* the Internet. References to it have started to appear in advertising and other media, and the Web is set to become as important as television, radio and traditional print publishing.

A large part of the Web's appeal is that it is extremely easy to use, whereas many other facilities on the Internet, such as those described in Chapter 7, require moderate to advanced technical skills and knowledge. Complete newcomers can learn how to use the Web in ten minutes or less, and it takes only another ten minutes to learn how to use its search facilities (see page 65). Understanding how to publish your own material on the Web takes longer, but the countless examples of web sites produced by people with limited computer experience demonstrate that this is also relatively straightforward (see Appendix 5).

A web publisher creates a set of pages which contain text, images and perhaps sounds, animations or video clips. These are posted on the Web and remain there until the publisher decides to change them. To see the pages on a web site, users need to view them with a special piece of software called a 'browser', which is either free or available for a relatively small outlay. Both ISPs and on-line services include one of these in the introductory packages they send out when you become one of their customers.

The biggest difference between web pages and more traditional forms of publishing is that web pages can contain 'links'. A link appears as an underlined word or phrase, or part of an image. If you click on one with a mouse it leads you to a new page, and this can be anywhere on the Web (publishers are not limited to creating links only to their own pages). Following links is like following a train of thought: for example, a page created by a bungee-jumping enthusiast may contain links to pages about other dangerous sports, which in turn may be connected to the pages of an insurance company, and so on. This process is known as 'browsing' or 'surfing' the Web.

Because they always give you the option of jumping to related information, links provide an environment which appears to respond directly to your interests. Browsers keep a note of the links you choose as you visit various pages. This facility enables you to backtrack easily if you find you have followed a large number of links and want to return to a page several stages further back.

Another strength of the Web is that its pages do not have to be fixed in the way that printed pages are. This means that they can include forms for visitors to fill in – popular examples include product orders and 'visitors' books' – and links to email addresses and other Internet facilities. Pages can be set up to change automatically according to the time of day or the time of year and to display a counter that shows the number of people that have visited the page. Some sites also include a search facility to help you find your way to information more quickly.

Using the Web

To find a page, you need to know its address. Web addresses are known as URLs (Uniform Resource Locators) and typically look something like this:

www.somename.some-extension/someword/etc1/etc2

To view this page, you simply type the URL into the 'address' line in your browser. The browser then finds the page for you, copies the information to your computer and displays it on the screen. Once the page has appeared, you can either follow its links to other pages or type in a new URL to see a completely different page. Some URLs include characters such as the tilde '~' or long strings of numbers. It is important to type in a URL exactly as it appears, adding no extra spaces, and including all the punctuation – no matter how strange it looks.

What is on the Web?

In terms of content, web pages divide neatly into two groups. The first group includes pages of business and professional information, created by organisations, magazines and newspapers, small and large businesses, schools and universities, towns and cities, government offices, and so on. These pages often have advertising or free information which is related to the organisation that maintains them; some have both.

A typical example is Railtrack's site *(www.railtrack.co.uk)*. These pages include the usual corporate public relations material but also feature an electronic train timetable. Visitors to these pages can type in a starting station, a destination and a preferred travelling time, and the timetable will then calculate and display the best route.

Another good example is the site maintained by *New Scientist* magazine *(www.newscientist.com)*. Instead of simply repeating the information already provided in the paper version, these pages include a searchable archive of features and back issues, additional background information, and other facilities such as job advertisements.

The editors of some magazines create pages where their readers can offer instant feedback and comments about the articles. Ziff-Davis is one the world's largest technology magazine publishing companies. The Ziff-Davis web site has readers' comments appended to articles by many of the regular columnists. Although the readers often disagree with the editorial point of view, their inclusion makes for a much livelier and more informative source of information than is usually possible in print.

The other group includes private and hobby pages which are maintained by amateurs who have created them for fun. These people either have a burning interest and want to share it, or simply want to tell everyone something about themselves. The pages vary hugely in both quality and content; some are extremely inept, while others are very impressive and professional. The range of content is vast, and often the sites include links to rich sources of background information that could take hours or days of research in a library.

The Web does have other uses, some of which are quite unusual, for example 'WebCams' – video cameras which produce an image that can be seen over the Web. One of the earliest was created to show whether a coffee machine in a Cambridge college was full or empty, so that students did not need to make the journey down the hall to find out in person. Since then hundreds of WebCams have appeared in all kinds of locations: it is now possible to check the surf off the coast of California, watch various people around the world while they work in their offices, examine the state of the sun as viewed from Australia, check skiing conditions in a Swiss resort, and look out over the frozen wastes of the Antarctic. The site at *earthcam.com* maintains a list of active WebCams, so you can see which ones are likely to be worth looking at.

CASE HISTORY – Simon

DJ Optik – real name Simon James – works in various dance music clubs and pubs around the country. He uses the Web to keep track of the latest news and also to order records and other items that would be impossible to obtain locally.

'One of the main sites I look at is called Hyperreal – *www.hyperreal.com* It has a complete list of everything to do with dance culture. One of the best things about it is that there is a huge list of links to other music and dance sites. The dance scene isn't just about the music, it's about the culture – the clothes, the news, the people and the attitude. By following the links I can see what's happening in the dance scene throughout the world, browse through a clothes store's site in San Francisco, order records from Australia, or find out what's happening at a local club. Hyperreal is maintained by volunteers, so no one makes any money from it. And it's bigger than most sites. There's a lot of interest in dance music which doesn't get covered in any other way.'

Finding the information you want

There are three ways to use the Web. The first is to follow links to wherever your interests take you. Although doing this can be entertaining, it is not a particularly reliable way of finding specific information, and it is very easy to run up a huge bill this way. A typical surfing session can easily take an hour or two, so regular random browsing is not recommended unless you can afford it.

The second approach is to find URLs in magazines and other media. Many have web directories that list the best sites dealing with a particular topic. Although these lists are useful, sites do appear and disappear without warning, and this means that the directories can

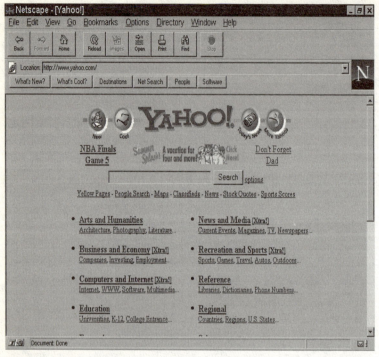

Yahoo! is one of the most popular Internet indexing search engines.

become out of date very quickly. Nevertheless, they do provide useful jumping-off points for further exploration.

The third and best way to find information is to use the Web's own search facilities. Known as 'search engines', these are special sites which link to a computer that maintains its own directory of web sites. (For a list of the most popular search engines see page 261.)

These search facilities fall into two groups. The first is a collection of topic lists, divided and subdivided by category and sub-category. The best-known example is the Yahoo! site at *www.yahoo.com* The main Yahoo! page has a selection of category headings, which appear as links. At the time of writing these are:

- arts and humanities
- business and economy
- computers and Internet
- education
- entertainment

- government
- health
- news and media
- recreation and sports
- reference
- regional
- science
- social science
- society and culture.

Beneath each heading is a short list of three or four of the most popular subheadings. For example, under science you might find:

- computer science
- biology
- astronomy
- engineering.

Otherwise, if you click on 'science' itself you will find a long list of further subheadings. Picking one of these – for example 'nanotechnology' – will lead to further subdivisions of the subject, which eventually lead to a list of links to relevant web sites.

The second kind of search engine uses 'keywords' to find information on the Web. The most popular example is the AltaVista site at *www.altavista.com*

A keyword is simply a word that the engine looks for in all the sites in its index. If a match is found, the site will be listed, together with its address and the first sentence or the first few words. Keywords can be combined in various ways. In fact, combinations are usually essential to get useful results. For example, searching for a common word such as 'money' will produce a list of millions of sites, which is far too many to be useful. So it is vital to make the search criteria more specific. You might choose to look for 'currency exchange rates' or 'stock prices', for example.

You may need to practise to get the best results from a keyword search engine. All of them include help pages which explain how to search for keywords more effectively and how different words can be best combined. It is well worth taking the time to read these pages and do some experimenting to master the system. When looking for specific information, choosing the right keyword combinations and using the

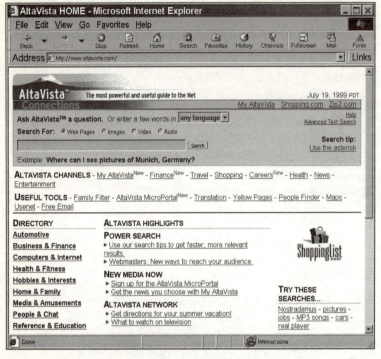

AltaVista offers keyword searches for both web and newgroup information

various advanced search options can sometimes save you hours. (For more information about using search engines see page 217.)

Agents

Agent software, which is starting to be sold over the counter, enables you to create your own personal web search without using any of the existing search engines. You tell it what kind of information you want to look for, then leave it to roam the Internet on your behalf. At this point you can disconnect from the Internet and do something else. As the agent finds information it creates a list of URLs, complete with short descriptions. The next time you connect, it copies this list to your computer.

One of the most popular agent systems is called Autonomy, which has been designed to be very easy to use. As soon as you start up the software it appears on your screen as a friendly dog that needs to be 'trained'; you do this by typing your requirements on a blackboard. The words or ideas you are looking for can be typed in plain English, although Autonomy's understanding of what you want is still relatively crude. As you continue to use Autonomy, the dog appears to 'learn' or 'understand' what you want more quickly. Although it is not perfect, the system can be understood by anyone, and is a good example of the attempts being made to make the Internet less technical.

Portals

Portals are a Web buzz word. A portal is a search engine that also offers news, email and chat facilities, and access to newsgroups. Many of the large search engine sites (such as Yahoo! and AltaVista) are currently reinventing themselves as portals. The theory is that visitors will be so attracted by the all-in-one features of the portal that they will return again and again. In effect, it becomes their 'home' on the Internet. The owners of the portal can use this hold they have over visitors to persuade advertisers to part with significant sums of money.

While in theory portals are an interesting money-making idea, in practice there's no obvious reason why people should use them. Getting email directly from an email account maintained at a portal is no more convenient than getting it from an account maintained by an ISP. In fact, in many cases it is rather less convenient. If you find that the community that develops around a portal is one with which you feel an affinity, then this kind of service may have something to offer you. Otherwise it's tempting to write it off as nothing more than a clever piece of marketing.

The Web's limitations

Although the Web can be extremely useful, it is not perfect. The most obvious problem is that it can work very slowly; it is not unusual for pages to take a few minutes to appear. The speed depends on two things: the number of people trying to look at a site at the same time; and the speed of the connection between the web site and your computer. At the time of writing an updated version of HTML – the system that holds the Web together – is being considered which will make this connection more efficient. However, lack of speed is likely to remain a problem for the foreseeable future. Anyone who uses the Web can expect a slow service some of the time and should budget for the bills caused by this.

Search engines are useful but not infallible. Sites such as Yahoo! have to be maintained by hand to a certain extent, and if a site disappears or a new one appears, it can take a while – perhaps a month or two – for the new information to appear in the listing.

Similarly, keyword searches can date quickly, resulting in 'broken links' – listings that appear as a result of a keyword search, but lead to a message that tells you the information has either moved or disappeared entirely. Keyword searches rely on special programs called 'spiders' which crawl over the Web looking for changes. But, as there are millions of pages to look through, collecting the information is a neverending process. It is also possible to hide pages from these spiders – either deliberately or by accident – so the index is rarely complete. You need to think laterally when looking for particular information on the Web. For example, when looking for one word, you might also need to look for other words that might lead to it.

File Transfer Protocol (FTP)

The Web has subsumed the features of a number of older Internet information distribution systems and can now be used to obtain information from them without the need for the old-fashioned software and working methods they require. A facility known as FTP (File Transfer Protocol) makes it possible to access and copy information from various computers called FTP 'servers' anywhere on the Internet. FTP is a simple copying system. It does not attempt to display the information or do anything useful with it.

FTP servers are most often used as libraries of free or trial software; many companies offer these systems to allow visitors to get hold of new and updated versions of their products directly over the Internet. This is better for the companies, as they no longer have to copy the information on to a floppy disk and send it through the post, and better for their customers, who can have the software delivered directly to their computer and start using it immediately. Other kinds of information are also available; books, bibliographies, FAQs for newsgroups (see page 12), photograph archives, and sounds can be copied to your computer using FTP.

FTP works in one of two ways:

- **Anonymous FTP** is open to everyone. All FTP computers – known as FTP servers – require a password and an identifying name before they will allow visitors to copy the information they hold. In the case of anonymous FTP, the identifying name is 'anonymous' and the password can be anything. It is common practice to use your email address as the password, so that the computer's administrators know who has been using the facility.

- **Secure FTP** can be used only if you have a suitable name and password. You will need to obtain these from the administrators. If you do not have a suitable name and password, you will not be able to receive the information.

Web browsers hide the complexities of FTP away behind a single mouse click. Where FTP facilities are offered on a web site, all that is usually required is a click on a specially labelled link; everything else happens automatically. However, for situations where more control is needed special FTP software is also available, often free. For more details see page 133.

CASE HISTORY – Janet

Janet Anderson subscribed to an ISP but decided soon afterwards that she needed email software that was better than that provided by the ISP. She decided to look for it on the Web and found something suitable very quickly.

'I found out about this site called Tucows from a magazine. It's a huge list of all kinds of free software, decorated with a picture of two cows. The software is rated so you can see how good it is. It's also divided up into categories to help you find your way around.

'The site has copies – called mirrors – all over the world, so the first step was to find a local one with the same information. You are given a long list showing where the copies are, so it was easy to find the ones in the UK. I had no idea whether any were better than the others, so I picked one at random. Apparently some sites respond more quickly than others, but I can't say I noticed any difference.

'The list of categories came as a bit of a shock. I didn't have any idea what most of them were – what's a "DNS server" or a "finger client" – but one of the buttons had "email" written on it in big letters so I clicked on that one.

'The rest of the process was surprisingly easy. There's a long list of the different kinds of software with a brief description of each and its "cows" rating. Eudora Lite had a good mark, so I thought I'd try it. To get hold of the software all I had to do was click on a link and tell my computer where to file it. It took just a few minutes to copy. There were no bills to pay, and I didn't need to give a credit-card number to anyone.

'Eudora – there's a "Pro" version as well as a "Lite" version, but you have to pay for the other one – is much better than the original software I was using. It files mail from different people in mail boxes and maintains my address book.

'Installing the software was easy, setting it up wasn't, so I had to ask for help from my ISP. Luckily they're used to people like me asking them awkward questions and they sent me a help sheet, which answered most of the questions.

'It's strange – I seem to have become some kind of computer expert now. I never would have thought I could do something like this, but it's been much easier than I imagined.'

Chapter 5

Getting support and sharing interests on-line

Usenet comments on itself

```
Subject: Re: Orrie answers the woodchuck question!
From: Nathan Sullivan <alfonso@cegt201.bradley.edu>
Newsgroups: rec.humor.oracle.d

kirsten@spike.wellesley.edu (Kirsten Chevalier) writes:

> Indeed. It often seems as if the majority of Usenet
>traffic is composed of various rephrasings of the
>command "go stick your head in a pig." Understanding
>this fact would be crucial to any high-level
>understanding of Usenet; whether such an understanding
>would be possible or even desirable is a question
>I'll leave open for discussion.

And if anyone were to ever gain such an understanding,
Usenet will instantly disappear and be replaced by
something even more bizarre and inexplicable.

Some say this has already happened.

Most say it isn't possible.
```

Because of its interactive and open nature, the Internet enables people with similar interests or problems to find, talk to and help each other. Mailing lists (described in Chapter 3) can be used to do this, but a system called Usenet is also available. Where mailing lists use email technology to pass messages between people, Usenet has a special system of its own, which is an important component of the Net. Various on-line services provide their own equivalents of Usenet, which work in much the same way but are for the exclusive use of their subscribers. The information and comments that appear in them are not available to users of the Internet as a whole.

Newsgroups are used in two ways: as a source of entertainment; and for finding answers to specific questions. For entertainment purposes, newsgroups provide access to groups of people with the same interests. As a source of help, they offer the chance to obtain information from people who are experts in their field.

To get the best from the newsgroup system, it is essential to understand the culture of Usenet. Newsgroups have their own traditions, some of which are common to the whole system, while others are specific to individual groups. Newcomers who understand and respect these traditions will find Usenet much more entertaining and informative than those who do not. It is possible to annoy people in newsgroups if you do not behave in the expected way; in return they may well act in an unpleasant manner towards you.

CASE HISTORY – Alan

Alan Marks has an interest in unusual phenomena and was delighted to find plenty of information relating to his hobby on the Internet. But his enthusiasm soon turned to disillusion when he discovered the low quality of much of the debate in newsgroups.

'I have a strange hobby – I'm interested in UFOs, aliens, crop circles and other odd things. The Internet can be great for finding material about these sorts of subjects, especially on the Web and in the numerous newsgroups – the local religions seem to be *Star Trek* and *The X Files*.

'When I started using Usenet I saw a long list of groups which looked really interesting, and I got very excited. But when I started reading the messages, reality sank in.

'It was like stepping into a war zone. I was completely unprepared for the personal attacks in some groups. It seems that a number of people spend their time making sneering put-downs about anyone who disagrees with them. And then the replies are made in kind, and so it continues. I've since found out that sometimes the same arguments and the same insults have been carrying on for years, which is extremely strange but true.

'It wasn't just to do with my interests either – these personal attacks are not unusual and seem to be a common feature of lots of groups. I don't know why, but some people on Usenet are very aggressive. Everyone's postings get equal space, so if someone packs an emotional punch that posting will appear "louder" than the more reasonable ones.

'This seems to have a hypnotic effect on other people; they can't help getting hooked into the name-calling that follows. There are even Net celebrities – people with unlikely names like Archimedes Plutonium – who are cranks who get a lot of attention in the more serious science groups, where they're fair game for experts with time to kill.

'If I was starting now, I'd make sure that I got news software that can filter out the troublemakers and keep the endless arguments off my screen. I have that now, and it's made a big difference. I can watch the filter to see how many messages it kills, and sometimes that number has been a third of all the messages in a group. Is it censorship? Not really – on Usenet you have to look after yourself, and if you don't like someone or something you don't have to read those postings. If someone isn't happy with filtering out the disagreeable postings, Usenet isn't for them.

'And the point is, once you start filtering, life on Usenet becomes much more enjoyable. I've made some new friends in newsgroups, both locally and in other countries. One of them set up a mailing list recently which has been really great.

'Also, you hear about events before anyone else. The Internet had information about Hale-Bopp months before it was mentioned on TV. As soon as a rumour of any kind starts, a newsgroup devoted to it is formed, and someone usually puts up a web page about it too. But you do need to be selective about what you read and how seriously you take it. And life's a lot more peaceful if you stay out of the arguments.'

Usenet in practice

To use the newsgroup system with your Internet connection, you need two things:

- access to a **'news server'**, which is a big computer that deals only with newsgroup messages. All the main ISPs and on-line services have their own news servers, and you will be given access to one when you sign up with them.

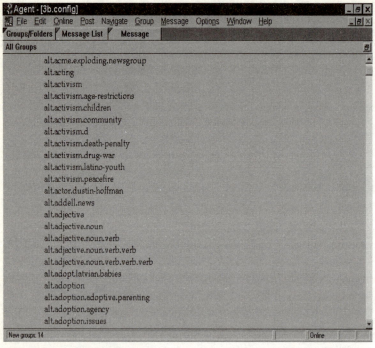

Usenet has tens of thousands of newsgroups, a tiny fraction of which are shown above.

- **suitable newsreading software** The most popular web browsers – currently Netscape Communicator and Microsoft's Internet Explorer – include basic newsreading features, but these are very poor compared with proper newsreading software, which can be bought in stores or copied from the Internet.

Subscribing and posting

Subscribing to a newsgroup is as easy as tuning a radio or TV into a particular channel. You do not need to send an email message requesting to join the group. (In fact, attempting to do so is unwise as it marks you out as being a beginner, and therefore very low down the pecking order that exists in some groups.) Usually you simply select one or more groups from a long list, and select a 'subscribe' option (or something similar) from a menu. The messages for the groups you have subscribed to will appear automatically next time you connect to the Internet.

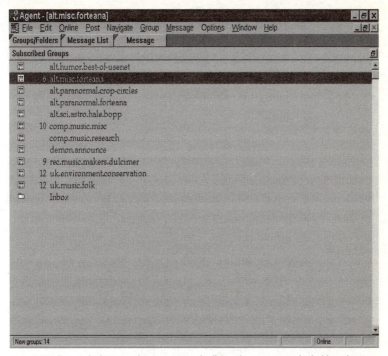

Once users choose which groups they want to read, all the other groups can be hidden. This software also shows the number of messages waiting to be read in each group.

To make life simpler, messages about the same topic are often grouped together. These chains of related messages are the Usenet equivalent of individual conversations and are called 'threads'. Most Usenet software manages threads automatically. Typically only the oldest message in a thread is shown, with the newer messages hidden away. If you select or click on the first message the others will appear.

A further enhancement offered by many newsreaders (the Internet jargon for newsreading software) is colour coding. Unread messages are shown in one colour, while those you have read are shown in another. This makes it much easier to keep track of the flow of conversations.

Posting a message to a newsgroup is very similar to writing an email, except that the 'address' of the message is the name of one or more newsgroups instead of one or more individuals. All software includes options that let you start off a new discussion in a group or add a comment to an existing one. For the latter, the existing message is quoted and edited in the same way as for email, and many of the same conventions apply (see pages 40–1).

The most significant difference is that the conversation includes more than two people, so it is very important to edit the messages in such a way as to make it clear which comment you are responding to and who said what. Most software has a 'quote phrase', which you set up when you use the software for the first time. This phrase then appears at the top of every message you write when replying to someone else's comment, and automatically includes the name and email address of the person you are responding to. A typical example is set out below.

```
On Mon, 06 Jan 97 14:42:36 GMT, badger@bolthole.lemon.co.uk
(Nick Badger) decided to entertain us with the following:
>In article <QyC$FgAC+hbzFw8M@gthomp.melon.co.uk>
>Gillian Thompson <gthompson@gthomp.melon.co.uk> writes:
>>In article <E9oKts.6yn@csa.bris.co.uk>, "Jai Helden"
>><pz0079@irix.bris.co.uk> writes
>>>I am afraid I can /never/ tell what others are
>>>thinking, which when I was younger led to a few
>>>embarrassments.
>>
>>A good rule of thumb is that others are thinking
>>exactly what you'd like them to be thinking.
>>Remember the world really only exists in your mind,
>>so make the most of it. HTH
>
>Unfortunately that doesn't help cases such as a certain
>person I used to know, who was insecure almost to the
>point of paranoia. If there was a possible negative
>connotation, she'd take it. If not, she'd invent one ...
>
Wow Nick - did we meet in a previous life?

Liz http://www.ginandtonic.melon.co.uk/Liz/
```

Although at first glance this can seem like a confusing mass of unrelated text, the result is relatively simple. The first six lines at the top are the quote phrases, which introduce the people participating in this particular exchange of messages. Quote phrases do not have a standard format. Some people use humorous introductions, while others use much simpler ones such as: 'In article <so and so> <such and such> writes:'. Perversely, quote phrases appear in reverse order, with the most recent listed at the top.

QyC\$FgAC+hbzFw8M@gthomp.melon.co.uk is the reference code produced by the various news servers to keep track of the administrative details of the message. This information is strictly for the benefit of the computers involved in passing this message through the Usenet system. It does not contain any information of interest to the people involved in the conversation. Although there is an '@' sign this is not an email address.

Under the last quote phrase is the first message in the exchange: Jai Helden explaining that he cannot tell what others are thinking. Then comes Gillian Thompson's tongue-in-cheek response, then Nick Badger's response to her response. Finally the newest message is Liz's response to Nick. The original message and the replies are shown in chronological order. Liz's response is not quoted because she is the author of the final reply – her 'sig' (see page 101), which includes the URL for her web site, appears at the end.

Although this may look complicated, it is much easier to use the system than to describe it. To keep track of who is saying what, you simply need to count the quote characters ('>') and match them to the person with the same number in the quote phrase. The smaller the number is, the more recent the message. When you post a reply of your own all the text has another quote mark added at the front. You can then edit out the very earliest messages if you think they are no longer relevant. Below is a reply from Steve Casey with the first couple of contributions removed.

```
>On Mon, 06 Jan 1997 17:39:16 GMT
>liz@ginandtonic.melon.co.uk (Liz Purdue) added the
following to the fount of human knowledge:
>>On Mon, 06 Jan 97 14:42:36 GMT,
>badger@bolthole.lemon.co.uk (Nick Badger) decided to
>entertain us with the following:

>>Unfortunately that doesn't help cases such as a certain
>>person I used to know, who was insecure almost to the
>>point of paranoia. If there was a possible negative
>>connotation, she'd take it. If not, she'd invent one
```

79

```
>Wow Nick - did we meet in a previous life?
```

Maybe we all did. Which is why we decided to live so far
apart this time around.

HTH,

Steve

Steve Casey
Skydancer Media Ltd - http://www.skydancer.com

Missing messages

One problem with Usenet is that not all groups, and not all messages, are available everywhere. The Usenet network is rather ramshackle and inefficient, so some groups and messages fall through the gaps. One way in which ISPs differ from each other is the varying quality of their Usenet connection. Some offer a relatively small selection of groups – perhaps a few thousand – while others offer 30,000 or more. Only a tiny minority of ISPs based in the USA carry every single message that appears in every single group. For a variety of technical reasons, UK ISPs do not manage to do this. Some deliberately restrict the number of groups their subscribers can see to limit the demands on their resources. ISPs will sometimes make a particular group available if asked, although this may not always be possible for technical reasons.

Some ISPs may not carry certain groups for moral reasons – for example, those controversial groups that are used for various illegal activities including pornography and software piracy. However, others do provide access to these, using the argument that they are simply carriers of information and cannot therefore be held responsible for the content. This is a legal issue that will remain unresolved for some time yet, although there are signs that the industry and various governments are moving towards a situation where ISPs can carry whatever they like unless they receive complaints from the police or the public.

For these reasons, newsgroup coverage can be patchy. This is not usually a problem as you are very unlikely to miss a group if you do not know it exists. And unless you have an interest in groups with illegal content, the legal restrictions should not bother you. A more common problem is that messages may be delayed, which can make conversations stall temporarily.

ISPs can also remove messages deliberately. They delete old newsgroup messages from their news computer for the same reason that people remove files from their computer at home: to save space. This is known as 'expiring' the messages. Typical expiry times vary from a few days to a fortnight, depending on the resources of the ISP. A full set of messages for every available group can take up enormous amounts of computer filing space (a few gigabytes a day), and the volume is growing exponentially. So ISPs sometimes set up different time limits for different groups; those with a lot of traffic will have their messages deleted more quickly than others to make way for newer ones.

Newsreading software also includes an expiry feature which performs the same task for your own computer. Typically, you can mark certain messages as interesting, and they will stay on your computer until you decide to remove them by hand. All the other messages will be deleted after a set time to save space.

You can also delete messages (both your own and other people's) once they have been posted to Usenet in an attempt to stop people seeing them. However, this requires specialised knowledge and remains the preserve of Usenet experts, who do this deliberately when they find messages they object to, particularly ones that are attempts to abuse the system. A person with the pseudonym of 'Cancelmoose' runs 'Cancelbot' – a system which automatically hunts down and removes 'spam', Usenet's version of junk mail – commercial messages posted simultaneously across hundreds of newsgroups. In one celebrated case, war broke out in a newsgroup when an organisation called The Church of Scientology had some of its secret documents posted anonymously. It tried to cancel these messages, but they were posted again immediately. After a day or two all parties involved were posting thousands of messages (all conflicting) in an attempt to make sure that the information either did, or did not, become public. A related example was the 'Netcom death penalty', which was enacted in late 1997 by a large group of disgruntled users who were unhappy with the amount of junk mail being sent by users of Netcom, a major US ISP. For a short period all news postings made by Netcom users were deleted as soon as they appeared, although normal service was restored after negotiations.

Groups and group names

When you link to Usenet for the first time, your newsreading software
will copy a list of all the available groups to your computer – to do this
you typically need to select an option labelled something like 'Get all
groups'.

Groups are arranged into categories. These in turn have sub-
categories, sub-sub-categories, and so on. Each name appears as a
collection of words separated by dots – for example, *uk.business.telework*
In this case 'uk' is the main category heading and is used for all groups
specific to the United Kingdom; 'business' is a subheading that
includes all the business-related groups; and 'telework' specifies one
particular group from this sub-category – in this case, a group for
people who work from home. The name as a whole often, but not
always, gives a good indication of what the group is about. When
verbally quoting the name of a newsgroup, the dots are not mentioned,

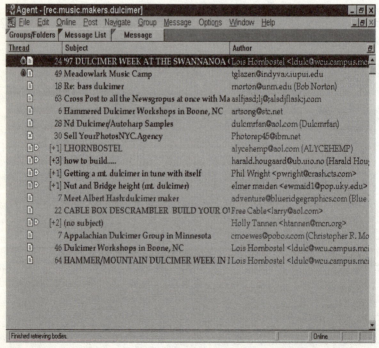

Each group contains a list of messages from individuals. A busy group may have hundreds of
these. The 'CABLE BOX DESCRAMBLER' message that appears near the bottom is an example of
spam.

so '*uk.business.telework*' is simply 'UK business telework'. Where it is relatively easy to work out the meaning from the context, group names may be abbreviated: '*uk.singles*' becomes '*uk.s*'

Originally, eight main categories existed, but there are now hundreds. Many of the newer categories are specific to certain countries or academic and research establishments, and this limits their usefulness for most readers. When looking for a newsgroup about a specific subject, it is advisable to explore the main categories and perhaps those under the 'uk.' heading before investigating the others.

The traditional category headings are:

rec. – recreation. Hobbies, pastimes, sports, and leisure

biz. – business. Investment and business advice

sci. – science. For scientific discussions and information

comp. – computing. For computers and computer users

soc. – society. For and about various cultures and social and ethnic groups

misc. – miscellaneous. Includes some buy and sell groups

talk. – Idle chatter and repetitive debates

news. – Useful (mostly) information about the Newsgroup Network

alt. – alternative. Anything – literally.

Most of the information on Usenet appears in these groups, and you will find plenty of them to keep you busy. Outside these headings, groups fall into a variety of category types, including the following.

- **Groups set up by ISPs for discussions, help and support for their members** Demon (demon.), Netcom (netcom.), Pipex (pipex.) and others have their own groups.
- **Groups for various countries** The UK (uk.), Canada (can.), Germany (de.), Poland (pl.), and Mexico (mex.) are typical examples.
- **Groups for various cities** London (lon.), Cambridge (cam.), Ottawa (ott.), New York (nyc.) and so on. Postings to these groups can sometimes get confused when there are cities with the same name in different countries.
- **Groups for various US states** California (ca.), Minnesota (mn.), and so on.

- **Groups maintained by companies or commercial organisations** These are anathema to traditional Usenet culture, but are starting to make an appearance. The ClariNet news service (clari.) contains groups which offer a paid-for subscription service for anyone who wants news of the more traditional kind. Computer software giant Microsoft (microsoft.) has a large number of groups devoted to its products.
- **Groups created by universities and colleges for their own use** uwarwick. groups are for the University of Warwick, utexas. for the University of Texas, and so on.
- **Other local groups** For example, groups for the Triangle area of the USA (triangle.), based around part of North Carolina.

Given these top-level categories, groups are sub-categorised by adding extra descriptive subdivisions separated by '.' Some examples are listed below:

- **uk.people.consumers** Devoted to consumer topics of all kinds. Mainly for UK readers, but available for anyone anywhere
- **uk.people.teens** Chat for UK teenagers. (Another subdivision of the uk.people sub-category)
- **demon.ip.support.win95** Support for Internet problems for users of the Demon ISP who are using Windows 95 (and despite the name, Windows 98 as well)
- **alt.family-names.jacoby** Genealogy and general chat for anyone who has this particular surname
- **no.typografi** Discussion of typography in Norwegian.

It should be obvious from looking at the above groups that the categorisation system is rather random. For example, it would make more sense for the London groups to be in the UK category, but in fact they are in a category of their own. Although attempts have been made to impose order on Usenet, the categorisation scheme is very much a free-for-all. This is likely to get worse as more and more people start using Usenet.

It is also difficult to tell what the different groups are about. The information provided above should help you to make an educated guess about many groups, but in practice even experienced Net users often have to experiment. It is not at all obvious what *cns.cbd.cbd-30* is about, for example. Often the only way to find out is to subscribe to the group and read a selection of messages – and even then it is not always clear.

To make matters worse, some groups flicker into life and then die again even though their names remain on the list. A group may be popular for a year or so, and then the messages dwindle till only spam (Usenet's equivalent of junk mail) remains. After a while postings may reappear, and the group becomes worth reading again. As before, the only way to find out if a group is alive or not is to check whether there are any worthwhile messages in it.

To further add to the confusion, some groups and their names are nothing more than running jokes, while others rely on specialised information that most people cannot be expected to know. An example of the former is *alt.adjective.noun.verb.verb.verb* which – rather bizarrely – consists entirely of postings which start with an adjective, follow it with a noun and add three verbs at the end. When this book was first published, this group was receiving hundreds of postings a week but now unfortunately it seems to have become another ghost group.

An example of the latter is the groups in the *alt.2600* collection, which is the home of various hackers who like to abuse computers and the telephone network. The name comes from the group's history: one particularly famous hacker discovered that a toy whistle, given away in a packet of cereal, produced a sound at 2600Hz when he tried blowing through it into a telephone receiver. 2600Hz happened to be the pitch of the signalling tones used by the telephone exchanges of the time to allow free calls. He then passed on this information to other hackers who started getting free calls in the same way, and the number passed into hacker folklore. This kind of obscurity is typical of some parts of Usenet.

Finding interesting groups

Fortunately, there are more direct ways to find useful groups than reading through the full list of names. Most newsreading software includes a search facility which can pick out groups that contain a particular word, or keyword. It is useful to do some lateral thinking when trying this. For example, when looking for 'hi-fi' you should also check for 'audio' and other synonyms.

Many web search engines also include the ability to search through archived newsgroup postings. These are invaluable when you are looking for conversations about a certain subject. Deja News

CASE HISTORY – David

David Payne decided to get an Internet connection installed at home. His first project was to find out the whereabouts of an old friend with whom he hadn't been in touch for over seven years.

'Paul likes to play with computers, so I thought that there was a good chance he would also be on-line. Fortunately, he also has an unusual surname.

'It actually took only a few minutes. I used Deja News to search for his surname, and it came back with a long list of his newsgroup postings. He'd changed his email address halfway through the list, but it was obvious which was the most recent because Deja News shows the date and time of each posting as well as the subject, the newsgroup and the author.

'He was a little surprised to hear from me, but we met up recently and it was great to see him again.'

(*www.deja.com*) is the best-known service. In addition, some of the web search facilities such as Yahoo! (*www.yahoo.com*) and AltaVista (*www.altavista.com*) include an option for looking through newsgroup archives.

All the search engines work the same way, offering simple searches for occurrences of a certain word or postings by a certain person. More sophisticated options can make a search more specific by including or excluding certain newsgroups, or by looking for postings sent between two particular dates.

Finally, if you want to see what a group is about, you can read its FAQ (Frequently Asked Questions document), if it has one (see page 12). FAQs can be invaluable for finding information or getting practical help about a subject. They are also available on the Web (search for the words 'FAQ finder' using any search engine).

Getting the best from groups

To get the most from newsgroups, it is vital to be familiar with Usenet's own peculiar culture, and, in particular, the culture in any group that you may be interested in. Some groups are much more polite and mature than others, so watch a group for a while to see how it functions.

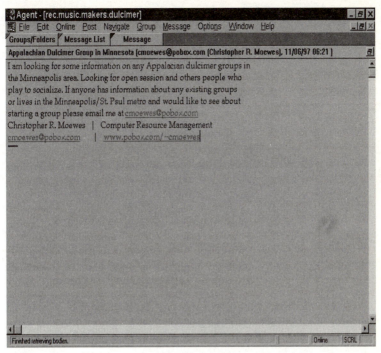

Individual messages in groups can be long and involved, or they can be short and to the point.
Here is a typical example. Note the included email address and web site URL.

Following are some useful dos and don'ts:

- **Do** read a group's messages before joining in. If you are looking for support or information, you will be able to see immediately if this is the right group for you. You can also gauge the atmosphere of a group, identify dominant personalities who may be either a problem or particularly qualified to help, and find out what kind of subjects make the other members of the group react in a hostile way.
- **Do** read the FAQ list if there is one. It will be posted at least monthly, and more probably weekly. If there does not seem to be one, it can be worth posting. 'Is there an FAQ anywhere?'
- **Do** read the charter, if one is posted. It is a formal statement of what the group is about and a summary of the kind of postings that are and are not acceptable. Charters are sometimes ignored once a group has started to thrive, but if one is available it helps to be familiar with it.

- **Do** keep calm under pressure and avoid taking things personally. Even if someone is being intensely annoying, it is best not to get drawn into arguments. If you familiarise yourself with the group before posting you will know who to be wary of. It is possible to make a mistake and ask for information in a way that annoys people. If you have done this, do not try to defend your position, as this will usually make matters worse. It is better simply to ignore the abuse and leave the group. If the mistake was genuine and you want to remain a part of the group, a brief apology can sometimes help. But, otherwise, getting involved in any violent verbal exchange – known as a 'flame war' (see page 102) – is usually a waste of time.

- **Do** edit other people's posts when replying. Reproducing a 500-line message in its entirety with a single short comment at the end is a guaranteed way to annoy people. As with email, it is common practice to leave in only the paragraphs or comments to which you are referring.

- **Do** keep it clear who is responsible for which comment when editing. It should remain obvious who said what, even if some of their comments have been pruned.

- **Do** use software that lets you read and write newsgroup postings off-line (see page 40). Trying to read newsgroup messages on-line is a guaranteed way to run up a huge telephone bill. Plenty of the better software works off-line. If you plan to do more than dabble with Usenet it is well worth either buying a good newsreader or copying one from the Net.

- **Do not** post the same message to more than one newsgroup unless it is absolutely essential. This is known as 'cross posting' and is not popular. Cross posting can start a conversation that spreads between groups, rather than remaining within the boundaries of individual ones. This can make it hard to follow the conversation that results, and also tends to increase the chances of a violent argument breaking out. If you receive a message that has already been posted to numerous groups, you can trim the header list (see page 243) so that your reply is sent to only one or two. Typically, software shows a list of the groups that a message appears in, and to trim the headers you simply delete all but one or two groups from this list.

- **Do not** post impassioned comments unless you want a backlash. It is a curious feature of Usenet that people respond more to the tone of a post than its contents. Even if your point of view is valid and you can marshal an encyclopaedia of facts to support it, impassioned rhetoric will infuriate some people.

- **Do not** reply immediately when someone has annoyed you. It is always better to write vitriolic ripostes but wait until the next day to send them. This gives you a chance to calm down, and then decide whether or not to send a more moderate response instead.

- **Do not** be tempted to edit someone else's posts creatively by changing words, adding new ones, or leaving some out. This is acceptable only in a handful of non-serious groups when it is done as a joke and is obvious. Otherwise, it is almost guaranteed to attract a flurry of rude messages.

- **Do not** sell anything in a newsgroup unless you are sure that it is acceptable to do so. Listing a pointer to a web site that tells everyone about you, and perhaps the products or services you offer, will not annoy anyone, whereas posting a three-page advertisement in a group which does not welcome them certainly will. Private sales seem to be more acceptable, but, again, only certain groups allow them.

- **Do not** post the wrong kind of information. If a group is for text-only messages, posting your holiday snaps to it will not endear you to the group. Similarly, if a group is dedicated to 'for sale' advertisements, having a discussion about something profound will irritate some people.

Good newsreaders software can also make a big difference to the ease and efficiency with which you can read and post Usenet messages. Look out for the following features:

- **Killfiles** These are filters that 'kill' (remove) certain messages according to rules that you specify. You can kill postings from particular authors, about certain subjects, or any other type of messages according to set specifications.

- **Off-line newsreading** If you use a browser for reading messages in newsgroups, you will have to read them on-line, with your telephone connection running and the phone bill increasing. Off-line reading facilities copy the most recent set of messages to your computer in one go, enabling you to break the connection and then read and reply to them at your leisure.

- **Email facilities** It is usually better to use a proper email package for email, but situations will arise in which you will want to write a follow-up to a newsgroup posting with a private message. Having email facilities included in the newsreading software makes this much easier.

- **News management facilities** Most newsgroup software includes an 'expire' option that deletes old messages after a certain period of time – without this your computer's entire filing space will fill up. It is also useful to have a 'keep' option which marks messages that are of particular interest, so you can keep them permanently without needing to copy and file them by hand. This feature also enables you to organise interesting messages, for example, filing them in folders under different subject headings.

- **Web links** URLs can appear in newsgroup postings. A useful feature of the best software is the ability to start a web browser and pass the URL to it automatically when you click on it, so the relevant web page appears automatically.

- **Threads** Messages are arranged into 'threads' – a long list of all the messages that refer to the same subject. Good newsreaders can show these threads, making it easier to follow one particular conversation all the way through. Some software even shows threads diagrammatically and indicates who has responded to whose comments.

- **Customisation** This facility allows you to change the colour, style and size of text to suit your screen and personal preferences, and also to change the way that unread and read messages appear. (For example, unread messages could be purple and read messages could be blue.)

Trolls, troublemakers, spam, scams and killfiles

Trolls are Usenet's equivalent of an April Fool joke, except that they can happen at any time of year. A troll is a posting that is deliberately provocative or outrageous and is intended to make anyone who responds to it look stupid.

They are not always easy to spot, however. Some postings that look like trolls are actually quite serious, while others that can appear serious are really trolls. A good rule of thumb is to ignore anything that looks too outrageous to be believable.

Troublemakers are a common problem on Usenet. These people repeatedly get into arguments or continue the same arguments for years on end. They are usually quite easy to spot, especially in the more popular groups, as there will be a crowd of angry buzzing messages around their postings.

The best way to deal with troublemakers is to ignore them. They thrive on attention, usually of the negative kind, and getting into an argument with them is a waste of time and quite stressful. It is hard for beginners to appreciate just how nerve-racking an electronic argument can be. More experienced users, who have learned this the hard way, refuse to be drawn in, no matter how outrageous or offensive the troublemaker becomes.

Spam is Usenet's equivalent of junk mail and is a perennial nuisance on Usenet. It is postings which are made to thousands of groups at the same time advertising goods and services. There is a constant battle between the people who send it – known as 'spammers' – and everyone else. Spammers are usually marketing and sales people who cannot resist the opportunity to send messages to a captive audience of millions for very little outlay. The best way to deal with spam is to use a good killfile (see below).

Scams are postings that claim to offer you instant wealth. They can usually be recognised by subject lines such as '$$$$$FAST CASH NOW!!!$$$$$'. These are electronic versions of the pyramid schemes that have been illegal for a few years, and have been given a new lease of life by the huge number of potential victims available on the Internet. The idea is that you recruit a number of other victims, each of whom sends you some cash. They, in turn, recruit others, keep some of their cash and send you the rest, and so on. The problem is that at the bottom of the chain you get nothing and can lose a lot of money. Participating in these schemes is outside the law. David Rhodes, who is often quoted in the preamble attached to these scams, was sentenced for fraud.

Killfiles are the solution for most Usenet problems. For anyone who uses Usenet regularly, a killfile option is not a luxury, it is essential. A properly set-up killfile can remove almost all of the most annoying and irrelevant postings that users are likely to come across, and make the experience of Usenet much more pleasurable and useful.

Special groups

Most newsgroups are used exclusively for text messages, but other types of information can also be posted on Usenet. Although the technology used to do this is not particularly sophisticated, millions of non-text messages are sent every day. These messages are segregated into special groups because they cannot be read in the usual way.

These groups pose a serious problem for the Internet because they take up valuable computer time and space that could be better used for other activities. Non-text information is very bulky, and as the volume increases, the whole Internet slows down. This may yet prove to have disastrous consequences. Some experts have warned that the whole Internet may collapse and have to be rebuilt from scratch. Whether or not this happens remains to be seen. For now, non-text groups are something of a liability on the Internet – even if they are extremely popular.

Non-text information is sent to Usenet using a system very similar to that used to add attachments to email. All non-text messages are known as 'binaries', although – rather confusingly – the name is also used to describe groups with certain kinds of content, specifically pictures, video clips, and sound clips.

If you try to read one of these messages as text, you will see a very long string of gibberish. To make sense of this, you need to 'decode' it (see Chapter 7). As with email, the better software does this for you automatically. It can also automatically start a 'viewer', a piece of software which will display the information in the most suitable way, for example, as a picture on the screen for images, in a small video window for video, and so on.

The main difference between binaries and attachments is that binary files are almost always sent in multiple parts. A typical binary appears like this: *<description> Some picture.type 1/5*. The first part, <description>, is a very short descriptive phrase, for example 'Balinese temple dancer'. 'Some picture' is the name of the image as it appears in your computer – perhaps 'BALIDANCER'. 'Type' is the type of information: for images and photographs it will usually be 'GIF' or 'JPG'. These are popular image formats that can be viewed on most computers. The '1/5' means that the message has been sent in five parts and this is the first message of five. Somewhere else in the group you will find '2/5', '3/5', and so on.

Usenet's unreliability can cause serious problems for binaries: not only do parts often arrive out of sequence, but sometimes one or more go missing. Out-of-sequence binaries are not usually a problem – the better newsreaders can automatically rearrange them, and at worst it is possible to cut and paste the sections together by hand before decoding them. But if a section is missing, the binary is ruined. When this happens it is acceptable in some groups to post a message that says 'Please re-post parts 1 and 2', for example. In others it is not. This depends on the culture of the group.

Sometimes a 'part 0' is posted. This is a short text message that introduces the binary and explains what it contains, both technically so that readers can decide which viewer software to use, and descriptively. A typical photograph can take a minute or so to appear, while a short video clip may take an hour or more.

Copying binaries from Usenet to your computer can be very time-consuming. A typical photograph may take a few minutes to appear, and a short video clip a couple of hours or more. This makes the binary groups expensive and of limited interest, except for those who are passionately interested in the content. However, binaries will become more popular as connection speeds increase.

The easiest way to work with binaries is to use good newsreading software. Without it, they can be too cumbersome to be worthwhile. With it, the whole process becomes very streamlined. For sources of software, see Appendix 7.

Binaries groups

Groups that have the word 'binaries' appear in two ways: either as a group (or collection of groups) that stands alone; or as a group associated with another group used for text messages. The 'catch-all' binaries group is *alt.binaries* Typically, someone will post a message to a text group saying something relevant to the discussion and explaining that they have copied a corresponding picture, for example, to *alt.binaries* Readers can then view the picture if they are interested in it, or ignore it if they are not.

As a rule, text and binaries are kept as strictly segregated as possible, and it is another unwritten Usenet 'law' that messages of one kind are not welcome in a group created for the other. This helps make the information clearer for everyone, although inevitably some people ignore the distinction, much to everyone else's annoyance.

Warez

The 'warez' ('wares') groups are the other family of binaries groups. They are best avoided because they are part of an illegal subculture on the Net that offers 'free' software. This has been pirated and is then posted for everyone in the group to use. *This software is not legal.* If you are caught with it on your computer you may be liable for prosecution.

If you try posting warez software, it is very easy for the software company in question to get your name and address from your post by obtaining the details from your ISP. Even disguising your message (see page 146) will not stop the company from finding your details. ISPs keep records of who posts what, when, and from where, and can be asked to reveal them to the software company or the police.

Another reason why you should avoid warez software is because it is often infected with viruses. You should always use a virus checker on any software you copy from the Internet, no matter where it comes from.

In addition, warez people are generally very aggressive and abusive, which again makes visiting these groups unpleasant. They use a language of their own called EliTe (the capitalisation is deliberate) which is a warped form of English that is hard for most people to understand.

'Newsgroups' on on-line services

CompuServe and AOL offer their own Usenet-like systems, although these work slightly differently from Usenet newsgroups. (Note that if you use an on-line service you can use these proprietary systems as well as Usenet itself.)

Instead of appearing as a collection of groups in a long list, these 'forums', 'discussion areas' or 'message boards' are usually linked to other related information. For example, a feature about alternative health will typically include a message board where people can swap their experiences and offer help and advice.

As with Usenet, the quality of information may vary from group to group, and a number of discussions that appear can be patchy. However, they are far less prone to name-calling than Usenet groups, and people seem much less keen to take centre stage and present their opinions forcefully. On the other hand, discussions can lack some of the vibrancy of their equivalents on Usenet. Each group has a relatively small number of regular contributors; people seem to visit a group only once or twice before moving on. Temporary visitors to Usenet newsgroups, however, tend to read a group without contributing anything.

Another important difference is that the low volume of messages means that some boards have comments that are a year or two old. As they do not have a formal expiry system, messages remain until they are deleted by the system's administrators – not a regular occurrence – or until the system suffers a technical failure and loses some of its archives. At best, this can make a board a fascinating historical archive, but at worst you have hundreds of messages to look through before you find the most recent and most interesting ones; and many of the original contributors are no longer with the service. (Note that the information in these areas is not archived by any of the Usenet archiving services.)

The great strength of on-line services is that they can offer technical support from various companies. Many computer companies have message areas on these services which relate specifically to their products, and these are read by their support staff. They give you a direct line to someone who knows the product and can answer questions about it. If you do not understand the answer, you can ask another question. Because the interchange is public, companies are aware that getting the answer wrong or appearing to be unhelpful in some other way is bad public relations. The exchange is much more direct than it would be on Usenet, which has a 'non-commercial' ethic that has made it impossible for companies to set up the same kind of service on it.

Because on-line service providers and Usenet offer such different services, they are complementary rather than competitive. The ideal situation would be to have access to both. Usenet is best for 'informal' support and debate. Groups have a much wider range of contributors, and the existence of FAQs (see page 12) is helpful. The on-line services are better for the 'formal' support mentioned above. When a Usenet-like group of regulars appears on an on-line service, it is usually much more tightly knit and dedicated than those found on Usenet. It is also easier to find related information, because the groups are closely associated with libraries of software, live chat and other resources.

Chapter 6

Internet secrets: people and culture

The Internet has a language all of its own. Because it is not possible to convey tone of voice or facial expression, various novel ways of communicating emotion and personality have evolved.

The Internet also has a culture of its own. People who use the Net seem to have more unconventional interests and values and express themselves differently. Any newcomers to the Net may find all of this bewildering, so what follows is a guide to those aspects of Internet life that are most daunting to inexperienced users.

Learning the language

Although English is the most widely used language on the Internet, it has been extended to include a variety of expressions and novel forms of punctuation which are not used anywhere else. The language also has certain conventions. These are used in much the same way that 'Dear Sir/Yours faithfully', for example, is used in letters.

Smileys and emoticons

Without the nuance of tone of voice, or the visual impact of body language, on-line conversations can easily give the wrong impression. To compensate for this, many Internet regulars add extra characters to their email messages and live chat to show what they are feeling.

These characters, known as smileys (and occasionally as emoticons – but apparently only in Internet books and never on the Internet itself) are made by combining punctuation marks to draw a picture. Of the hundreds of possible smileys, only a handful are used regularly:

:-) **Happy smiley** Used when someone is laughing, is happy, or has made a joke

:-(**Sad smiley** Used when someone is unhappy

;-) **Winking smiley** Used for sarcastic, ironic or flirtatious comments

;-(**Crying smiley** Used when someone is very unhappy

:) **Shorthand happy smiley**

:(**Shorthand unhappy smiley**

;-> **Biting smiley** Used for a very sarcastic comment.

:o) **Open-mouthed happy smiley**

:o(**Open-mouthed unhappy smiley**

Some can be emphasised by repeating them. So :)))))))))))) is a very happy smiley indeed. People either love smileys or hate them. In some of the UK newsgroups smileys are considered to be very un-English and rather gauche. (The reasoning is that people have managed to write to each other without smileys for centuries and do not see why they should start adding them now.) In other newsgroups, and in many emails, smileys are both popular and welcome.

Another way of expressing emotion is to spell out actions and comments between angle brackets, thus: <grin>, <sigh>, and so on. More popular examples are often shortened to single letters: <grin> to <g>. Actions are much more versatile than smileys and can be used to express anything: <kick>, <fires gun>, <opens window>, and so on. Some people use a more formal version; the letters 'fx' are added after the first angle bracket. This is short for 'effects' but again indicates an action: <fx: writes Internet book>.

Another similar convention is to put 'emotions' in pairs:

```
<bored>

That's really very interesting indeed.

</bored>
```

This is based on HTML, the system used to create web pages (see Appendix 5). The words in angle brackets work like a sophisticated form of punctuation, which sets the tone or emotion for the words they bracket. They apply to whatever text is written between them and are often used ironically. The first word 'turns on' the emotion and the last word (after the slash) shows where the emotion stops.

Adding emphasis

ON THE INTERNET, WRITING IN CAPITALS IS CONSIDERED SHOUTING. Although this is a rather arbitrary convention, using upper-case letters all the way through an email or newsgroup message can make the text hard to read and is considered rude. But capitalising a single word or phrase is a good way to add emphasis.

In print, emphasis can be added by putting words or phrases in italic or bold text. This is not possible on the Internet. To create the same effect words are placed between characters to give them extra weight, thus: /italics/ and *bold*. As with real italics, these effects are best used sparingly.

Abbreviations

Internet users tend to abbreviate common phrases to acronyms. These can be very confusing for newcomers because often there is no easy way to guess what the abbreviations mean. Popular examples include:

AFAIK	As far as I know
BFN	Bye for now
BRB	Be right back (used for on-line chat)
BTW	By the way
DK	Don't know
FOAD	Please leave quickly and quietly (or words to that effect)
FYI	For your information
DIMU	Did I mess up? (or misunderstand?)
HAND	Have a nice day
HTH	Hope this helps (not always meant literally)
IIRC	If I remember correctly
IMHO	In my humble opinion
IMNSHO	In my not so humble opinion
IMO	In my opinion
ISTR	I seem to remember
ITYMTP	I think you missed the point

IYSWIM	If you see what I mean
LOL	Laughing out loud
MOTAS	Member of the alternate sex
MOTOS	Member of the opposite sex
MOTSS	Member of the same sex
OTOH	On the other hand
POV	Point of view
ROTFL	Rolling on the floor laughing ('That was very funny.')
RTFM	Read the ******* manual
SO	Significant other
TLA	Three letter acronym
TTFN	Ta ta for now
YMMV	Your mileage may vary (i.e. your experience may be different)

In some quarters the more extrovert abbreviations, such as ROTFL, are considered gauche, but the less colourful ones, such as IMO, are used regularly by everyone.

During on-line chat, words are sometimes abbreviated to single letters. For example 'How are you?' becomes 'How r u?', 'Oh I see' becomes 'o i c', and so on. (Punctuation and capitalisation are often rather arbitrary when chatting, and it's not unusual for some people to type entirely in lower case.)

A popular newsgroup and mailing list convention is 'Ob:<some word>'. This is short for 'obligatory', and is used (ironically) to denote a comment which is relevant to the group after a long off-topic digression. For example, on a music mailing list someone who has just spent three paragraphs discussing the price of herbal tea might add 'ob:music' followed by a few lines of something more appropriate.

Sigs

A 'sig' – short for signature – is a short piece of text that is added automatically to each of your email or newsgroup postings by your software. Almost all software includes this facility, although you do not have to make use of it. You type the text that you want to appear into a designated space, and it will then appear at the end of your messages until you decide to remove or change it.

Sigs are used to include jokes, electronic and 'real life' contact details, URLs of personal web pages, and so on. They tend to appeal to novices who have not yet tired of the constant repetition of a sig. More experienced users tend either not to use them at all or to keep them very simple.

In certain newsgroups, long sigs are guaranteed to attract unwelcome attention. A 'rule' states that no sig should be more than four lines long, and some people – including whole newsgroups – will be very aggressive towards someone who has one that is longer than this. (An entire newsgroup – *alt.fan.warlord* – is devoted to the ruthless verbal abuse of people with long sigs.) The rationale is that long sigs waste Internet resources while they are copied from place to place. But given the huge volume of information that moves across the Internet every day, the truth is that this is often no more than an excuse used by some people wanting to pick a fight.

However, it is still a good idea to show consideration for other Internet users when creating a sig. The four-line rule can usually be relaxed slightly if some of the lines use spacer characters such as '-' and '|' to draw boxes. Very long sigs, especially drawings and sketches made out of letters (known as ASCII art), are definitely frowned upon. You should also avoid preaching, religious sigs of whatever denomination or belief, or anything that looks too much like aggressive self-promotion.

Below is an example of a sig that is unlikely to be popular:

```
                               \ _ /
                            -= ( _ ) =-
                               / | \
    .\/\/.              ,\/,   ,\/.//,                        ,~
   /o//o\\ ,.,.,  //o\ /o\\o\\                        |\
    |  |  /###/#\    |    |  |                         /|  \
    |  |  |' '|:|   |`=.='| |                         /_|__\
^^^^^^^^^^^^^^^^^^^^^^^^^^^^^^^^^^^^^^""""""""""""~~~~~~~~~~~~~~~~~~
   Tina Moriarty  Receptionist  email~ reception@anycorp.com
   Anycorporation   1234 Any Ave,  ZA 72043   215-1234-567
```

But this one will not cause offence to anyone:

```
Richard Wentk    Freelance Widget Services
richard@acompany.com http://www.acompany.com/rjw
```

Although the former may seem considerably more interesting and colourful, at least initially, it causes problems in two ways. The first is that long sigs become less and less appealing with constant repetition.

Once someone has seen a sig like this a few hundred times, the novelty value will have worn off completely.

The second is that it does not work on certain computer screens. On some computers, letters on the screen are all exactly the same width (fixed pitch fonts), while on others the widths vary (variable pitch fonts) to create a more natural effect. A sig that works well on one kind of screen will look incomprehensible on another:

```
                        \ _ /
                       -= (_) =-
                        / \
    .\/\.        ,\/,  ,\./,              ,~
   /o//o\\ ,.,.  //o\ /o\\o\\             |\
   | | /###/#\   | | |                   /| \
   | | |' '|:|  |`=.='| |               /_|__\
  ^^^^^^^^^^^^^^^^^^^^^^^^^^^^^^^^^^^^^"""""""""~~~~~~~~~~~~~~

   Tina Moriarty  Receptionist  email:reception@anycorp.com
   Anycorporation  1234 Any Ave,  ZA 72043  215-1234-567
```

A good way to make a sig more interesting is to include a link to your personal web site. You can put as much information as you like on these pages, and people can choose whether or not they want to read it. Another option is to use 'sig switching' shareware (the ideas behind shareware are described on page 259) which selects a different quote or comment from a long list for every message you post.

Sig regulars

Although sigs vary, certain ideas are used frequently. The first idea is the 'standard disclaimer'. For legal reasons, company employees who post from a company account are often asked to include a line that says 'This posting is my personal opinion and not in any way that of the company'. This has led to a spate of jokes and puns in sigs about who owns opinions, who pays for them, whether or not they can be hired for a trial period, and so on. The shortest example of a joke is: *#include <disclaimer.h>* which is programmer-speak for 'Include the standard disclaimer that everyone uses here'. (It is a feature of Internet culture that terms and ideas that come from computer programming are very popular, both in sigs and in Internet humour in general.)

Another sig standard is the 'geek code'. This is a shorthand way of summing up the personality, interests, and even the current romantic status of the author of a message. A typical example looks like this:

```
V3.12 GM/CS d s:++ a- C++ U+ p L !E W++ N++ o+ K W- O?
M- V- PS? PE? Y PGP- t- !5 X- R- !tv b+++ DI+ D- G e++++ h- r
z++
```

Each letter indicates something about the author, and the number of pluses or minuses shows how strongly this information applies. The '!' indicates that this particular interest is avoided, and the 'v 3.12' at the start shows that this information is shown using version 3.12 of the geek code.

In the example, 'a-' means the writer is aged between 25 and 29, the 'N++' means 'I read so many newsgroups that the next batch of news comes in before I finish reading the last batch, and I have to read for about 2 hours straight before I'm caught up on the morning's news. Then there's the afternoon...,' and 't-' means the writer is not a *Star Trek* enthusiast. The geek code is maintained by Robert Hayden, and details of the latest version, including a description of what all the letters mean, are available at *krypton.mankato.msus.edu/~hayden/geek.html* The code has spawned a number of variations, and it is likely that more and more of these will appear as the Internet increases in popularity.

Rot13

Rot13 is an old Internet tradition used to disguise messages of a dubious or potentially offensive nature. It is a very simple code – each letter in a message is shifted 13 letters to the right, so that 'A' becomes 'N', 'B' becomes 'O', and so on. To read the original message the letters are shifted back. Letters that fall off the end of the alphabet are rotated back via 'A'; hence its name – Rotate 13.

Most newsgroup software includes a Rot13 feature. Its use is generally announced in most messages in plain English before the block of disguised text. If you see a message that looks like a random collection of letters arranged in words and sentences, it is likely that it has been encoded with Rot13.

Flames

Flames are verbal abuse. For some reason, on certain parts of Usenet flaming is considered to be an acceptable, even worthy activity. The most serious flames escalate from newsgroups to private email. Flames do not follow any set rules, and most are not very sophisticated. In fact, the vast majority simply say 'I think you're really stupid', in various more or less colourful ways. A flame war is simply a major outbreak of flaming (the word can also be used as a verb in this way) between two or more Internet users.

Net culture

Some email addresses have much more credibility than others on the Internet. They are judged by the 'domain name' – the part of the address that appears after the '@' sign and identifies which business, institution, ISP or on-line service someone is using. Some domains are widely thought to be the homes of troublemakers. Others are not popular because their users rightly or wrongly have been stereotyped as being 'clueless'. (On the Internet, being called 'clueless' is the worst insult that can be levelled at someone. It implies an embarrassingly naive gullibility, a lack of tact and understanding of Internet culture, and ignorance about the technology.) Some people go so far as to killfile all messages that come from these domains.

The main implication is that beginners should choose their ISP or on-line service carefully. However, the prejudice against the less popular services can be surmounted, and if you contribute to discussions in an intelligent way you will eventually be welcomed as 'one of the crowd'.

The distinction between 'undesirable' and other addresses has its roots in the history of the Internet. Politically, there are two groups on-line and these exist in a state of perpetual tension. The first group comprises the old-timers, the academics and the administrators of the Internet's computers. The other consists of the ordinary users – everyone else. This second group includes a surprising spread of social groups and people with varying interests, including a significant number of users at or near retirement age (who have the time to explore the Net), and a much larger number of women. Originally, this group consisted mainly of students and – mostly male – computer professionals, but this has now changed dramatically.

Initially, the Internet was not designed for the general public. Because of this its original users sometimes show resentment towards the newcomers, whom they see as interlopers, especially if they do not understand the system or show no enthusiasm about computer technology. From this point of view, the Net can be unashamedly elitist – an exclusive gathering of technocrats who would prefer the system to remain as it was in the early 1990s, before the general public started using it.

These original users left their mark on the culture of the Internet in two ways. The first is Usenet's intolerance of commerce. The Net was built as a not-for-profit facility which was subsidised with public money. Because of this, no one is supposed to use the Net for private gain, and doing so is seen as an immoral abuse of the system. This is one reason why 'spam' (see page 91) is considered such an outrage. It is not simply an irritation but a deliberate misuse of public resources. The second is to do with the limited resources that were originally available. 'Bandwidth' – the Internet's ability to carry information – was scarce, and activities that wasted it were frowned upon.

To some extent both of these ideals are being marginalised as the Net 'goes public'. Large amounts of bandwidth are now wasted every day on completely trivial activities. The Web is not particularly efficient, and, to make matters worse, many web publishers are now experimenting with sound and video, which can use hundreds of times as much bandwidth as text does. At the same time, the most popular newsgroups are also being used to exchange binaries of a distinctly dubious nature (see page 93), and again these take up inordinate amounts of bandwidth and so waste resources. Flat-rate pricing for users encourages this abuse. The situation is even worse in the USA, where local calls cost a nominal amount, and anyone can create a permanent Internet connection for themselves by installing a separate telephone line and leaving it constantly connected to his or her computer.

To summarise, the Net is changing and shifting from an environment in which users impress each other with their intelligence, knowledge and computer skills, to one that is more open and to which anyone can contribute. The uses to which the Net is put are also changing – less time is spent on research, and more time is spent on mundane activities such as chatting and shopping.

However, the qualities and values that have influenced Net culture remain the same. These are discussed below:

- **Constant innovation** Both Netscape and Microsoft have released new versions of their software annually, adding major new features each time. Older versions of the software do not show sites that make use of these new features correctly.

- **Pranks and practical jokes** The Internet has a tradition of pranks and practical jokes which are designed to make the unwary and inexperienced look stupid. A typical example is newsgroup 'wars', in which one group decides to invade and subvert another. These campaigns can be quite subtle. The invaders start by posting peculiar, but not quite unbelievable, messages to the target group. Then they try to engage their victims in a flame war, either by insulting them or appearing to be so ridiculous that they draw insults themselves. Finally, they instill paranoia by slandering their victims and trying to get them to mistrust each other. Once the group has dissolved in flames and recriminations they announce themselves and say words to the effect of: 'Well, don't take it so seriously – we were only joking'. Some – although fortunately not many – web sites have similar 'gotchas'. This kind of humour is very widespread on the Net.

- **Frank and vigorous debate** At best Internet debates can be fruitful and interesting: for example, *uk.politics* has changed the voting intentions of quite a few people during its short life. But at worst they can degenerate into name-calling and abuse. There is an Internet 'rule' – only half tongue-in-cheek – which suggests that as soon as one person accuses the other of being a Nazi, the debate ends. More experienced users know how to avoid getting into an argument that gets this heated but often only because they have learned what to avoid the hard way. Debate is always informal and people show their private faces much more than they might in the letters pages of a newspaper or in a live radio phone-in. Sometimes the language in debates is frank and explicit. While this may shock some people, these debates provide perhaps a more accurate picture of how most people really are than the rather formal and stylised pictures that appear in the traditional mass media.

- **Tolerance for unconventional ideas** Some of the information available on Usenet and the Web is remarkable by anyone's standards. It is possible to find automatic Shakespearean insult generators, shops that advertise time machines (guarantee not included), big red buttons that do nothing at all, galleries of grotesque art, lists of the contents of people's desks, and even stranger things. Anyone who does not have an open mind or an appreciation for surreal humour may find Net culture difficult to come to terms with. It is possible to avoid these quirkier facets of life on-line by using only email, and ignoring the Web and newsgroups. However, most people would consider this to be something of a waste.

- **Rough justice** Anyone who infringes the unwritten rules of the Internet, such as using Usenet for commercial purposes – especially knowingly and deliberately – can expect retaliation. Net technology can be used in offensive and aggressive ways (such as those discussed in Chapter 8), and these can cause a lot of inconvenience to anyone who finds themselves on the receiving end. Because no central authority exists, there is no one to give a final verdict on what is and is not acceptable. ISPs and on-line services have the last-resort option of 'pulling someone's account' – denying them a service, with prejudice. But individuals and groups also take the law into their own hands at times. Fortunately, random attacks are rare, happening mainly to celebrities, and mistakes and flame wars on Usenet do not usually lead to more than a heated exchange.

Survival tips

A number of other on-line survival tactics can prevent unpleasant experiences. All of these are very straightforward but can help avoid some of the more common and petty annoyances of on-line life.

Local variations

One curiosity of the Internet is that it cannot cope with certain letters or characters. Unfortunately, one of them is the UK pound sign '£'. This character appears differently on various computer systems and can cause a number of other problems. To get round this, an acronym for 'UK pounds' – 'ukp' – is generally used instead. This can be read correctly on any computer.

A similar problem will be caused by the symbol for the Euro when it starts to be widely used. So far no acronym has appeared, although there is no doubt that one will – if only because many computer systems have no ways of showing the correct symbol.

Another source of confusion is the difference between UK and US date formats. In the UK dates are always shown as day/month/year. In the USA they appear as month/day/year. It is also helpful to remember that many UK words have completely different meanings in the USA – and *vice versa*. Again, these differences can be a source of confusion or embarrassment, depending on the circumstances.

Staying out of trouble

All ISPs and on-line services have a document called an Acceptable Use Policy (AUP) or Conditions of Service (COS), which lists in detail what is and is not acceptable on the service. The content of these documents is not particularly controversial – they consist mostly of commonsense requests not to waste Internet resources or harass other users. Typical points in an AUP are:

- do not attempt to send spam or junk mail, especially for profit
- do not attempt to hack into the ISP's computer systems
- do not attempt to forge email or otherwise misrepresent yourself
- do not attempt to annoy other users in any way.

ISPs differ in the severity with which they treat transgressions. Some will – remarkably – turn a blind eye, even if they have had complaints from other users. Others will terminate their agreement with a user as soon as trouble is reported. It should go without saying that it is best to respect the guidelines in these documents.

Dealing with junk mail on Usenet

Junk mail is unwanted and unsolicited email that advertises a product or service. It can be a serious problem for anyone who posts regularly to Usenet or subscribes to on-line services. It is sent by companies who use the Internet's search facilities to find the email addresses of their intended victims. Once the companies have a list, they simply mail the same message to everyone on it. This can be a good way for them to generate new business. Even if only a tiny proportion of people reply, they will still get more leads for less effort than with almost any other advertising technique. Unfortunately, for most of the Internet population junk mail is simply a nuisance.

It is possible to avoid it. On Usenet, many people now post using a false address, for example by adding an extra word such as 'nojunkmail', together with a message in their sig that explains that this word should be removed. This is very quick and easy – the false address is set in the newsreading software the usual way. For example, instead of *sara@sara.demon.co.uk* the address would be *sara@nojunkmail. sara.demon.co.uk* Almost any extra words can be added. For best results, use a word that doesn't include 'spam', as the address-collection software used by spammers has become intelligent enough to filter out obvious spam-blocking additions. The object of the exercise is to deliberately create a bad address, so that mail sent to it is not delivered to your mailbox. However, it can be helpful to use a word that makes it clear that the address has been modified in some way so that legitimate readers will be reminded to remove it before they attempt to send you email.

With this technique, the unwanted mail will usually be sent straight back to the sender. If enough people did this, junk mailers would be deluged with a flood of returned mail. Unfortunately, some are clever enough to use false addresses of their own. Instead of coming back to plague them, the returned mail disappears into a black hole on the Internet, having wasted the resources of various computers along the way.

Note that even if you do everything you can to keep your email address off the spammers' lists, this still doesn't guarantee that you will receive no spam at all. The latest popular tactic is to target popular ISPs and on-line services, such as Hotmail and AOL, and send spam to email addresses that have been created at random electronically. If your address is at all obvious (for example, *mary1@hotmail.com*), spam will still appear in your mailbox, even if you have done everything you can to ensure your privacy.

And so a complementary next step is to use a 'mail kill' facility. This is the email equivalent of a killfile (see page 89), but is available only with mail services that use the POP3 system, explained in Chapter 7. Mail kill gives you the chance to see who has sent you mail before you copy it to your computer. Unwanted mail can be deleted before you waste your time and money copying it and reading it.

Mail kill is not as effective an option as not getting the mail in the first place, which is why it is suggested that anyone who uses Usenet frequently should opt for using a false address. The problem with this approach is that some people find it annoying, because they have to change the address by hand when they want to reply to you.

Another way of dealing with junk mail is to include a piece of legalese in your sig which says something like: 'Unsolicited mail is not welcome. All such mail will be charged a proof-reading fee of £500. The sending of such email constitutes agreement with the terms of this contract.' Some people even go so far as to cite a section of the US legal code to justify their claim. The main problem with this approach is that it does nothing at all to stop the mail. Junk mailers do not bother looking through sigs – they simply collect email addresses automatically, and the software they use ignores the rest of each posting. The other problem is that the legal background to such a claim has yet to be tested in court. If someone takes a junk mailer to court and wins because of non-payment, the whole junk mailing system will collapse very quickly. Unfortunately, this has not happened yet.

One final way of dealing with junk mail or spam is to 'mail bomb' the offender. This means sending them one or more huge and inconvenient messages. Although this may be tempting, it can also be counterproductive. You may incite the person at the other end to return the favour, and even if they do not, you will still be making work for a system administrator, who will have to clear up the mess.

Junk mail on on-line services

Users of on-line services do not have the option of changing their address. In any case, when preparing for a mailing, junk mailers compile on-line users' mail addresses in a slightly different way. Instead of searching through postings in the archives, they create their lists by checking to see who is on-line at any one time, and – where available – by checking user profiles (described on page 122) for keywords. This can mean that the more you use the service, the more likely you are to get junk mail.

On-line services take junk mail seriously and make some attempt to block it at source. This means that their subscribers never see the mail – much of it is deleted *en masse* by the administrators of the service, who use software that checks for multiple postings. Unfortunately, some mail still gets through. However, the software offered by these services enables you to check mail before it is copied to your computer. It is relatively easy to delete junk mail before it wastes any of your time.

Complaining about junk mail and spam
If junk mail and spam are sufficiently annoying, you can send an email complaint to the ISP that seems to be the source of the trouble. Some

ISPs are genuinely unaware that certain customers are abusing their service and are only too happy to be told so that they can terminate the offender's access to the Internet with extreme prejudice. But other junk mailers have direct Internet connections that do not go through an ISP. Any email complaints will go straight to them in person, and they will, of course, ignore them.

To complain, you need to find out which ISP, if any, the offender is using. Sometimes this is obvious – you will be able to tell from his or her return address. Sometimes it is less obvious, especially if an attempt has been made to disguise the name of the ISP used. All countries have a few dozen ISPs which get most of the Internet business between them, and once you start to recognise these you will have a good idea of where to send the complaint.

The complaint itself should be addressed to an administrator at the ISP. The most widely used addresses are
postmaster@(isp's domain name) and *abuse@(isp's domain name)*
To complain, make a copy of the offending message, including all the headers, and add a short note that explains why you think the message is out of line – whether it is spam, junk mail, and so on. A stronger message is not usually required.

Although this appears to be a slightly hit-and-miss method, it can work very well. You will often get a message back explaining that the offender has had his or her access to the Internet revoked. (For more detailed information about headers, and how to find someone's email address if he or she tries to disguise it, see Appendix 6.)

The future of spam

Spam will continue to be a major problem on-line until Draconian steps are taken. According to some estimates, spam now accounts for as much as 10 per cent of all email traffic. In the UK there are no plans to introduce anti-spam legislation. However, it is likely that the only long-term solution to spam will be a legal one, and as more and more people begin to depend on the Internet for their livelihood and for their links with others, appropriate legislation will begin to appear.

Banner ads and 'pop ups'

While spam is an annoyance that can be avoided, at least to some extent, banner ads and pop-ups (tiny web pages produced by services such as Geocities which contain a single advertisement and appear automatically on top of pages that people are trying to see) are a more serious nuisance. Banner ads can make pages very slow, since they are copied from central advertising computers that produce advertising for hundreds of different web sites. These are inevitably overstretched, which means that any page that includes a commercial banner ad takes an extra few seconds to appear while the ad is prepared and displayed. In some cases this delay can be as long as 10 or 20 seconds. Taken individually this is negligible, but over the course of a month or a year of surfing, the impact on a phone bill becomes significant. Because banner ads are 'legal' there is no outcry or public criticism of them. Unfortunately, this doesn't prevent them being a nuisance.

Banner ads can be blocked in a number of ways. Apart from saving money, blocking these ads can make the web appear much faster. Losing a wait of 10 seconds for each web page visited can make browsing a much more pleasant experience. Note that the blocking is entirely legal, and that you have every right to prevent this information appearing on your computer's screen. It is particularly useful for businesses, whose employees would otherwise waste time and money waiting for banner ads to appear.

An example of a banner blocker is available at *www.junkbusters.org* This is a simple, free program that can be started automatically whenever a computer is switched on for the first time. It checks banner ads against a list of banner sources, and simply removes any that it finds. The list of sources supplied with the software is not comprehensive, but can easily be changed. (As a side-effect, this means the program can also be used to filter out unwanted web sites, and make them invisible to children – although note that intelligent older teens will not find it hard to turn off this filtering.) While effective, the software is perhaps a little technical for beginners to set up and use. For information about alternative free or low-cost software that performs a similar task, search the web for 'banner killer'.

Chapter 7

Internet secrets: a technological survival guide

Technology is unavoidable on the Internet. Although it is possible to get by with only a minimal interest in how the Internet works and what it can do, it is helpful to know about the ways in which technology can be used to make life on-line more interesting and productive. At the very least it is useful to know something about the technology in order to 'beat the system', if only to get the least frustration from its quirks and deficiencies.

The Internet is evolving continuously, and some of the facilities discussed below are no longer at the cutting edge. Others are used only by more experienced Internet users. However, all are included here for reference purposes and for the sake of completeness.

Counting the cost – how to make the best of your connection

An Internet connection is rather like a water pipe. The better the connection is and the wider the pipe, the more information that can flow through it. However, all pipes have a limit and once this is reached a backlog forms, and information trying to get through the pipe has to wait. On the Internet, the amount of 'pipe space' that information takes up is known as the bandwidth. Text needs a small bandwidth, still images and sounds need slightly more, and live video needs the most – enough to be impractical for a typical home connection.

Bandwidth is a limited resource. The most central parts of the Internet – which are known as the 'backbone' and connect countries to each other – use extremely fast connections and have plenty of spare bandwidth. However, traffic becomes congested at the slightly slower connections between the backbone and each ISP, and more so again over the much slower links between ISPs and their customers. On-line services tend to have much faster links to the Internet, and faster links within their own systems. However, they also have far more users to contend with simultaneously, and all suffer from obvious speed problems at peak times.

Wasting bandwidth on the Internet is a 'crime', and – as mentioned in Chapter 6 – flagrant misuse can attract unwelcome attention from other users. The source of the problem is that traffic on the Internet has been increasing exponentially since the mid-1990s. Before the Internet became available to the general public, research scientists were able to transfer large amounts of information across it relatively quickly. This is no longer possible, even though the technology has improved and there is more bandwidth. It can now take days to copy information that used to take a few hours.

The Internet has its own 'rush hours', and if you want to minimise delays and perhaps also telephone charges it is useful to know how to avoid them. Most traffic on the Internet comes from the USA, and once the people living on the East Coast start to wake up – at about lunch-time in the UK – it takes noticeably longer to view certain US web sites. By the time those living on the West Coast are awake as well, three hours later, the whole network has slowed down significantly. The situation is made even worse once everyone in the USA leaves work and goes home to check their email, play on IRC and read their favourite newsgroups. By about midnight in the UK it is almost impossible to access some web sites at all. This USA evening rush hour corresponds to peak traffic in the UK, which happens between about 11pm – after the pubs shut – and midnight.

During these peak periods, Internet access can be four or five times slower than during less busy times. Although this applies to web sites in particular, the same can be said, albeit to a lesser extent, about email and newsgroups. Some ISPs have developed a system whereby newsgroup messages are queued during the peak times, and then processed later in the night, when far fewer people are using the service. Similar delays may also apply to email sent during these busy periods, although ISPs tend to make email a priority in an attempt to make sure it gets through quickly.

The Internet is also very busy at weekends. Although corporate traffic is less heavy, there is much more personal information being sent in the form of email and 'after hours' newsgroup contributions. The peak tends to last slightly further into the night than during the week

– people stay on-line longer because they do not need to get up early the next morning.

The best way to avoid the rush is to use the Internet during the early hours of the morning, typically between 3 and 5am, although this is clearly unacceptable for the majority of people. To avoid this problem, many home computer systems, if left switched on, can be set up to send and receive waiting email and newsgroup messages during this period. Windows 95/98, for example, has a 'scheduler' program which can be set up to start email and newsgroup software at a certain time.

The next best option is to do whatever you can to limit the amount of time you use the Internet during the peak periods. For example, email and newsgroup messages will arrive in your computer much more quickly first thing in the morning than last thing in the evening. Even though the telephone charges are higher in the morning, you may find yourself needing to spend less time on-line to get the same information, so that it becomes cheaper overall. Of course, the length of time depends very much on the volume of information involved. It can be useful to time a typical call at both times of day to see which works out cheapest.

Beware of bank holiday telephone rates; depending on which telephone service you use, the costs may be charged at the weekday rate rather than the cheaper weekend rate.

Speeding up your connection

You might think that using the latest fastest modem would be enough to guarantee you the fastest possible connection. The reality is rather different. For web use especially, *the factor that determines the speed of your connection is the speed of your ISP or on-line service*. Tests prove that there are huge differences (up to 500 per cent) between the speeds at which different ISPs can deliver the same information to your computer. This has an obvious effect, both on telephone charges and on the usefulness of the Internet in general. Choosing a fast ISP is very, very important to your overall experience of the Internet (for more information on how to do this, see Appendix 1).

Speeding up email

Although you cannot do anything to make email reach its destination any faster – apart from switching to a different ISP, perhaps one recommended by a friend, if mail seems to be taking far too long – you can improve the speed at which email is transferred to and from your ISP. The speed limit is set by the speed of your connection, and this depends on the hardware used by your computer and your ISP (see Appendix 2). Even with this limit, there are still a number of things you can do to make the most of the speed available.

The first and most important step is to make sure that your email software works off-line (see page 40); this will make a large difference to your monthly bill, and will also provide you with a more relaxed environment in which to read and write messages.

Text messages are very fast to post, and unless you send hundreds at each sitting, the amount of text you send will not make a big difference to your bill. This is not true of attachments. The secret here is to 'compress' attachments before sending them. A common solution is to use software such as PKZIP to squeeze the information down to the smallest possible size. Doing this can reduce some information to an eighth of its original size.

Before you compress an image you should save it in the least bulky format possible. This is done using an image editor which converts it from one image format to another. (Image formats are different ways in which the same picture can be stored in a computer.) Some formats take up much less space than others. For more details of these formats and the best one to choose when sending pictures across the Internet, consult the help documentation supplied with your image editor – and do not forget that good image editors are available on the Internet.

Speeding up newsgroups

Although killfiles (see page 89) are indispensable, they can also slow down the speed at which information from Usenet is copied to your computer. A killfile needs to check each and every article against its 'kill' criteria, and this can take a noticeable and sometimes even an objectionable amount of time. Make a point of checking your killfile settings frequently to see if any can be removed: some spammers change their email addresses regularly to avoid killfiles, and old killfile settings created to get rid of them will no longer apply. Some killfile software has an 'expire' option for each setting, which will automatically search for a certain person or subject after a set time. It is worth getting into the habit of using this feature whenever you know that the setting will be temporary.

Another problem with newsgroups is that your list of groups can proliferate. Every month or two, look through the list to see if the groups in it really are indispensable. You may find that you are no longer interested in some of them. If you find yourself spending an hour a day reading and replying to news, you may want to consider whether all the newsgroups are really worthy of your attention.

It is tempting to read every single message that appears in case you miss something important by not doing so. However, if you miss a week's worth of messages, you will find that in most groups you can pick up where you left off. If something really is essential you can read about it in the various archive services. These last two points also apply to mailing lists (see page 49).

Some news software includes a facility for copying only the titles of messages to your computer. These are known as *headers* and provide a useful summary of the information in a group. To read the content of the messages (which are known as the *bodies*) you simply select the ones you are interested in – perhaps by highlighting them with a mouse – and then use an option that is labelled something like 'Get bodies of selected messages'. This copies their contents to your computer. Apart from making it possible to weed out spam, this option can also be especially useful in binary groups, where copying all the information might take hours. At worst it provides an excellent way to filter your news manually so you can concentrate on discussions and information that genuinely interest you.

Speeding up the Web

The key ways to speed up the rate at which web pages appear are: to choose your times carefully, as described above; and to use a variety of tricks and software extras to manage web information.

Images take much longer to appear than text, so one very useful technique is to select 'text only' versions of web pages wherever these are available. Unfortunately not all sites offer these, but for those that do it is well worth ignoring images and graphics – especially of the decorative kind – when you are trying to keep your costs down.

All browsers include a 'new window' option which you can call on while waiting for a slow site. This opens another window that can be used to look at a completely different site at the same time. In fact, you can have three or more windows open simultaneously. However, this may start to slow your computer down unless you have plenty of memory installed. Many pages contain more than one link, and by following two or more links in parallel you can save yourself minutes, or even hours.

Another useful feature of web browser software is the 'cache' facility. This keeps copies of web pages in your computer's own filing space. When you backtrack, pages are read from this local copy instantly. This saves you from having to wait for them to appear over the Internet again. However, the size of the cache is finite, and the oldest information is always removed to make way for the newest arrivals from the Web; this happens automatically.

To get the best from the cache you should set it to the maximum possible size. This can be demanding of filing space and memory, so make sure you have plenty free. Another advantage of the cache system becomes clear once you start creating your own web pages (see Appendix 5). The cache contains the words, images and page layouts used to create every site you have visited recently. Copyright permitting, you can use all of these in your own designs.

'Off-line' browsers are an extension of the cache idea. As well as caching information, these browsers index it automatically and create internal links so that you can view pages as if you were still on-line. You will need a lot of free filing space to get the best from an off-line browser, as web pages can take up a lot of room. Examples of this software are available for free on the Internet, although you can also buy commercial versions.

Speeding up access to on-line services

There is very little you can do to speed up access to these services. You are locked into a proprietary system which gives you minimal opportunity to change anything. Connection speeds vary significantly from service to service, so by trying out different ones it may be possible to find a cheaper service whose connection is faster. This is one reason why free trials of the on-line services (as discussed in Chapter 2) can be so useful.

Speed tips for Windows 95

At the time of writing, Windows 95 has some rather serious problems in dealing efficiently with the Internet. These manifest themselves in two ways. Firstly, modem connections are extremely slow and inefficient. This means that phone bills are much higher than they need to be. Secondly, some web sites are actually inaccessible from within Windows 95 – they appear not to exist or to be busy, even though they are working properly and should be just as visible as any other site.

The roots of the problem are too complex to explain here in full, but in essence the dial-up networking facility offered as part of Windows 95 has been set up to work best over a small local network instead of the Internet.

Fortunately, there is an easy remedy for this. A large number of web sites offer free or very cheap shareware which can change the relevant settings within Windows 95 and improve connection speeds. For details try searching the Web for sites that contain all of the following words: Max, MTU, RWIN and Win95. (These are the names of the relevant settings within Windows 95.)

While it is possible to fix the problem by hand within Windows 95, this requires expert technical knowledge. The available shareware makes it possible for everyone to improve the speed of their connection without needing to know exactly what needs to be changed or why. These problems have apparently been fixed in Windows 98.

'Secret services'

Apart from the most popular Internet services (email, the Web, newsgroups and IRC), there are a number of others which, although less widely available, are nevertheless useful. They all require special software, which is often available for free, or perhaps as shareware (see page 259), from any of the many software archives on the Internet.

Finger

Finger is a more direct version of the email autoresponders discussed in Chapter 3. Instead of sending a request for information by email, Finger lets you ask a computer for information directly. For example, if you are using a large computer system, such as one at a university, and know someone's email address you can 'finger' that address; in return you will receive some information about him or her. This typically includes the time and date the person last used the computer, and whether or not he or she has any email waiting. Finger may also retrieve a special collection of information called a 'plan', if one is available. Despite the name this has nothing to do with planning. It is like a sig but does not have any length restrictions. Internet users create plans to tell other users about themselves or to include humorous quotes and other information.

Some ISPs use the Finger facility to provide details about the status of their services. Users can Finger a specific address to receive an up-to-date maintenance and status report. Another common use is to provide a list of people who are using a large computer system.

Finger is only sporadically useful. Although you can perform Finger requests from any computer, many computers on the Net are not set up to offer Finger information when asked for it. Often this is done deliberately for security reasons; a curt 'access denied' message will be given.

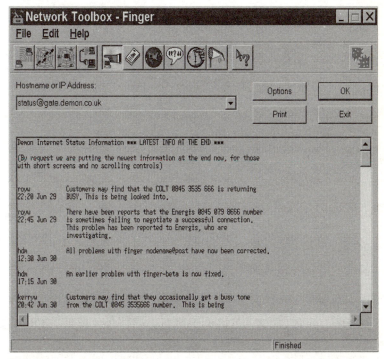

To use Finger you need special software. This example shows Finger being used to get the latest connection information from Demon Internet.

Telnet

Telnet is used to play computer games in which many players take part at the same time, to connect to certain large libraries of information, and is also sometimes required for IRC. When you type something on your keyboard, the information is passed to the other computer, which then responds as if you were typing into it directly. Similarly, information from the other computer appears on your screen as if you were connected to it directly.

As with Finger, the service has two components: software on the destination computer that accepts remote connections from other computers and gives them access to its facilities; and software on your computer that allows you to connect to them remotely. Although it is possible to install the first kind of software on a home computer, it is more often found on large computers which are designed to have many users, such as the computer systems owned by universities and large companies. The second component can also be installed on any computer.

Ping

Ping is an 'are you there?' message which is sent over the Internet to check the speed and reliability of a connection to a distant computer; perhaps one you would like to connect to using Telnet. Ping sends five messages, which are known as packets, and measures how long they take to return. If the round trip takes a long time, or if any packets go missing, you know that the connection to a particular computer is too slow to be useable. Ping also enables you to see if a distant computer is working, and to check on the speed at which information will flow between your computer and the other one. Although once obscure, Ping has become widely used by on-line gamers who use it to assess the speed of a connection to a central gamer's computer (see page 171) and hence to other game players. This 'ping time' has a direct influence on the playability of an on-line game, and can literally make the difference between winning and losing.

Traceroute

Traceroute is an extended version of Ping which lists all the steps the Internet takes to make a connection between your computer and another. These appear as a list of computer names, together with 'ping' timing information for each one. You can use Traceroute to make an educated

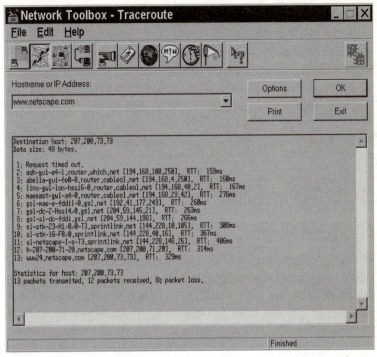

Traceroute shows all the computers that work together to make a connection between your home computer and any distant computer, such as a web site.

guess about the geographical location of an unfamiliar email address. It can also show up problems. To give an extreme example, if you check a computer in the USA and the route shown goes via South Africa, then the Internet is obviously in difficulty, and traffic will be very slow.

Whois

This is a more sophisticated version of Finger. Instead of fingering an individual's information, you can check the state of a sub-network. Whois can list all the administrative contacts at an ISP, which can be useful when you are planning to complain about junk mail or spamming.

DNS lookup

DNS lookup converts Internet addresses made up of words into the numbers which the Internet itself uses. All computers on the Internet – including those that are not for public access – have an address made up of four numbers each between 0 and 255 separated by dots (e.g. 128.0.0.1). The word equivalent exists to make life easier for humans. As a tool it is really of interest only to system administrators, and has only been included here for completeness.

Time

This sets your computer's local time to your ISP's clock. Many ISPs use clock signals transmitted by one of two atomic clocks: one in Rugby in the Midlands, or one in Germany. Your computer's internal clock will then always be accurate to the nearest second. For details on how the year 2000 date-change problem may affect date- and time-keeping on the Internet see page 252.

On-line 'secret services'

Similar 'secret services' are also available on the on-line services. For example, AOL offers 'Profiles', which are a much-improved version of the Finger/plan idea, and 'buddy lists' which let you create a list of favourite people and show you when they are on-line. There is also a 'locate' facility which shows you the name of the chat room someone is using, so that you can join him or her there immediately. All of these features are built into the AOL software.

Profiles are like index cards that users fill in, listing their name, location, date of birth, interests, and so on. Some people have turned their profiles into an art form by ignoring the suggested categories and filling the space with poetry or other unusual or surprising information. It is not unheard of for people to lie in their profiles, creating a completely different persona from the one they have in real life.

Buddy lists are a very useful adjunct for anyone who likes to chat or send instant messages to people on-line. You can add and remove people from your list at any time, create sub-lists for different situations or times of day (for example, at work during office hours) and also block other people's buddy lists so that you do not appear in them. The locate option simply shows a chat room name and is included as a sub-option within the buddy list feature.

More about email

The Internet has two types of email system: SMTP (Simple Mail Transfer Protocol) is an old-fashioned and rather crude system which is still used by some ISPs; POP3 (Post Office Protocol 3) is a more modern system which offers a number of advantages over SMTP.

Using SMTP is very simple. When you check for mail, your ISP's mail computer copies it to your computer immediately. SMTP works by checking if you are the owner of the mail. It will then copy the messages that match up with your username/address. There are no facilities for managing mail more comprehensively, although some ISPs include a feature which lets you check if mail is waiting.

POP3 is more complex and has two major advantages:

- You can **read and reply to email that arrives in your mail box using any computer with an Internet connection** – so if you are on holiday abroad and find a cybercafé you can check to see if there are any messages waiting for you. Instead of checking who you are electronically, POP3 asks for a password, and as long as you know the password and the Internet name of your ISP's mail computer (which it will be happy to tell you before you leave) you have the 'key' to your mailbox.

- If you have suitable software you can **delete messages that you do not want to read before they are copied to your computer** – this is useful for dealing with junk mail or other kinds of unwanted email attention, such as mail-bomb attacks.

New mail systems are being developed that will expand on these facilities and make it even easier to manage a mailbox, but these are unlikely to become standardised until after the beginning of the twenty-first century. Plans are even being drawn up for communications systems that use satellite technology to follow you wherever you go by tracking your portable computer or mobile phone.

More about MIME

MIME is best avoided for text messages. One example of a MIME problem is the way that it handles letters that are specific to certain countries. Keyboards are arranged differently throughout the world, and various countries use variations on English roman lettering by adding accents and other extras such as cedillas. Although it is possible to send these variations in a MIME message, attempting to do so may cause more problems than it solves.

Other 'odd' characters, such as the '£' pound sign, also cause problems. MIME treats them in a strange way: it replaces them with a code that starts with an '=' sign and is followed by a two-digit identifier. This can ruin sigs that use these special characters and is also an annoyance on mailing lists, where messages arrive broken up by countless '=' signs which appear at the end of each line because they are inserted in place of the invisible 'carriage return' characters at the ends of lines.

If you need to include a special character in a MIME message, use a work-around (such as 'ukp' instead of the '£' sign) or write it out in words if you possibly can. Most software will warn you against using special characters if you try to do so when sending the message. If a warning appears while you are typing an email, rewrite it, avoiding the troublesome characters. Alternatively, if you never use attachments, most software includes an option which will turn off MIME altogether.

More about audio

Live audio over the Internet is available using the RealAudio system – a feature of the RealPlayer described on page 128. Another system, called MPEG3 (shortened to MP3) has also become very popular. This allows sounds and music to be copied from person to person via email attachments or by way of FTP. MP3 is now regularly used by fans to distribute snatches of favourite music. It is also used by up-and-coming composers and would-be pop stars who want to give their music a wider airing. CD-quality music requires a lot of filing space (around 10Mb/minute for stereo). The MP3 system makes transfers more efficient by cutting down drastically on the amount of space required, albeit with some loss of quality.

To use MP3 you will need to copy the music to your computer using email or FTP. You will also require a special player to make sense of the information. Players are available for all major computer systems. For example, users of Windows 95/98 can use a player called WinAmp. As with much software, players are available on the Internet for free. Large libraries such as Tucows (listed in Appendix 7) often include a selection. MP3 information can easily be converted to other popular formats such as WAV (for PC users) and AIFF (for Mac). If you have a CD-writer, you can create CDs of your favourite MP3 music (copyright permitting).

Converting your own recordings to the MP3 format is rather harder. Converters tend to be difficult to use and to set up, and the details are too technical to be included in full here. However, the relevant information is widely available on the Web and in the relevant music-technology newsgroups, such as *comp.music.misc*

DIY binaries and attachments

You will not usually need to decode binaries by hand. However, for those situations in which your software does not have the facilities to do the job automatically, it is useful to know what steps to follow. Binaries are sent using one of three systems, each creating a different kind of message. If you know what to look for you can identify very easily which system has been used, and will then know how to decode them.

Uuencoding

The most popular format is 'Uuencoding' (uue), or sometimes 'Uucoding'. The two 'U's are short for 'Unix to Unix'. This is one of the oldest systems in use, but also one of the most reliable. It is widely used for sending binaries on Usenet – in fact someone who tries to use a different system may well be flamed (see page 102). Uuencoded binaries look like the one overleaf.

A typical example may be anywhere between a few hundred and a few thousand lines long. The lines at the top define the section/part number of a multi-part file, then the version of the software, and then the name of the file that has been encoded (overleaf, as an example, the file is called 'RW2.JPG'). The 'Begin' statement tells the decoding software where to start.

To restore the original information you need to copy the different sections together into a single file, then put the result through uudecoding software. Copying sections together by hand can be a chore, but it is sometimes the only way to retrieve the information. This can be done using any standard word processor, although remember to make sure the results are saved as 'plain text', or 'text only' with no page-layout information (i.e. bold, italics, indentations etc.). Anything other than plain text will confuse the decoding software.

```
section 1 of uuencode 4.21 of file RW2.JPG by R.E.M.

begin 644 RW2.JPG
M_]C_X``02D9)1@`!`0$`8`!@``#_VP!#``$!`0$!`0$!`0$!`0$!`0$!`0$!
M`0$!`0$!`0$!`0$!`0("`0$"`0$!`@("`@("`@("`0("`@("`@("`@+_
MP``+"`%<`-P!`1$`_\0`'P```04!`0$!`0$``````````$"`P0%!@<("0H+
M_\0`M1```@$#`P($`P4%!`0```%]`0(#``01!1(A,4$&$U%A!R)Q%#*!D:$(
M(T*QP152T?`D,V)R@@D*%A<8&1HE)B<H*2HT-38W.#DZ0T1%1D=(24I35%56
M5UA96F-D969G:&EJ<W1U=G=X>7J#A(6&AXB)BI*3E)66EYB9FJ*CI*6FIZBI
MJK*SM+6VM[BYNL+#Q,7&Q\C)RM+3U-76U]C9VN'BX^3EYN?HZ>KQ\O/T]?;W
etc.
```

BinHex

'BinHex' is popular with users of the Apple Macintosh. It is not as robust as Uucoding because it does not have any built-in checks for garbled transmission, and this makes it more prone to errors. If you send a photograph using BinHex, it may end up looking disjointed in places. In addition, BinHex may not work properly if you use the wrong version of the BinHex software – the version you should use is listed at the start of the information. Below is an example of the first part of a BinHex file.

The line at the top identifies this as a BinHex file and tells you which version of the software (here 4.0) you need to use to be able to decode the file successfully.

```
(This file must be converted with BinHex 4.0)

:#$!`-$)ZDR"R!%T348Fi3NP0"3!!!+lr!!!L4B-MrpMri!!35NC*4J!"!J%!5!"
)!!$rl3'i8'K[G'pcD'p`)$-Z-!!i3NP0!qN!!!!!!(J!!`!!!%J!5!!!!!!#fJ)
Srq(ri3,j!N8$4`8S!r`!!J!!!%J!5!!!!!!#f!)S!!%!!!"N!!!!!3!$!`-!!!!
"*`m!!3!"!!!!!!!!!!!!!!!!D!J!'3'3!!!!!!!!!!!!!!!!!!!!!!!!!!!!!!!
!!!!!!!!!!!!!1%**632Y!!!!!!!3!%J!!!!"!!%!5!!!!!%!!6K#58d$m`!!!!!
!#!!!!!!!!!!!1%**65F3!!!!!!!+!!%!!!!!!!!!!!MK#58d$p3!!!!!!5!![CQB
!!3"XCQB!"J!!!!!!!3![CQB!!3#KQCS!"J!!!!!!!3!b!!!!!3"D!!!!"J!!!!!
!!3!e!!!!!3!Y!!!!"J!!!!!!!6K#58d$q!!!!!!!F!!!rrrrrrrrrrrrrrrrrr
rrrrrrrrr`2S!!!!!2rrrrrrrrrrrrrrrrrrrrrrrrrrrm$k!!!!!$rrrrrrr
etc
```

Base64

Base64 is not a favourite with the Usenet community. As a general rule, do not use Base64 unless you know that the person, or people, to whom you are sending the information are going to be able to decode it. If you are using MIME, this decision is made for you automatically, because MIME tends to use Base64 as a matter of course. For other uses, especially posting to Usenet, Uucoding is much more popular and is also more likely to work successfully. Below is part of a Base64 transmission; the identifying line at the top is present in any Base64 file.

```
Content-Transfer-Encoding: base64
```

```
/9j/4AAQSkZJRgABAQEASABIAAD/7QGhQWRvYmVfUGhvdG9zaG9wMi41OgBIA
AAASAAAOEJJTQPpAAAAAAB4AAwAAABIAEgAAAAAyoCQP/x//cDOQJJKgIFeA
PeAQAAAAEsASwAAAAADS8JYAABAAAAZAAAAQEAAQAAAAAAScPAAEAAAAAAA
AAAAAAAAAAAAAAAAAAAAAAAAP/C/9oNbQmGAAgBAAAAAAAAAAAAAAAAAA
OEJJTQPtAAAAAAQAEgAAAABAAEASAAAAAEAAThCSU0D8wAAAAABwAAAAAA
AAAOEJJTQP1AAAAAABIAC9mZgABAGxmZgAGAAAAAAAAC9mZgABAKGZmgAGAA
AAAAADIAAAABAFoAAAAGAAAAAAAAADUAAAABAC0AAAAGAAAAAAAOEJJTQP
4AAAAABwAAD///////////////////////A+gAAAA
etc.
```

Although all of these methods may be hidden away by newsgroup and email software, it is possible to find and use software that works with them directly. Such programs are usually awkward to use and old-fashioned; for example, on a PC only a DOS, not a Windows, version of the relevant software may exist. However, anyone who uses the Internet a great deal and needs to be able to use binaries reliably will find that having this software to hand can save a lot of time and trouble and can rescue information that might otherwise be irretrievable. (For more information on binaries see Chapter 5.)

Getting more from the Web

Although the Internet can deal with any kind of information that can be stored in a computer, individual computers and the software they use may not be quite so versatile. This can usually be remedied with the appropriate software. For example, all the popular web browsers can handle most common kinds of information found on a web site: specifically text and certain kinds of images. But, although other information, such as sound clips, can be copied to your computer, a browser may not be able to do anything useful with it.

To solve this problem, web browsers can be extended with software 'plug-ins'. These are small programs – usually free, and almost always available for copying from the Internet – which 'plug in' to the browser and enable it to work with more specialised kinds of information. Hundreds of plug-ins are available, although many use proprietary systems which work only on certain computers or with certain other software. The most popular plug-ins are discussed below.

RealPlayer

RealPlayer, a plug-in from RealMedia, plays video as well as audio and is the replacement for the original RealAudio player, which was introduced in 1995 and was audio-only. Both sound and video are 'compressed' so they can be sent more efficiently. The disadvantage of this process is loss of quality. Anyone using a modem at home can expect radio quality from the sound, and tiny clips resembling a patchwork quilt from the video. There will also be gaps and pauses, because RealPlayer 'streams' the information across the Internet. If the traffic is heavy on the Internet, the information being relayed will appear in bursts.

RealPlayer makes significant demands on computer hardware. Any machine built before about 1996 will be too slow, and will introduce gaps of its own as it tries to reverse the compression process. Despite the drawbacks, however, RealPlayer is worth using. It is the most popular way to offer sound and video over the Web, and makes it possible to take advantage of the multimedia extras now offered on some web sites. For example, the BBC news site at *news.bbc.co.uk* now regularly includes sound and video in RealPlayer format. As connection speeds increase, the quality will improve, and within the next few years CD-quality audio and reasonably good video will become possible.

Shockwave and Immedia

Shockwave (made by Macromedia) and Immedia (made by Quark) are both software packages that attempt to expand the facilities that web pages offer. These plug-ins enable you to look at ornately designed pages, with complex animations, sounds and other special effects. (Professional, non-free versions of Shockwave and Immedia are used to create these pages.)

VRML

VRML – Virtual Reality Markup Language – may prove to be the core technology used to create web pages in the future. Instead of a flat image with simple text and graphics on it, which is created using HTML (the current system), VRML creates a three-dimensional environment, in which objects can be animated, and enlarged so that they can be examined in detail. At the moment, a VRML plug-in on a personal computer needs too much computer power to be anything more than a curiosity, but as computer speed and power increase this may change. For now, very few pages offer VRML information, although the system offers an interesting taste of what the future may hold.

Other types of plug-in

- Microsoft's Video for Windows and Apple's Quicktime plug-ins play video clips in one or more of the common personal computer formats.
- MIDI plug-ins can play MIDI files (the computer world's equivalent of the barrel organ).

These two types are not as standardised as RA, Shockwave, Immedia and VRML, and when you look for suitable plug-ins on-line there will almost certainly be more than one that you can use. Note that more recent web browsers include MIDI playback facilities as standard.

Adding plug-ins to your browser

Plug-ins are usually free, although you may be asked to fill in a registration form which asks you for your email address, and perhaps other personal details. (Information about where to find plug-ins is included in Appendix 7.)

To add a plug-in to your browser follow these steps:

- **Copy the software to your computer** This is usually straightforward. If your browser needs a plug-in to show the information on a certain page, you will usually be asked if you want to 'get the plug-in'; you will then be taken to the page with the plug-ins listed on it automatically. Generally, the only difficult part of the process is deciding which version of the plug-in to use. Sometimes different versions are available for different computer systems and different locations. (Some plug-ins are language-specific.)

- **Start up the software** This will usually start an installation process, which works in exactly the same way as any other software installation. When the installation is completed your browser will be ready to use the new plug-in, which is then available whenever you use your browser in the future.
- **Restart your web browser** The plug-in will then be ready to use.

Using File Transfer Protocol (FTP)

To use FTP you can either rely on your web browser or you can use proper FTP software. Although the former option is much more straightforward, it is not guaranteed to work properly in every situation – browsers sometimes make mistakes which prevent an FTP connection from working properly. True FTP software is intended for more experienced users of FTP, who are not frightened of dealing with a slightly more technical version of the system and who need the extra flexibility that proper software offers.

Using FTP with a browser

It is possible to use FTP with a browser without even being aware of it. This is because FTP is often disguised as 'downloading' – copying information from the Internet to your computer. Whenever a web site has the words 'Download now!' (or similar) with a link, the link will usually lead to an FTP facility. To copy the information, you simply click on the appropriate link, and then tell your computer where to put the information on your hard disk. (It is sensible to create a separate folder, or directory, on your hard disk to put these downloads in, so that you always know where they are. Otherwise, they can get lost after the download.) The FTP process then starts automatically. The popular Netscape Navigator and Communicator browsers shows that the download is working properly by displaying a cryptic message that says 'Saving location', together with a bar graph which shows how much of the information has been copied.

Downloads can take varying amounts of time, from a minute or two to a number of hours, depending on the quantity of information being copied and the speed of the connection between your computer and the Internet. Most browsers show a progress indicator which estimates how much time is left before the process is complete. It also shows the speed at which the information is being transferred. You can use this information to decide whether or not to continue with the transfer – if the process is taking too long you might decide to try at a different time, when the Net is less busy.

The larger and more popular FTP sites have 'mirrors' – copies of the same site on computers in different locations. In theory it is always quicker to access the pages on the computer that is geographically nearest to you. For example, if there is a mirror site in Europe as well as in the USA, it should be quicker to get the information from the computer in Europe (if you live in the UK). In practice, however, this is not always the case. Internet connections to Europe from the UK can

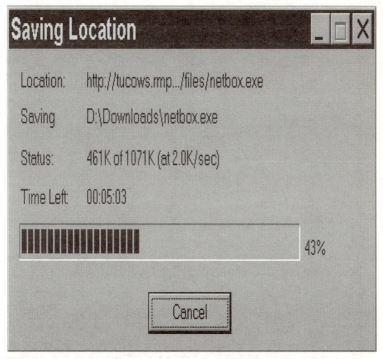

When using a browser for FTP you will usually see a progress display like this one. The 'time left' is an estimate that changes as the speed of the connection varies.

be noticeably slower than those to the USA. Sometimes connections within the UK itself can also be slower than those to the USA.

Where mirror sites are available, they are always listed clearly. To get the best possible connection it is often worth experimenting to see which mirror offers the fastest transfer speed. To do this start a download, wait a minute or two for the speed to stabilise, and then check to see whether it is faster or slower than the download from another computer. This is not so important with small chunks of information that can be copied relatively quickly, but with much larger amounts, which can take hours or more to copy, it can save you a lot of time.

FTP is very prone to rush-hour delays, and it's worth downloading software during off-peak periods, such as weekend mornings. The speed of the link is shown as a number of 'K' on the progress indicator and is short for 'thousands of characters per second'. Any speed less than 0.5K (or 500 bytes/sec) is abysmally slow and not worth waiting for. Rates between 0.5K and 1.0K are barely acceptable – but in some cases are the best possible at the time, in which case it might be worth making another attempt later. Rates between 1.0K and 2.0K are average, and any speed that is faster is good.

Browsers often include a 'time-remaining' estimate, which uses the measured connection speed to guess how long the rest of the download will take. It is a curious quirk of FTP that speeds are rarely constant. This in turn means that time-remaining estimates can vary too. Typically the speed takes a minute or so to settle, and then slows gradually towards the end of the process. A download starting at less than 2.0K may well have slowed to half this speed by the end. It is worth taking this into account when estimating how long a download will take.

You can continue to use the Internet while downloading. Web access, email and news will all work in the usual way – there is no reason to stop what you are doing and wait for the download to finish.

Sometimes so many people are trying to use a particular FTP site at the same time that access is denied completely; instead a message appears asking you to try later. Unless you need the information immediately, you should try again during the early hours of the following morning, when the Internet is likely to be less busy.

Once the software has been copied to your computer, you can use it as you would any other. Software obtained from an FTP site is exactly the same as that on a floppy disk, except that you will not generally get a printed manual to refer to. However, if a web site offers a 'shrink wrap' version of the software, it means you are buying a box full of disks and a manual that will be sent to you using the letter post. You can usually download the software anyway – although of course the box will arrive much later.

Using FTP software

If you want to use FTP software, you will need to know slightly more about how computers work and how to find information on them; in particular, you should know how to use directories and how to move up and down through a list of directories both on your own computer and the one at the FTP site.

It is also helpful if you know something about the different kinds of computer systems that are used on the Internet, such as UNIX, VMS, and so on. FTP works very slightly differently on each system, although most software includes an 'auto' option which works out what kind of system you are trying to link up to, and adapts accordingly.

If none of this sounds daunting, the rest should be straightforward. To start an FTP session you need to type in the location of the remote computer. This appears as a typical Internet address, with words separated by dots. These addresses are listed on web sites and in magazines. You may also need a username on the remote computer and a password. These will be necessary if access to the information you are trying to copy is restricted to certain people for security reasons. (To get a username and password you will need to email the administrator of the FTP computer you are trying to use. He or she has the right to decline your request. For information about 'anonymous' FTP, which uses a password and username but offers information with no restrictions, see Chapter 4.)

You can then attempt to make a connection between your computer and the remote one. The progress of the connection is usually shown in a tiny message window, although information appears here too quickly to read. The different stages the process goes through are indicated here as cryptic numbers and messages. Fortunately, you do not need to understand these to use the system successfully.

Once the connection has been made, most FTP software is designed to show two 'windows': the one on the left lists the contents of a

directory in your computer, and the one on the right shows a directory
on the remote computer. You can navigate through both these
directories in the usual way. To copy a file from one location to the
other you highlight the one you want then either click on the 'copy'
button or drag the name of the file between the windows.

One final point to watch for is the difference between 'binary'
transfers of information, and 'ASCII' transfers. The latter is used for
text, the former for images, photographs, artwork, sound and video.
All FTP software includes an option to set one of these transfer types.
It is important to choose the right one, otherwise the transfer will
produce gibberish. When it has finished, click on a button marked 'log
out' or 'exit'; your connection to the remote computer will then be
broken.

Although FTP is generally used to copy information from a remote
computer to your machine, it can also work the other way. This is
important if you decide to publish your own web pages (see Appendix
5). The final stage of the publishing process consists of copying your

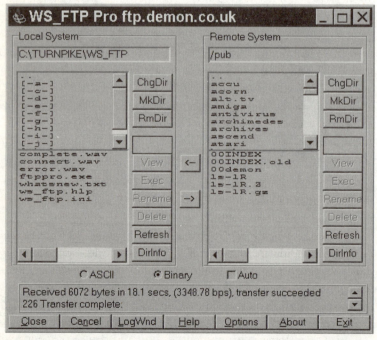

FTP software can often make for much faster transfers of information, even though it is rather
harder to use than the web browser equivalent.

pages to a web server so that they are visible on the Web. FTP software is often used to do this, although if you are using high-quality web publishing software, the process will be hidden away in much the same way that a browser hides away FTP.

Easy FTP?

The easiest way to use FTP is to avoid it altogether. Internet magazines frequently produce compilations of popular software which appear on CD-ROMs that are stuck to the magazine. It can be worth keeping a regular watch on these, as sometimes you will be able to save yourself a few hours of downloading by copying the information from a CD instead. This can be particularly useful when updated copies of browser software appear, as these are invariably huge downloads that would literally take hours to copy using FTP.

Archie and other Internet antiquities

A number of older systems exist to help find information that can then be copied using FTP. However, these are rapidly being made obsolete by the World Wide Web, which offers the same features but is more attractive and easier to use. They are only included here for completeness and reference. Very few people still use them regularly now.

Archie

Archie is a keyword-based search facility for FTP sites. About 40 Archie computers throughout the world regularly check through 1,500 FTP sites to see which files are available. When you access the Archie system it works its way through this file list and shows the ones it thinks you may be interested in. The relatively small scope of the search makes it much more focused than a web search, which has millions of computers to look through. However, the Archie system is not as comprehensive, and of course it will not find files on any FTP computer that is not connected to it.

To use Archie you can either use special Archie software – a web search using a search engine should return a list of possible candidates – or you can Telnet to an Archie site, such as the one at Imperial College in London at *archie.doc.ic.ac.uk*

Once connected, you simply supply a keyword and Archie will reply with a list of files and the FTP servers they are located on. You can then use FTP to copy these to your own machine. Some Archie software includes proper FTP facilities, which make the process even more straightforward. Archie searches can be slow, so expect to be on-line for a few minutes for each search.

You can spend your time more efficiently by performing an email Archie search. This has the advantage that you can start a search and then disconnect from the Internet. To do this you send your request to *archie@name-of-server-here* Leave the subject line blank. In the main text of the message you need to specify one of the Archie search methods:

- **set search sub** This search asks Archie to find any file with the keyword in the name, ignoring differences between upper and lower case. It will then return all files in which the keyword appears, even if it is not a whole word. For example a search for 'water' will return 'watermelon', 'Waterloo', 'water quality', 'waterfall' and so on.
- **set search subcase** This search will have the same preferences as 'set search sub' except that capital letters have to be matched exactly.
- **set search exact** If you search for 'water' using this method, only files with the whole word 'water' will be found.
- **set search regex** This method uses a variety of special characters to narrow the search. For example '^' in front of water will return all files where 'water' is at the front of the name, but not in the middle or at the end.

You then type 'find' followed by a keyword to search for, and the word 'quit' at the end of the message. A complete search email might look like this:

```
To: archie@archie.internic.net
Subject: <blank>
Message body:
set search sub
find money
quit
```

After a while – usually more than ten minutes but less than a day – you will get an automatic response from the Archie computer with a list of matching files. Of course, this is not quite as interactive as doing the whole search on-line, but unless you are in a hurry it can be just as effective.

Gopher

Gopher is a precursor of the World Wide Web. It is a text-only system that classifies information into headings, subheadings and so on, in much the same way that a search engine like Yahoo! does (see pages 66–7). Gopher information is kept on special computers – called Gopher servers – which tend to be maintained by governments and universities. Because of this, Gopher information is generally of a more serious nature, such as academic research and government reports, and carries no advertising. Because Gopher is a text-only system, it can be much quicker to use than the Web.

There are three ways of accessing Gopher information:

- **with a web browser**: addresses start with 'gopher://' instead of 'http://'
- **through Telnet** (see page 120) – *gopher.tc.umn.edu* is a good address to start from
- **with special Gopher software**, which is free and available from many archives on the Internet.

Once the information has been found, it can be copied using FTP.

Veronica is a keyword search system for the Gopher network. Most Gopher servers include this option, which works with web browsers as well as with the special Gopher software. When you type in a keyword Veronica responds with a list of Gopher 'addresses' which include that particular word.

WAIS (Wide Area Information Services) is an extended, more useful, version of Veronica that searches the text of a document instead of just the description. To keep a search simple it is also possible to look through information categories rather than for keywords. The WAIS network is limited to a handful of academic computer systems, making it of marginal use to anyone without an interest in academic subjects.

Chapter 8

Electronic bandits and superhighwaymen

Far from being a superhighway, the Internet is much more like a seventeenth-century mud track. Apart from being slow and inconvenient to use, it can also be dangerous. The perils are financial and intellectual, and in extreme cases even moral, and Net users should know how to take suitable precautions.

Internet security is a complicated issue. It has two facets: keeping private information away from prying eyes; and avoiding on-line scams and other unwanted attention, such as mail-bomb attacks. The Internet was never designed to be a secure system, and few safeguards against malice and trickery have been built in. However, there are a variety of steps anyone can take to improve security, and these are discussed in this chapter.

Hackers and crackers

Like any other human activity, the Internet has its own bandits, criminals and con-artists. 'Hackers' and 'crackers' are the words used to describe Internet users – usually teenage and male – who attempt to abuse the system. (The word 'hacker' was originally used to describe any unusually gifted computer programmer, but the public has now come to regard it as meaning the same as 'cracker' – an Internet criminal. 'True' hackers are understandably offended by this, but the terminology remains widely used.) Typical hacker exploits include:

- breaking into secure computer systems and stealing information
- reading email that is supposed to be private
- collecting credit-card information sent via email
- taking over a web site and vandalising its original information

138

- attacking an Internet computer so that it becomes overloaded and stops working properly.

A particular class of hacker, known as a phone phreaker, specialises in hacking the computers that operate the public telephone network. Hackers often become phreakers to feed their Internet habit without having to pay the bills. In fact, this class of hacker is less of a nuisance on the Internet itself than others. Apart from illegal access to free calls – at an estimated cost in the UK of £400 million between 1990 and 1996 – phreakers are also fond of listening in on private conversations and playing pranks. A favourite trick is to change a neighbour's settings at the local exchange so that it treats their phone system as a pay phone; it will then not let them use it unless they insert some change.

Keeping hackers out

The only way to create a completely secure computer system is to disconnect it from any networks and severely vet the people who use and supervise it. Some military systems maintain security this way, although even this supposedly fail-safe system is potentially open to bribery and blackmail.

Disconnection is not an option for Internet users, and so a much simpler and more convenient security device is used instead – the password. Unlike more sophisticated systems – such as those that rely on physical keys, for example magnetic cards – passwords do not require extra hardware and are easy to use. But it is important to be aware of their security limitations. A password becomes useless if someone can guess it or work out what it is by trial and error. So it is essential to choose passwords carefully, especially if sensitive information is at risk.

Some service providers, such as Pipex, supply a computer-generated password, saving you the trouble of creating one. However, most leave the choice of password to you. The best passwords are easy to remember but impossible to guess, either through psychology or with mechanical aid, such as the war dialler described overleaf. It is not advisable to use names of children, spouses or pets, addresses, phone numbers, maiden names or words related to favourite hobbies. A hacker who is familiar with a person will try all of these first, as well as other words that they know their victim is likely to have chosen.

Picking a word at random is safer, but even this approach has its drawbacks. In the USA in particular, where local calls are either free or cost a negligible fixed amount, it is easy to create a piece of software called a 'war dialler' – an automated password-cracking program. A war dialler will work its way through an entire dictionary of potential passwords in a matter of hours, trying each word in it (which will typically be the list of words in a word processor's spell checker) until the password is found. Home users are unlikely to be targeted like this without good reason, but business users who have a permanent connection to the Internet should choose a password that offers a higher level of security.

Random letter and number combinations are reasonably secure, providing they have not been devised with the help of the standard password-creation software which is widely available on the Internet. Dedicated hackers will have copies of this software and will again combine it with a war dialler if they are determined to get in. The search process is more time-consuming than a straight dictionary-based attack, but hackers can be very patient people. Some are happy to spend weeks or even months trying to hack a computer if they think the information it contains is worth it.

Perhaps the best passwords are those made from a random combination of words from a dictionary and numbers – for example, a password such as 12ARTICHOKE59COTTON would be very hard to crack, even with a war dialler. For maximum effectiveness the number of digits should vary randomly. Of course, the longer a password is, the harder it is to crack. Combined passwords also have the advantage of being easier to remember than completely random strings of numbers and digits.

Password solicitations
Having gone to considerable trouble to choose a secure password, you should, of course, make sure that no one knows what it is. This advice is obvious, but one form of hacker attack – the password solicitation – causes regular grief for the unwary. To solicit a password, a hacker simply asks for it, perhaps by pretending to be someone from the police or from higher up an organisation's hierarchy. Some of the most successful hackers have been able to attack supposedly secure computers by calling someone inside the building and asking for a password.

For business users, the way to avoid this is to make sure that everyone who knows the password also knows who is and is not to be trusted with it. In addition, they must understand that it should be revealed only under very clearly defined circumstances. In a busy office, passwords should never be written down, except in secure areas which are open only to authorised staff. It may be tempting to keep a PostIt of the password under the desk – or worse still, on the monitor – but this is not recommended if security is important.

Password solicitations are a particular problem for users of on-line services. One favourite hacker technique is to access a chat room and send messages to newcomers which suggest that something has gone wrong, and that the user needs to reconfirm his or her password and credit-card details. This kind of message always ends with the threat that if the user does not do this, he or she will not be able to use the service any more. Anyone who falls for this trick can expect to receive a crippling credit-card bill at the end of the month because the hacker will use the password at every possible opportunity. Below is a typical example, copied from an AOL chat room:

```
AOLService: Sector 4G9C of our data base has lost all I/O
functions. When your account logged on to our system, we were
temporarily able to verify it as a registered user.
Approximately 94 seconds ago, your verification was made void
by loss of data in the Sector 4G9C. Now, due to AOL verification
protocol, it is mandatory for us to re-verify you. Please click
'Respond' and re-state your password. Failure to comply will
result in immediate account deletion.
```

This kind of attack can be extremely effective. With the right tone and convincing use of made-up jargon, this message could easily catch out inexperienced users. AOL (the on-line service provider) makes a point of reminding its users wherever possible that AOL staff will never ask for password or credit-card information on-line, but novice users often forget this. Once a hacker has one person's password he or she can then collect more, and it becomes almost impossible to evict that person from the system. If you receive a solicitation, copy the message and send it to the service's administrators; it makes their job much easier and also helps prevent attacks on other people.

Password solicitations are also sometimes sent as email messages. These work in exactly the same way. Victims receive an official-looking message that suggests they have to supply their password and credit-card details by return. A recent variation on this approach is a message that suggests passwords and credit-card details should be stored electronically at a web site 'for convenience'. Again, the message itself can appear official enough to convince the inexperienced (although a closer reading usually shows a few spelling mistakes and grammatical errors). All of these should be ignored, or reported to the ISP or on-line service. Reputable ISP staff will be suitably circumspect about asking for password information. Anyone who does ask for this information is most likely attempting to perpetrate an on-line fraud.

Email security

Internet email is not secure. If someone with the required skills deliberately sets out to try to read your email messages, their contents are less secure than those of a standard letter. Fortunately, the tools and the knowledge needed to do this are very advanced, and it is certainly not something a casual Internet user sitting at home with a PC can do easily.

In a number of instances in the USA, 'private' email messages have been intercepted and used as evidence in a court case. It has also been suggested that some hackers have created systems that scan passing email for credit-card details, which they then file away for future use. But it is not just hackers who have an interest in email. A web site has details of an alleged US Government email-scanning system called Echelon, which can read a sizeable proportion of the world's email traffic and can be set up to look for certain target words – presumably those related to national security concerns.

Note also that if you use email at work, *the email belongs to the company.* You have no legal rights to privacy of any sort. Anything you say may be used in legal proceedings without your permission. It is also perfectly legal for employers to read your email, and to check if you are using it for non-work purposes.

It is possible to improve email security by using a secret code. (For more about this see PGP on page 145.) At the time of writing, banks and shops are experimenting with a number of different systems which appear to be secure enough for general use.

Email viruses

Email viruses are an Internet myth that regularly catches out the inexperienced. *It is impossible to damage a computer or the information on it by downloading and reading a message made of plain text.* Information contained in an attachment can only be dangerous in one of two ways: if it is a piece of software infected with a computer virus, or if it is a 'macro virus' designed to cause problems with a certain kind of wordprocessor (for more details, see page 153). Images and other kinds of information, such as video and sound, sent as attachments are completely safe.

The situation is more complicated on on-line services which use their own proprietary email systems. Hackers have been known to take advantage of loopholes in the process that copies attachments between users. If you use an on-line service, do not download attachments unless you are sure that the email is safe.

Mail bombs

Apart from trying to read email messages, hackers and other Internet 'undesirables' can abuse the email system in other ways. A 'mail bomb' is a collection of huge and/or numerous messages, which is sent to your email address and clogs up your connection. A mail-bomb attack can be disastrous. You will not usually be able to receive any more email messages until your ISP or on-line service provider sorts out the mess by deleting the unwanted messages.

A more insidious form of mail-bomb attack is the mailing-list subscription ploy. If you are the victim of one of these you will suddenly find that you have been subscribed to thousands of mailing lists, and will then receive thousands, perhaps even millions, of messages a day. A person who calls him- or herself the Unamailer (after the US Unabomber) perpetrated mailing-list attacks on a number of famous people late in 1996. Ironically, he or she did it to protest against the lack of security on the Internet. It took many weeks to deal with the results of the Unamailer's actions, who was never traced.

Because it is so simple to forge email on the Internet, even a novice hacker can launch an attack such as this relatively easily. More experienced hackers can do it in a way that leaves no trace at all, making it almost impossible to track them down. Apart from being careful about who you annoy on-line, you cannot – unfortunately – protect yourself against this. However, as new and improved ways to manage email become available, attacks will become less destructive and easier to deal with.

Email forgery

It is hard, although not impossible, to forge a handwritten letter. But it is very easy to forge an email message well enough to fool an inexperienced Internet user. With a little thought, it should be obvious how this can be done using almost any standard email package.

However, this simple forging technique will not confuse more experienced users. All email arrives with a long list of information at the top called a 'header'. The information in the header is used to route the message to the correct destination, and it includes the name of the computer system the email originated from. If this does not match the suggested return address in the header, then there is a chance the email has been forged. It is possible, but certainly not easy, to forge headers. (For more information about headers see Appendix 6.)

If you need to identify the sender of an email message with absolute certainty, your best option is to ask for a 'digital signature'. This is a special code which contains information that identifies someone as the only possible author of a message. Digital signatures are available when using the PGP system described below. Some US states are beginning to look into the legal implications of digital signatures, and it is likely that by the beginning of the twenty-first century all email will be authenticated with digital signatures as a matter of course.

Encryption

Encryption uses secret codes, which rely on complex mathematical techniques that make them virtually unbreakable. Both US and other governments are keen to make sure that encrypted email can still be read by government agents, using special electronic keys that bypass the encryption process. This raises interesting questions about who should and should not have access to 'private' information.

In theory these keys would be made available only to the government and under the strictest conditions – for example, if there is reasonable suspicion of terrorism. A more sophisticated system called DES is widely used but may also not be completely secure. Many Internet users worldwide distrust the US Government's motives for having access to private information and would prefer to use an alternative system which is secure from all prying eyes, authorised or otherwise.

PGP (Pretty Good Privacy)

At the time of writing, PGP provides the most secure encryption available but is at the centre of complex legal and patent wrangles, which makes it difficult to obtain outside the USA. It is not hard to find on the Internet, although you may, depending on its current legal status, have problems obtaining a copy from a software company in the USA. PGP is very secure and can also be used to encrypt information on a computer's hard disk, but it is rather complex.

Most secret codes are flawed because at some point the person sending the message has to tell the recipient how the code can be cracked. This is usually done with a 'key' – the information that defines how the code works. If there is no way to communicate a key securely, the code is useless, no matter how difficult it is to crack. PGP gets around this problem by using two keys: a private key, and a public key. The private key is known only to one person. As long as he or she keeps it secret, the code will be secure. The public key is made available to anyone. The sender needs to find out from the recipient what his or her public key is and then uses it to encrypt the text of the message with the PGP software. The message is then secure and can be sent in an email in the usual way. The recipient runs the message through the PGP software with both the public key and his or her private key. This process deciphers the message and reproduces the original text.

The reason this system works is because the two keys are mathematically related. If just one key is known, the only way to find the other is to perform billions of calculations. With current computer technology this would take many times the lifetime of the known universe.

Fortunately, you do not need to understand the theory to use PGP. Since 1996 new and improved versions of the program have started to become available. These have 'wrappers' which hide away the technicalities and make the software easier to use. You can buy PGP extensions to popular email packages (such as Eudora) but at the time of writing, for the reasons mentioned above, these are not widely available over the counter in the UK. As an interesting aside it is possible to use PGP to secure other kinds of communications: a version designed to work with WebPhones can secure private voice conversations.

Interest in privacy, security and encryption has led to the rise of a small subculture on the Internet – the self-styled 'cypherpunks'. The existence of uncrackable encryption systems has brought about a new situation in which citizens can be sure of communicating with each other without government interference. To date, governments have taken it for granted that their agents can listen in to 'private' telephone conversations, open letters and take whatever steps they consider essential to maintain national security.

Cypherpunks consider this unreasonable and make a point of using whatever technology is available to help ensure privacy. The situation is a complex one. PGP is used for illegal communications as well as innocent ones. Unless governments ban PGP – and such a ban may well be unenforceable in practice – its use will continue to grow. It is impossible to say what the implications of this are. Some countries – notably Russia, France, Iran and Iraq – have already announced bans of 'unsupported encryption systems'. Anyone who tries to use PGP in some of these countries may suffer serious legal, and perhaps even life-threatening, consequences.

It is important to bear in mind that codes that are unbreakable today will not be so tomorrow. At the time of writing PGP is literally unbreakable – with today's technology, the computer power required to break the code would tie up all the world's computers indefinitely. But because computers are continuously becoming more powerful, it is unlikely PGP will still be secure in the 2020s. New computer designs which work very differently from today's machines are already being proposed, and it is likely that they will be exceptionally good at the kinds of calculations needed to break a PGP code. If you have information which needs to be kept secure for a long time, it is best to take other non-electronic precautions to keep it safe, such as using a physically secure storage facility.

Anonymity

When using email and newsgroups it is sometimes useful to be able to post anonymously, so that the recipient does not know who you are or where you are posting from. A number of 'anonymous remailers' offer this service. These are special email computers which separate the text of your message from its 'header' (the Internet's equivalent of an envelope), give it a different one and then send it on to its final destination. Normally, headers contain information about your name, the time and date you sent the message, the computers your message passed through, and sometimes the software you are using.

'Anonymised' headers replace this information with details that say very little about you.

To use an anonymous remailer, you email a special address and in return receive a unique mail identifier. This is your 'anonymous address'. It works just like a normal email address, except that whenever you send email through it, your true address is hidden. A reply sent to your anonymous address will be forwarded to your true address, although again this process keeps your true address hidden. In effect the anonymous address acts rather like a PO Box, except that you can send mail from it anonymously as well as receiving it.

Anonymous email cannot guarantee total security. One of the most famous and widely used anonymous remailers – which used the address *anon@penet.fi* – was closed by its owner when he was served with a controversial court order, brought by the Church of Scientology, requesting full details of its users. (At the time the Church of Scientology was involved in an Internet 'war' with the members of a certain newsgroup, who were posting its secret documents anonymously, see page 81.) This is a problem that affects all remailers – if your name appears in a raid like this one, your anonymity will be compromised, even if you have been using the remailer for completely innocent reasons.

It is also possible to track email into and out of a remailer, rendering the anonymising process ineffective, but the skills and equipment needed to do this are beyond the capability of most Internet users.

To increase the security of a message, you can send it through multiple remailers. This reduces the chances of having your details handed over to a third party because only the remainder at the end of the chain will have your true address. However, doing this does not make your email any harder to trace electronically. If you do use multiple remailers, you can be sure that the only people who will be able to trace you will be dedicated government agencies who have the kind of computer facilities – if not necessarily the expertise – to track someone in this way. Most people do not need this level of security, but those who do can combine anonymous email with PGP to create an almost totally secure communication channel. For practical information about using remailers, search the web for 'anonymity' or 'anonymous remailer'.

Newsgroup security

From the point of view of security, the main problem with newsgroup postings is that they are archived for posterity. This has some surprising implications. Archiving enables total strangers to see a complete record of everything you have posted on Usenet. This can give them more information about you than you may feel comfortable with. One Internet revenge technique is to look through the archive, pull out postings that might be embarrassing and re-post them in a different context. Many people have suddenly found their more colourful peccadilloes unexpectedly brought to light in this way.

In the longer term, it is worth bearing in mind that the stated aim of the archive services is to make all postings available indefinitely. This means that anything you post on Usenet will remain available there perhaps for hundreds of years. This can have implications for your relationships and family life. Some people have already taken to vetting prospective romantic partners by searching for and reading their postings on the Web. Thinking further ahead, your argumentative Usenet postings will still be there for your children to read when they reach their teens; could this affect your relationship with them? Similarly, you will be able to read their postings, once they start making them.

The same applies to a lesser extent to mailing lists. It is not unheard of for someone to pick a posting from a mailing list and put it up on a web site without asking for the original writer's permission. As a result, a number of your comments may be posted publicly without you knowing. Given a selection of these, and your Usenet postings as well, a complete stranger can form an impressively accurate picture of your hobbies, interests and private life. (Note that if you have a popular surname this becomes harder.) Because of this you should never post anything that could attract unwelcome attention or which says more about you than you would like other people to know.

To maintain your privacy on newsgroups, you can use an anonymous email address, as discussed earlier. This should work well but has the disadvantage of appearing odd in the social setting of some groups, in which it would be the equivalent of trying to hold a conversation while wearing a brown paper bag over your head. In others, however, especially those that deal with more dubious information, it is actually expected.

Fortunately, a less demanding form of anonymity is also available. It is possible to bypass the archiving process by including a line that says: 'X–No–Archive: yes' at the start of each posting. This tells the various archiving services to ignore your message and guarantees that it will not be saved for posterity. Note that your posting will appear with your contact details intact, although once it expires, your message will disappear for good. Doing this may also help you avoid junk mail, but is perhaps better thought of as a way of avoiding the attentions of nosy strangers – possibly including your descendants and relatives.

An issue that applies particularly to newsgroups, but also to a lesser extent to unencrypted email, is their relevance to existing laws regarding libel and slander. In 1999 the Demon ISP was successfully sued by an individual who claimed that defamatory remarks made in a newsgroup had not been removed from its news computers, even though he had sent in a formal complaint. Many newsgroup users, especially in the UK-specific groups, have seen this as a blow against free speech, but are nonetheless being careful about what they say in public to the individual who brought the charges.

Security on the Web

There are three security considerations on the Web – the security of web transactions, the security of web systems, and various questions about privacy raised by current web technology.

Web transactions

Web transactions, like email, are not very secure. In some situations – such as buying software on-line – you will be asked more questions than you really need to answer. If you are unhappy about giving away your address and phone number you will often find you can leave these parts of the form blank. If the creator of the web page complains when you try to do this, you can supply false information. It is not normally used for anything more sophisticated than sending out information about new products, which you will probably receive via email anyway.

Some web sites are secure (their address starts with 'https://' instead of the usual 'http://'). The system that they use to make them secure is called SSL – Secure Sockets Layer – and encrypts information before sending it to the site. When you look at one of these web sites, your browser will display an icon or some other form of information that tells you it is secure. For example, Netscape Navigator shows a solid key in the bottom left-hand corner when a transaction is secure and a broken one when it is not.

The SSL system is not completely secure. It can be hacked fairly easily, although, again, this requires computer power and skills which most people do not have. It is safe enough to be thought reasonably secure for on-line credit-card transactions. In practice you are less likely to have your credit-card number copied this way than you are to have your card stolen.

At the time of writing, more secure systems are being developed that can be used commercially with complete confidence. These will solve the transaction problem and make using the Web for transactions as secure (perhaps more secure) than giving your number to a mail-order company over the phone. In practice, any site that offers a 'secure server' is likely to be relatively safe. A hacker with access to plenty of computer time can hack messages to these sites, but the pay-off would not be worth the time and money he or she would have to invest to do this. So, while secure servers cannot offer perfect security, the security they offer appears to be 'good enough'.

The latest web technologies such as Java and Active X are not completely secure. To protect yourself from security problems, you should always use the latest version of any browser, as long as it is known to be secure. For more details see your browser's home page; this will always contain information about the very latest security issues.

Web site security

Web sites themselves are not always secure, but this affects you only if you are planning to develop a site of your own, and especially one for business purposes (see Appendix 5). Some organisations – including the CIA and the US Air Force – have had their sites vandalised by hackers, who take the existing pages and replace them with pages of their own design which typically have more eye-catching and controversial content than the originals.

For simple home pages, this is not something you should worry about. Your web pages will be kept on a computer run by your ISP or on-line service provider, and if your site is vandalised – which is very unlikely, as hackers usually concentrate on high-profile sites – the attack becomes their problem. Apart from keeping a back up of all the information on the site, there is little you can do.

However, professional web developers who rent space on a commercial web server should always check the security arrangements of their chosen host before signing a contract. A professionally run web site will be able to offer the security features listed below:

- **At least one security expert** He or she should keep track of all the latest security updates posted on the Internet and have modified the existing software used on the server to remove all the common and well-known security risks. This is an ongoing process. Much of the software used by the larger computer systems on the Internet has gaping security holes, which are familiar to hackers. These holes need to be closed by a computer security expert. A computer system that does not do this and continues to use the software in the form it was originally supplied, will be vulnerable to attack.

- **A properly installed 'firewall'** This is a piece of software that attempts to isolate secure parts of a computer network from the parts that are accessible from the rest of the Internet. It takes a reasonable level of expertise to install a firewall properly, and a bad installation can be worse than useless. The existence of a firewall is not enough; there should be evidence that it has been installed in a thoughtful and professional way and that all the potential security loopholes have been accounted for. For example, even the best firewall is rendered useless if someone on the network it protects installs a modem and uses a standard dial-up connection to the Internet.

- **A site policy that follows a document called RFC 1244** This lists sound security practices, and it should be evident that these practices are being adhered to. (If the staff managing a site are unfamiliar with this document it is very unlikely that they know anything at all about practical Internet security.)

- **Regular security checks** These should include checks on personnel and physical security arrangements as well as the software and hardware that make up the web server. Anyone dealing with very sensitive information should have an unblemished security record. Professional hackers and criminals sometimes attempt to bribe key employees instead of hacking in from outside; it is much quicker and easier for them to get in this way. Physical security is important for similar reasons, so keycards or other physical systems should be used to keep strangers out of the most secure areas of the building.

Internet security is not a straightforward topic, and for larger computer installations it is advisable to hire a security consultant to perform a full security audit. The issues are much more complicated than choosing suitable passwords and making sure these are known only by specific trusted people. Questions need to be asked about physical access, backup and recovery procedures, and even the management structure of an organisation. Organisations that do not insist on answers that guarantee security are leaving themselves wide open to attack.

Web privacy

Whenever you look at a web site you leave a record that shows who you are, which page or pages you looked at, which software you used, which web site you came from, and so on. Usually these details are clumped together and analysed statistically to provide information that can be used to improve the site. But they can also be used in other ways; it is possible to find yourself on the receiving end of junk mail by inadvertently leaving your contact details with a site you have visited.

You can make your web browsing more secure by using an 'anonymiser'. This is a web site that renders the personal details that are usually supplied by your browser 'invisible'. You can then continue to browse as before, without leaving your personal information at any web sites. Anonymisers are very easy to use – you simply visit the anonymising site, and then carry on browsing as before.

'Cookies' are a related problem. These are notes that are passed from web sites you have visited to your web browser and can contain information about the choices you made while you were at the site. The cookie system was created to save users from having to type in the same details whenever they revisited a site. But they can also be used in more underhand ways. For example, some sites use cookie information to change advertising to suit your interests. While not everyone finds this offensive or intrusive, it remains a rather devious way to attract your interest. And cookies can also be used to make a note of all the sites you visit during a browsing session – again, you may not want this information made available.

It is easy to dispose of cookies. They are created and kept in a file called 'cookies.txt' in your computer's filing system. If you edit this file or delete it at the end of each web-browsing session, your web usage will be cookie-free. You can find software to manage cookies for you, and this is available from many sources on the Net. A search for 'web cookies' should provide a list of plenty of places to look.

Viruses

Software that is downloaded from the Internet should be checked for viruses before it is used. While there are no risks from the downloading process itself, security-conscious computer users should get into the habit of testing any downloaded software with a virus checker before using it for the first time. These are available for a relatively small outlay and can save hours or even days of despair caused by a virus that has removed all the information on a computer's hard disk.

Documents prepared on a word processor and sent as an attachment can now also contain viruses. Users of Microsoft Office are particularly vulnerable to these. Instead of taking over a vital part of your computer, they rely on the fact that Office is so widely used, and that it contains automation tools, called macros. (Macros are typically used to create big changes in a document that would otherwise need to be done by hand repeatedly. An example would be converting a table of measurements from feet to metres.) These viruses can be included within a document when it is saved to disk, and will then start to work whenever anyone tries to read or edit it.

An 'autorun' macro will do something every time a document is loaded into a word processor to be read or changed. Because macros can do whatever their creator wants them to, it is very easy to create an autorun macro that deletes all the information in your computer. More playful variations on this theme include a virus that inserts a silly word at random into a document. Some variations are fiendishly clever. The Melissa virus, which caused so many problems in 1999, takes advantage of the integration within Microsoft Office to scan through a user's address book when it is first started. It then creates and sends convincingly authoritative and official emails to everyone in the address book, attaching itself to them first. If any of the recipients are also using a version of Office, they too become infected. The virus itself does no damage to individual computers, but can bring an office network to its knees very quickly. Since many companies now rely on email, this can prove very expensive.

The latest virus-checking software can deal with macro viruses as well as those of the more conventional kind. It cannot be emphasised enough that a good virus checker is essential whenever you try to download and use any potentially dangerous information from the Internet.

Following are some points to remember to help you stay virus-free:

- All plain-text messages are safe.
- Check attached software for a virus before using it. If the software is unsolicited, and you do not know the person who sent it, simply delete it.
- Where possible, check all messages sent as attachments before opening and reading them.
- In a business setting, watch out for the latest virus updates in the sources opposite.

Good Times and variations

The 'Good Times' virus is an email message that travels round the Internet, taking in the unwary and inexperienced, and perpetuating itself indefinitely. The Good Times email claims to be about a virus called Good Times that can be sent via email. The virus is supposed to cause fatal damage to a PC by overheating its chips, and anyone who receives information about this dangerous virus is encouraged to pass it on to warn their friends.

It is impossible to send a virus as part of an email message, unless it is hidden in some attached software or buried in a document as a macro. The Good Times virus is actually the warning message itself and is a typical example of an Internet prank and not a dangerous computer virus.

Good Times has spawned a number of imitations such as Join the Crew, Valentine's Day, Win a Holiday, and so on. These all work in exactly the same way and are just harmlessly irritating. In a cunning twist one message claims that email with the title 'RETURNED OR UNABLE TO DELIVER' is also a virus – in fact this is the standard Internet form email produced by a computer when it is impossible to deliver an email message because the address is incorrect.

Another variation is the BETA hoax, which suggests that Microsoft will offer $1,000 and some free software to the first thousand people who forward the message to someone else.

For the latest information about current hoaxes see these sites:

Department of Energy Computer Incident Advisory Capability at
ciac.llnl.gov/ciac/ciachoaxes.html

IBM's Hype Alert web site at
www.av.ibm.com/breakingnews/hypealert

Datafellows Hoax Warnings at
www.europe.datafellows.com/news/hoax.htm

Trojan horses

'Trojan horse' (also known as Trojan) software is a more dangerous
version of the Good Times virus. This is software that claims to do one
thing but actually does something very different and destructive. In the
Spring of 1997 a piece of software called AOL4FREE appeared on the
Internet. This was supposed to be a PC version of a similar program
with the same name that had appeared a few years earlier for the Apple
Macintosh. The Mac software was an AOL piracy program that gave
people free access to the AOL Service. The PC software was really a
Trojan horse and deleted all the information on the hard disks of any
computer it was installed on.

Virus-checking software cannot spot a Trojan horse, because
technically the program is not a true virus. As far as a virus checker is
concerned, a Trojan horse looks like an ordinary piece of software and
has none of the tell-tale signs that give away a virus. The only way to
avoid a Trojan horse like this is to watch out for rumours and public
announcements on the Net. Software that is associated with piracy and
other illegal activities is much more likely to cause trouble than
ordinary software.

Scams and con tricks

A classic Internet con trick was perpetrated on a number of victims
during the autumn of 1996. Some users in search of thrills found
themselves at a certain web site which promised them access to illegal
pornography. To use this site they were asked to download a 'special
viewer' on to their computer.

The viewer was really a piece of software that broke their existing
Internet connection and reconnected their modem – by way of an

international call – to a special number in Moldova, which was set up to charge by the minute. The first that most victims knew of the scam was when their enormous phone bill arrived. As with Trojan horses, the more illegal or dubious the activity on the web site, the greater the chance that some kind of trick will be involved.

The Web also suffers from the problem of commercial verification. How can you tell if someone is who they claim to be? This is a particular problem for share broking and investment services. If you visit one of these in a high street, you at least have the security of knowing that there is a real shop front that has real people working behind it. They may of course be dishonest, but if you ask the right questions you at least have a chance of avoiding fraudsters.

This is not so on the Internet, where anyone can create a 'shopfront' which gives a totally misleading impression. A good rule of thumb is that if an investment opportunity seems to be too good to be true, it probably is. To keep out of trouble, it helps to remember the following:

- **Never deal with unregulated companies** These may trade 'outside the law', and you will have no chance of getting compensation if they turn out to be fraudulent or dishonest. To find out if a company is regulated, look for information about its membership of a recognised professional body on a web site.
- **Do not invest in anything you do not understand** If something looks appealing, but you are not clear about how it works, get independent advice from an expert.
- **Always do your own research into possible investment opportunities** You can use the Internet's search facilities to check for company names and the names of directors, to see if they have ever been involved in litigation or come under some other kind of legal scrutiny.

General computer security

Can a hacker get into the information inside a home computer from outside? Fortunately, most of the time the answer is 'no'. Without external access software, there are no 'hooks' inside a home computer which can be used to delete or copy the information stored in it from outside.

The situation is less clear if the computer is being used with a web browser. Some browsers have very obvious security flaws which malicious hackers can exploit. But they can do this only if the browser is used to read the information on a site that contains special hacking instructions. In other words, you will have problems only if you find the site by accident, or are deliberately led to it. As a further safeguard, this applies only to certain versions of the popular browsers (such as Internet Explorer 3.01).

In general, it is impossible to make web browsing completely safe. But to date there have been a negligible number of instances where hackers have deliberately caused problems, and these have usually been staged to demonstrate that a security flaw exists.

The situation is more complex with business computers that are permanently connected to the Internet. These usually have obvious security flaws that hackers can take advantage of, and in many cases they do. This is why this kind of installation needs a thorough check by a security consultant.

Children on-line

The Internet can cause something of a dilemma for parents. On the one hand, it can be an extremely effective way to inspire enthusiasm for learning and making contact with others, but on the other hand, some of the information on the Internet is most definitely not suitable for children. At the time of writing, the problem of restricting access to unsuitable material has yet to be solved. Although systems are available that attempt to censor what children can see, none is perfect, and all have the unfortunate side-effect of accidentally barring wanted as well as unwanted information.

On the Internet, the most obvious way to tackle the problem is to use 'Net babysitter' software which attempts to check web sites for inappropriate content, including sexually explicit material, graphic violence, racism and so on. The software can look for certain words in the text at the site or can use one of the Net's own classification systems, which work very much like film ratings.

The problem with keyword searches is that they are rather unintelligent. While it is easy to get rid of most 'four letter words', a ban on the word 'sex', for example, may make it impossible to read completely innocent sites that refer to certain English counties.

Meanwhile, Net ratings are still in their early stages. There is no single standard rating system, and only a minority of sites – ironically often the ones with the most explicit content – bother to give themselves ratings. Many sites aimed at children do not do this, and unfortunately some software bars sites that are not rated. As a result, the sites that might most interest children 'disappear'. The latest web browsers are starting to take notice of ratings but until a system is agreed upon and everyone begins to use it, ratings will remain a patchy and unreliable way to restrict access. (In 1999 Australia announced legal measures to curb the spread of pornography and other illegal or dubious information, especially with a view to protecting children. While laudable and widely supported, it remains to be seen exactly how ISPs can follow the law in detail. If nothing else it is likely to result in a number of interesting legal test cases.)

The situation is slightly better on the on-line services, which have a more family-oriented approach. Some services, such as AOL, offer separate account names for each family member, and these can be set up from the 'master account' so that certain features of the service are unavailable. Access to the Internet can also be controlled from the master account.

One problem is that these controls are set up using a password system, and enterprising youngsters can look over their parents' shoulders so they can 'borrow' their password later. For some children, being left in a special children's web site is not enough, and it is usually very easy to escape and follow links that lead to more adult content.

Chat rooms and IRC can present difficulties of their own. You should explain to children that they should never give out identifying information, including names and addresses, school names, passwords, and so on, to anyone without your permission. Nor should they arrange a face-to-face meeting with someone they have met on the Internet without asking you first. Finally, if they come across upsetting messages which are aggressive and verbally abusive or suggestive, you should insist that they tell you immediately.

In practice, the best way to avoid inappropriate information is to rely on active forms of parenting. Finding a balance between effective concern and intrusive paranoia can be difficult here, and the whole subject needs to be handled with tact. Useful possibilities include:

- moving the PC to a living room where you can watch what children are using it for
- checking bookmarks and your browser's history file to see if any explicit or inappropriate sites have been marked. (For the latter, search the filing system for files or folders which contain the word 'history')
- checking new information that may have appeared in your computer's filing system – especially image files (names ending in .gif, .jpg, .tif), video files (.mov, .avi) or archives (.zip).

One problem that is particularly severe on the Web is the prevalence of manipulative advertising aimed specifically at children. Some 'kids' sites' are really thinly disguised corporate attempts to brainwash youngsters into an inappropriate enthusiasm for products and merchandising. It is useful to review these sites in the same way that you would check for information of a more explicitly inappropriate nature. Apart from being better for the children, you will also save yourself the effort needed to dissuade a determined youngster from pressuring you into buying something that neither of you really wants or needs. Parents who would like more advice should try the NCH Action for Children web site at *www.nchafc.org.uk*

Other Internet scams to avoid

The following is a list of other popular scams and con tricks typically sent out indiscriminately as junk mail messages. Generally, *any message that appears unsolicited from a complete stranger is most probably dubious.*

Bogus freephone numbers An email arrives that claims to include important information about a family member, or that the recipient has won a prize, or in danger of legal action over an unpaid bill. The email includes a 'free' phone number that can be dialled for more information. This number is really a high-cost premium rate or overseas number.

Unnecessary millennium bug tests Many companies and individuals are now preying on the insecurity of computer users with tests and 'fixes' that cost anywhere between £20 and £200 – even though test software is available on the Internet for free.

'Free' prizes As with the postal equivalent, the 'free' prizes only become available when an up-front payment has been made.

Chapter 9

Using the Internet for profit and fun

Although the Internet was originally designed for researchers and academics with advanced computer skills and high IQs, it is now becoming as easy to use as the telephone and television. The uses it is put to are changing accordingly, from software development and the exchange of academic information to commercial applications and entertainment. These new uses are still relatively undeveloped, although, even with the limited technology of today, the Net can already be used as an extremely effective business tool, as well as a wonderful source of diversion.

The Internet for business

Although more sophisticated business tools – such as up-to-the-minute stock quotes and portfolio management services – are only just beginning to become available, it can be surprising how much is already possible with the creative use of email, newsgroups and the World Wide Web. Their power is most obvious when all these tools are used to support each other. Because they are all available to the general public, the facilities they offer can be used by any business, no matter how small.

The Net's great strength as a business tool is that it provides easy access to information and other people. It can take the place of a library full of contact numbers and directories and can make it much easier to find customers and new business partners and *vice versa*. Sometimes this leads to new business opportunities that would not have been possible with more traditional media.

CASE HISTORY – Jacey

Jacey Bedford is a member of the folk group Artisan and used the Internet almost exclusively to arrange a US tour for the group. Her story is a good example of the way the different parts of the Net can be used together to accomplish a task that would not be possible with any one of them in isolation.

'Our most recent US tour was arranged via email. Using my PC and working from my office at home, I made contact with venue organisers, negotiated fees and dates and even enquired about airline tickets and car hire.

'To start off, I found a web site which lists American folk venues, state by state. This gave me addresses, phone numbers and, where available, email addresses. Once I found a site with good links it was easy to find other sites very quickly, and I used those links to find still more contacts. I also looked around in the *rec.music.folk* newsgroup and came across a few folk-related North American mailing lists. One of these was for radio DJs who present folk music, so I emailed them offers of free albums for airplay. The response time is very fast, and lots of DJs said they'd like to have albums. The DJs on the list have listings of the records they play in each show, so we were able to confirm whether they liked the records and if they were playing them a lot.

'Next I sent out emails to appropriate venues listed on the web venue database, introducing myself and the trio and offering to send out promotional packs and CDs. At the same time, I posted messages to the mailing lists and to *rec.music.folk*, asking if anyone else would be interested in having us. Then I sat back and waited. There were a few promising enquiries, and I traded emails with venue organisers to negotiate dates and fees. Once I had a few gigs confirmed, which took about a month, I posted again to the newsgroups and mailing lists to say "These are the venues already committed to our tour, does anyone else want to come on board?"

'At that point, with the area narrowed down to specific states and dates, I got enough fill-ins to complete the tour. We ended up with 13 dates in 15 days and travelled from Vermont to Pennsylvania, Delaware and then New Jersey. Only two nights on the whole tour were arranged by contact other than email.

'To co-ordinate the travelling, I looked up airline schedules on the Web (using search engines to locate airline web pages) and also checked car hire and prices. In some cases you can actually make your reservations or hire a car on-line. It's easy to turn virtual travel to real travel arrangements on the Web. All you need is nerves of steel and a credit card.'

CASE HISTORY – Samantha

Samantha Eddington discovered that business on the Internet can take on a life of its own, and the Net offers opportunities for new kinds of work which are entirely unique to it.

'It started when I decided to create my own web site. I was aiming for something that would help women in business – partly a reference guide, partly an e-zine (an electronic magazine published exclusively on the Web), partly a site where women could get together and talk about the issues involved.

'I mentioned the idea to a few friends and business contacts. I hadn't even got the pages published when I started getting attention from people who were interested in buying advertising space. It was all a bit of a surprise – there was just such a lot of interest and enthusiasm out there. Really, it's obvious why when you think about it. A full page ad in a glossy magazine can cost a few thousand pounds a month, but on the Web, where anyone can publish pages for next to nothing, amateurs can sell advertising for maybe £50 a year and still make a decent profit. The Web offers a captive, affluent audience, so advertisers love it.

'In the end I turned the offers down because I didn't want advertisements to affect the integrity of the site, and it felt completely wrong for the type of site I was wanting to produce. But I know that other people have started to make themselves a tidy little second income from taking advertising on their pages.

'I should be honest and say that the requests for advertising have slowed down now. There's so much on the Web these days that you'll only get serious attention from advertisers if your site is really popular. That's how the big sites like Yahoo! and AltaVista make their money. The advertisers know they'll get millions of visitors, and they're prepared to pay for that. The big search engines can also offer ad tracking – the ads they display will change to match the words the visitor is searching for, so the advertising is more effective. It's had the effect of squeezing out the little start-ups and the beginners, who either don't want to or can't play in that part of the market. But there's still money to be made if a site caters for a small niche market that can carry suitable ads for a low cost.

'But it's not just advertising that's selling. Once I had published my pages, I got a couple of offers of more web design work. And a friend of mine who started by putting up her own web pages just for fun has set up her own web design and consultancy company. She used to be a graphic designer but now spends her days writing HTML. That's a weird market – you can get "one man and his dog" outfits working from back bedrooms competing with multimedia consultancy houses that perhaps have a background in corporate video or CD-ROM design. Quotes for the same piece of design work can quite literally range from £750 to £10,000. And paying more doesn't necessarily get you a better product either. For anyone with design skills, it's been a bit of a gold rush – although, again, I'm expecting a shake-out over the next few years because, as the market consolidates, there will be less work to go around. On the other hand, it's likely that more and more ordinary businesses – the kind that usually advertise in the *Yellow Pages* – are going to want their own sites, and it's possible that there will be a whole new market for designers there.

'Unfortunately, I had to give up on my own site after a few months because maintaining it was taking up too much of my time. I really started it as a hobby, but it was becoming a full-time job keeping it running. But I learned a lot by doing it, and it was a very interesting experience for me.'

Many businesses make the mistake of treating the Web like an electronic version of a display advertisement or brochure. Although this can work well, it is not necessarily the best way to use the technology. The most effective sites offer the following advantages over traditional advertising:

- **Detail** You can get a lot more information on to a web site than you can in a typical paper brochure, and this gives you plenty of scope for doing things that you would not otherwise be able to do, such as offering a free service or free information which will attract visitors to your site. A good example would be an ISP that provides a free introduction to the Internet on its web site. The 'free extra' attracts visitors who would not otherwise want to see the site, and many of these people will then go on to read the advertising material. An outstanding free extra may even receive a 'web award' – these are rating systems developed by various companies and individuals to mark out particularly good sites. The amount of room on the Web makes it easy to publish large amounts of information in your site. An estate agent, for example, could include details of all the homes currently on the market in a format very similar to the paper flyers that agents currently produce. The extra overhead required to add full floor plans to an electronic flyer is minimal, and the web site serves to distract time-wasters who request flyers or even visits to properties they have no serious interest in buying.

- **Interactivity** Traditional publishing works only one-way (from publisher to reader), but on the Internet all activities can be two-way. Games, email, customer surveys, free prize draws, and so on, can all be interactive. Companies with sites on the Internet can support their customers, either with a mailing list (see page 49) or on the web site itself. Customers can ask questions of the company's support staff, and the answers are then made available for public scrutiny. This saves everyone time, because common questions can be answered once instead of again and again. Another useful by-product of this process is that the support creates a captive audience for the company's advertising.
- **On-line orders** A virtual shopfront has lower overheads than a real one and is open 24 hours a day, seven days a week. Although it may be wiser to give credit-card details over the phone (at least for the moment, see Chapter 8), customers can give details on-line of what they want to order and where they want it delivered without requiring any personal attention.

The Net and money

At the time of writing, the Net's relationship with money is uneasy, although this situation is showing signs of improving rapidly. The biggest problem is the lack of guaranteed security. Once this is solved – as inevitably it will be – the Internet will become as important to business as the high street and the retail park.

On-line share dealing

The Internet can help with share dealing in three ways:
- it can be used to supply information about share prices and the past and present performance of companies
- email can be used to send buy-and-sell orders to a broker
- help, tips and support are available on-line from other investors.

Up-to-the-minute share information is available from a number of subscription services, such as ESI (Electronic Share Information) at *www.esi.co.uk* These offer a range of options, from free trading summaries at the end of each day to up-to-the-minute share prices direct from the London Stock Exchange. A variety of news and other services – for example, full summaries of a week's trading, supplied in a form that will work with various popular financial software packages – are also available. These can be copied to your computer and analysed in your own time. Much of this information is also available in paper form, but many people seem to find the electronic option more useful and easier to work with.

The business of buying and selling on the Internet is done via brokers, who accept email requests and provide email confirmation of a trade. Many brokers on the Internet charge a flat fee of around £25 instead of a percentage commission, and this makes them good value for large transactions. The general public is not yet allowed to cut out the middlemen and trade 'on exchange' directly – to do so one would need a very secure connection, which the Internet is not yet ready to offer.

For help and support with share dealing, on-line services are the best choice. At the time of writing, there seem to be no UK-specific newsgroups devoted to share information, although a number of more general groups (such as *alt.invest.penny-stocks*) are available. However, on AOL, the Motley Fool pages provide some useful hints and tips for beginners, as well as suggestions for investment opportunities.

The combination of instant access to prices, speedy buy-and-sell facilities and plenty of on-line help and support make the Internet an unusually potent way to play the markets. The international nature of the Internet also makes it easy to build up portfolios in markets beyond the UK – especially the USA, where it is possible to use US brokers to trade shares on the US markets from the comfort of one's home in the UK. However, investors should be aware that, because the Internet is still not totally reliable, it is perhaps best thought of as a useful addition to existing trading facilities, rather than a replacement.

On-line banking

Since it was introduced in 1997, on-line banking is taking off quite rapidly. Many banks and building societies now offer an on-line service. Some use proprietary software; others offer widely available packages, such as Microsoft's Money. The security issues and technical teething troubles that plagued the earliest on-line banking experiments seem to have been largely cured. The charges (nominal) have to be set against the convenience of being able to check balances and make payments at all hours of the day or night. In short, Net users will find these services are well worth experimenting with.

On-line shopping

The Net is an ideal medium for selling certain kinds of goods and services (non-perishable luxury items, such as books and CDs) but not so good for others (perishable goods, such as foodstuffs). Its international nature (and, at the time of writing, the strength of the pound) make buying from overseas traders particularly attractive. On-line CD shops, and bookstores can carry a spectacularly diverse range of titles and also offer search facilities to make it easier to find specific items. One of the most successful bookstores is Amazon (*www.amazon.com*), which sells internationally and can supply obscure titles that many bookstores cannot even find. CD Now (*www.cdnow.com*) offers a similar service for CDs. In the UK some high-street stores are beginning to take advantage of the Web: Innovations, which sells gadgets (*www.innovations.co.uk*); and Argos, which sells domestic goods of all descriptions (*www.argos.co.uk*). Amazon has a UK-only branch at *www.amazon.co.uk*. The widest range of goods is available on web sites in the USA. These sell all kinds of items, from the mundane – mattresses, for example – to the extremely strange and unlikely – plates that protect the owner from 'harmful negative vibrations'. When you order from abroad, carriage and freight costs are usually reasonable, providing you do not want your purchase urgently. Deliveries can take anywhere between a few days, for companies that use an international courier service such as UPS, to a few months for items sent by ship. Always check delivery costs before buying, especially for heavy and bulky items. Watch out also for customs and VAT charges, as these can be considerable on some goods. (If an item is being sent by UPS, you can ask the supplier to send you a tracking number. You can then check its progress on the UPS web site at *www.ups.com* This details the movement of a package through the various depots and customs facilities involved in the shipping process.)

For the second category of goods, supermarket chain Tesco (*www.tesco.co.uk*) has pioneered electronic stores which serve the area around some of its branches. Goods are ordered on-line and, assuming you live within the required area, are then delivered to your door for a minimal charge. At the time of writing only 11 areas (ten in and around London, one in Leeds) are covered, but the scheme seems to have been well received, and Tesco has plans for virtual stores in other areas. Other supermarkets have been less keen to experiment. In general, many sites are still rather disappointing. Either they are simple electronic brochures with no ordering facilities, or they do not offer the full range of products available from the company.

Safe shopping

On-line shopping often makes use of credit cards. Credit-card companies have apparently had to deal with a number of complaints about unauthorised orders. However, it seems that a significant proportion of these have been complaints about orders placed with 'plain brown wrapper' web sites, run by companies that are perhaps not among the most reputable that trade on the Net. In general, credit-card trading on the Internet seems reasonably secure otherwise. (As a further security measure, deliveries are usually only possible to the card-holder's own address. This on its own goes a long way towards preventing fraud.)

To minimise any risks when shopping on-line, follow these tips:

1. **Look for 'secure' web sites** These either transmit card numbers to a business using a secret code, or else take care of card transactions themselves, acting as a trusted third party which uses card information to move money from one account to another, but never actually passes a customer's card details on to the business they are buying from. Secure web sites are usually clearly marked as such. While the code they use isn't totally secure, it is secure enough to make it time-consuming and inconvenient for anyone who wants to steal credit-card details.

2. **Choose your sites carefully** Any offer that appears too good to be true, most probably is. If there are no postal or telephone contact details, be on your guard. You may also want to ask for a paper catalogue, just to be sure that they have at least the beginnings of a legitimate business.

3. **Check the returns and refunds policy** This can be a particular problem if buying from abroad. If there is no returns or refunds policy, again, be on your guard.

4. **If you do decide to send a card number via email, make it hard to read in some way** This can be done by writing the number in words rather than as a string of digits, or by splitting the number across two or more emails, or by some combination of the

above. Some thieves use 'sniffer' programs which scan passing emails looking for anything that features a card-number-like string of digits. These measures will bypass most sniffers.

5. **Keep a record of all emails and other transactions** Some companies, such as CD Now, will send you regular updates that let you know what is happening with your order. *Always* keep any order numbers and other reference information. Check credit-card and bank statements as soon as you suspect there might be any discrepancies or other problems.

6. **Keep a special card with a low credit limit for Internet shopping** If your purchases never amount to more than a few hundred pounds, the safest thing is to ask for a special credit card with a very low limit, which you can use exclusively for on-line transactions.

7. **Use traditional methods including phone, fax, and even posted orders** to avoid having to give card details electronically. Processing non-electronic orders are less convenient and slower, but for non-urgent items this is still a perfectly legitimate way of doing business.

Note that Which? is now offering its own WebTrader certification scheme, which aims to make on-line shopping as safe as possible. Participating traders agree to a code of practice, and customers are protected as far as possible from fraud and other problems. Although WebTrader certification applies in the UK only, consumer organisations running similar schemes in other countries have agreed to work together to offer a similar service for consumers shopping outside the UK.

On-line selling

You can of course use the Internet to sell items, as well as buy them. Doing this professionally is known as ecommerce, and is outlined elsewhere (see page 232). But you can still use the Net to sell second-hand items you no longer want or need.

Newsgroups can offer a good way to do this. Currently the uk. newsgroups only include groups for selling books, computer equipment, and announcing stolen goods. However, you can sometimes still sell items relevant to other groups – such as old folk music CDs in *uk.music.folk* – providing that you attempt this only once or twice, and it is clear that you are not selling anything as a business. What is and isn't acceptable depends on the culture of each individual group, and if you check the archives or subscribe to a group for a while first, it will soon become obvious whether the attempt will be worth any flak you may attract.

On the Web, on-line auctions are becoming increasingly popular. The most widely used is eBay, at *www.ebay.com* (a UK version is available at *www.ebay.com/uk*) Sellers register for a small fee, and in return are able to offer anything from a £1,000 pair of recording studio speakers to a hobby pamphlet about building a bird bath. Buyers 'bid' whatever they think an item is worth. Auctions are time-limited, and if an item isn't sold it can be auctioned again immediately. Otherwise, the highest bidder wins. Buyer and seller then communicate by email to arrange delivery times and charges, payment method, and so on.

Although the process is supposed to be insured, there have been glitches, such as the case where a young teenager didn't appreciate that real money was involved, and committed his parents to spending more than $15 million on a variety of luxury items. In practice, the system is only variably successful. Typically it is rare and esoteric items that sell well. Everyday bric-a-brac seems less popular. Note also that the UK version of eBay still quotes prices in dollars. However, the relatively low cost makes it worth considering for anyone with odds and ends to sell.

Finally, you can of course list items for sale on your own web site. This is something that people seem oddly reluctant to do, but there is no reason not to take advantage of any free web space your ISP may supply in this way.

Meeting people

A lot of the fun of the Internet comes from meeting people. Newsgroups, mailing lists, chat rooms and IRC are the best places in which to make new friends. But other, less obvious, opportunities also exist. The Net has a strong tradition of on-line games and offers users the chance to create and participate in imaginary electronic worlds. These can be intensely social, and for some people the chance to meet other like-minded people is so important that they do not mind the fact that contact takes place at a distance, by way of a keyboard and computer screen.

Another good way to meet people is to publish a 'home page' – an autobiographical web site which lists interests, experiences, and so on. Home pages are often set up as a result of pure vanity, albeit usually of a rather mild kind, but are nevertheless an extremely popular part of Internet culture. The best home pages are shrines to the interests of their authors and attract copious attention from visitors who share those interests.

Finally, it is also possible to create your own newsgroup. This is a rather more advanced pastime than the others mentioned in this chapter, but it can also be a very good way to meet electronically a group of like-minded people on a regular basis.

On-line games

Computer games tend to be solitary affairs, but the Internet can remove the isolation and add a new dimension to games by enabling people to play with real opponents. Games fall into two categories:

- **Virtual worlds** are imaginatively social. The main object of the 'game' is to make contact with people and play-act different experiences
- **Networked games** are more limited and simply offer the chance to play a computer game – usually of a rather violent type – against human opponents instead of computer-generated ones.

Virtual worlds

These are completely imaginary environments on the Internet. They are used as a backdrop for participants who can pretend to be someone else for as long as they choose to remain there. MUDs (Multi User Dimensions, or sometimes Multi User Dungeons), MUSHs (Multi User Shared Hallucinations) and MOOs (Object Oriented MUDs – the acronym is always shown the wrong way round) are the areas of the Net in which game-players can create virtual playgrounds for themselves and for each other. In MUDs (the generic name for all of these environments), people can battle against the forces of evil, chase dragons, build futuristic cities and create imaginary communities. MUDs vary greatly in character and atmosphere: in some it is bad form to attack other inhabitants, while in others it is absolutely essential. Many are set in a Tolkienesque atmosphere familiar to readers of fantasy fiction. Some settings are based on other literary references, TV programmes or films. In some, the landscape and its features are fixed, while in others players can make their own additions to the imaginary world.

The MUD community is a small but vibrant part of the Net, which attracts a few thousand fanatical people each year. Some players live more of their lives on-line than in the real world. Even imaginary MUD-based marriages have been performed between couples who have never met in person. However, MUDs can be useful and educational too: some host writers' workshops or offer other kinds of virtual teaching.

You do not usually need special software to try a MUD. Some are on the Web, but many rely on vivid textual descriptions instead of graphics. The latter types are used via Telnet (see page 120). While the lack of graphics can be limiting, it can also free the imagination and make it possible to create environments – such as a 600m-high spiralling pink whirlpool – that might look less convincing if presented graphically. (At least without a sizeable special-effects budget and more time than most MUD designers have to spare.) For UK users, telneting to USA-based MUDs can sometimes be unbearably slow. However, with a wide variety of MUDs to choose from, it should be possible to find one more locally that responds much more quickly.

Everyone should try a MUD at least once, just for the experience. Although they may not interest everyone, by creating environments which nurture fiercely bonded communities, MUDs represent a taste of what the Net may have in store for all Internet users in the future. However, they also encourage a lot of time-wasting on-line. Long-term exposure is definitely not recommended for anyone who is accessing the Net from home – at least not without limitless financial resources.

Networked games

Networked games are conventional computer games that can be linked together over the Internet. A typical example is Quake, which features a gory and violent surreal environment populated by monsters and other players. Most networked games are 'shoot-'em-ups' which rely on killing or disabling opponents. Unlike MUDs, which rely to some extent on imagination and on-line social skills, networked games do not offer much in the way of personal interaction. The attraction comes from having one or more real, as opposed to computer-generated, players to contend with. Very popular games, Quake among them, are sometimes made available on special server computers which are maintained by an ISP. If there is enough demand, ISPs may set up these services on request.

Setting up a networked game is usually fairly straightforward. The games themselves include information on how to do this, and the most popular games always have newsgroups devoted to them. Anyone who is having problems or is unsure about how networking works in practice can typically find all the answers they need in these groups.

A system called Wireplay is often used for networked games. Once run by BT, it is now a free service that can be used by anyone. Wireplay provides high-speed connections for gamers in the UK, and also access to Internet gamers worldwide. For someone who concentrates solely on games, it can be a good way to take advantage of social gaming without necessarily going to the trouble of installing a full Internet connection. More details are available at *www.wireplay.co.uk*

Publishing your own web pages

To publish your own pages you need two things: access to space on a web server, and suitable web publishing software. Many ISPs and on-line services have their own web servers, and customers are allowed to use these at no extra cost. This facility is described as 'space on a web server' because customers are given a small part of the storage space on the server's hard drive. Typically, this is about 5 megabytes, which is enough to publish a couple of books like this one, including the text, the cover art and all the illustrations. Alternatively, you can sometimes find free space on a web server elsewhere; a good example is the Geocities Project (*www.geocities.com*), which is an attempt to create a collection of on-line communities arranged according to different themes and interests.

When looking for space for your pages, check the speed with which existing pages on that site appear. Some of the popular 'free' locations can be notoriously slow, which is obviously counterproductive if you want your pages to be seen by as many people as possible. Another point to watch for is the contractual details involved. Some free hosting companies require you to sign an agreement that effectively gives them full legal rights to any material you use on your site. This includes any creative work of your own. Artists, musicians, writers and anyone else who works creatively may wish to consider hosting companies with contracts that are more flexible. To find a selection of suitable sites, do a web search on 'free web hosting'.

When publishing pages you need to check whether the type of information you are allowed to present is restricted in any way. Some

ISPs and other web server facilities only allow information of a non-commercial nature. If you are publishing for a hobby these restrictions are not usually relevant.

The choice of web publishing software is endless. Pages are created using a simple computer language called HyperText Markup Language (HTML). HTML uses standard English letters and characters arranged in special ways to specify how text, links and other information appear on a web page. It is possible to write HTML by typing text into a simple word processor – although this is not recommended, as doing it this way is something of a chore. A better approach is to use HTML editing software (see Appendix 5).

CASE HISTORY – Eileen

Eileen Herzberg, a freelance journalist and author living in Cornwall, found that creating her own pages was far simpler than she thought it would be.

'It was surprisingly easy to put up my home page. I did have to phone my service provider a few times to ask some questions. If I'd known it was this easy I'd have done it ages ago. The package I used – HomeSpinner, a shareware package for the Macintosh – was very straightforward, although to be honest I just stuck to the absolute basics. Publishing was very interesting though. One thing I found was that doing something simple like making the page a different colour had an enormous impact but didn't take much effort.

'To start with I thought I had to put '<CR>' marks at the end of each line to break the text up into paragraphs, but then a friend showed me that putting '<P>' at the start of a paragraph and '</P>' at the end of it worked just as well and had the added benefit of making paragraphs the correct width no matter what size the screen was.

'But that's been about the only problem. So far it's been great. I've had a lot of feedback, which has been useful, and it's really fun getting email from complete strangers who read my pages.'

Creating a newsgroup

Although this is not usually something that most Internet users are likely to attempt, it can be surprisingly straightforward to do. The hardest part is dealing with the politics that surround newsgroups. If your newsgroup is to be successful, it needs to be available on as many newsgroup computers (news servers) as possible. This means you have to persuade the news administrators on the various servers that they should carry your group. Some carry all of them as a matter of course, while others are much more selective. To make the creation process easier for everyone, there is a fixed procedure that you have to follow. If you stick to the procedure, most administrators will carry it, if you do not, your group may be deleted ('rmgrouped' in the jargon) and made unavailable on many news computers.

The procedure is simple. Someone interested in a new group has to post a proposal called an RFD (Request for Discussion) in a special group called *news.announce.newgroups* Everyone who visits this group then says whether or not the group, and the group name, are a good idea. If the proposal gets lots of support, the proposer calls for a vote (CFV). If the vote is carried, the new group is created (newgrouped) by a designated news administrator. Following this procedure means that it is unnecessary for you to know about the technical details involved in creating a group – in effect, it is up to you to sort out the politics, and then someone else who is more technically minded creates the group on your behalf. (While the technical process required to create a group is straightforward and can be done from any computer, a group created without going through the discussion process will be considered a 'rogue' group and not treated seriously. As mentioned above, this typically means that it will be rmgrouped on most news servers, rendering it useless.)

This process applies specifically to international groups. However, a similar procedure is followed to set up more local ones. For example, to create a UK-only group (specifically, one that starts with 'uk.'), votes and discussions are posted to *uk.net.news.config* instead of *news.announce.newgroups* Otherwise, the process is identical.

Proposals for both local and international groups need to be formal in character and carefully thought through. It is best if the proposed group has a full charter, which lists what can and cannot be posted and also says whether or not someone has editorial control over it.

Discussions about new groups can be quite heated, and anyone who wants to create one should be warned that some of the comments – especially in the *uk.net.news.config* group – can seem rather petty and narrowminded. Much of the discussion centres around the names of groups and whether they match their intended function. UK news administrators are very keen to make sure that group names make sense, and their motives are not always understood by outsiders who simply want to create a new group to support a hobby or personal interest. For example, the group *uk.lifts* was removed because the name was supposedly ambiguous. In the event, a group called *uk.transport.ride-sharing* was created in its place. However, soon afterwards, one prankster set up an unauthorised group called *uk.vertical.people-transporters* presumably to make the point that some people might prefer a more relaxed approach to the naming of groups.

In the UK it is important to remember that many news servers are based at universities. (In fact, the UK academic network – JANET – is a major part of the Internet in the UK.) This has implications for the kind of groups that are acceptable. One reason why the UK does not have a collection of *uk.sex.* groups in the way that other countries do, is because academic news administrators worry that students will waste time and computing resources on something that is not relevant to their studies. Similarly, any group that is related to a commercial enterprise – even a book or magazine publishing house – is unlikely to be accepted because of the Net's tradition of allowing only non-commercial use.

These political considerations can be a minefield for anyone attempting to create a group, and, unfortunately, there is no easy way to find out what will or will not offend the people who run the UK's news servers, short of actually going through the process and learning the hard way. Full details of how to create a new newsgroup are posted regularly to *news.announce.newusers* and in the UK to *uk.net.news.config* Details are also available on the Web at *www.usenet.org.uk*

This process does not apply to the *alt.* collection of groups (see Chapter 5), and they are more or less out of control. A group called *alt.config* is used for a loose discussion of new *alt.* group subjects, but many news administrators either accept all new *alt.* groups without question or ignore them completely. Either way, it is much easier to create an *alt.* group than any other (proposers simply have to follow the steps that are posted there regularly), and the politics are not so prevalent.

Appendix 1

Choosing an Internet service provider

There are now hundreds of Internet service providers (ISPs) in the UK, ranging from those with tens of thousands of subscribers to those that have only a few hundred. Although they all do more or less the same thing – offer you a basic connection to the Internet over a telephone link – the level of service they provide can vary tremendously.

The information included in the publicity and advertising materials offered by most services is not detailed enough to base a choice on. The best ways to compare ISPs are to read magazine reviews and to ask for personal recommendations. (*Internet* magazine offers regular surveys and league tables of the best and worst performing ISPs.) You can also find out a lot about an ISP by asking the kinds of questions suggested in this chapter.

Unfortunately, irrespective of which ISP you choose, you will almost certainly have problems sooner or later. The Internet is still partly an experimental service, and because of this many ISPs seem to think they can offer appropriately experimental levels of customer care. The situation is improving slowly, but the reality is that your connection, together with the various Internet services at the other end of it, are unlikely to work flawlessly all the time. Even if it seems to start well, the service may get worse over time. ISPs tend to suffer from growing pains; for example, a service that was doing well with a thousand or so subscribers may start having serious difficulties when that number doubles, although after perhaps another six months the problems may be solved and its service may become dependable again. Computer systems can surprise the unwary in this way: once they are working near their limits, a 10 per cent increase in demand can create a 90 per cent reduction in service. Most ISPs do not have the experience to be able to predict situations like this, and they tend to deal with problems after they have started happening, rather than plan ahead to avoid them. In short, there are no absolute guarantees of quality. However, by following the advice below, it should be easy to spot some of the more reliable companies.

The arrival of free ISPs means that some people now subscribe to more than one ISP or on-line service. There is often no reason at all not to do this, although unless you are moderately computer literate you will sometimes find that installing one ISP's software will cause problems with that of another installed previously.

There is a way around these complications, but it may require expert help or prolonged research and head scratching before it can be persuaded to work as required. The trick is to use the same software for every ISP, and to create a different dial-up process for each one. This simply creates an Internet connection by calling whichever ISP you select. Once connected you will be able to check for email – from all of your ISPs, if need be – and use a web browser as usual. If one ISP is busy or seems slow, you can simply call another. (Note, however, that you will still only be able to *send* email, and use newsgroups, from your home ISP. While it is possible to circumvent this limitation, the steps required are beyond the scope of this book.) For more details on how this process works, see page 254.

What to look for in an ISP

It is possible to assess the level of service offered by an ISP objectively. When choosing between competing providers you should consider the following points.

Speed

The obvious measure of an ISP's speed is the speed of its modems. The simple rule of thumb is that an ISP's modems should be at least as fast, and preferably faster, than the one that you plan to use. Modem speeds are shown as a number – either 28.8k, 33.6k or 56k. The larger the number the faster the connection. The first two of these are now effectively obsolete, although some people still use 33.6k modems. (For more information about modems and modem speeds see page 191.)

But there is more to speed than the modem connection. Significant differences exist in the rate at which ISPs can access information from far-off parts of the Internet and deliver it to you. These differences can be very obvious – for example, with some ISPs it can become impossible to read certain web pages or copy particular software from the Internet because the information takes an unreasonably long time to get to you, especially during busy periods.

Unfortunately, you cannot check for these kinds of problems without first making a connection, and this means signing up for the service. However, some magazines publish objective tests which compare the performance of different ISPs. It is a good idea to refer to these before making a choice.

It can also be worth asking the ISP about its own connections to the Internet. Some smaller ISPs re-sell the services of larger ones through a slow and relatively cheap connection. If you come across an ISP that does this, it makes sense to cut out the middleman and go directly to its supplier to get your connection. A company that has a thousand-plus customers but is connected to the Internet over a single, relatively slow permanent connection will have serious problems keeping information flowing at a reasonable rate.

You should also check how long it takes for newsgroup messages to appear on a news server and for email to arrive at its destination. In this respect, some of the larger ISPs offer a very poor service indeed. Their facilities are permanently overloaded, and email messages can take hours to pass through the ISP's computers to their destinations. This is a serious consideration for anyone who uses the Internet professionally. If you are using email to deliver something to meet a deadline, using an ISP with a slow email service can be more trouble than it is worth. And of course, if someone sends you a message you should be able to read it almost immediately, instead of a few hours later.

As yet, magazines do not include tests of email and newsgroup delivery speeds in their surveys, because objective trials are quite hard to set up. So, unfortunately, the only way to test this part of a service is to do it for yourself. You can easily find out how long emails take to arrive at their destinations by arranging to send one to a friend and asking him or her to tell you when it arrives. Email headers (described in Appendix 6) also contain time and date information about how long the message took to get from your computer to its destination.

Another point to watch for is the time it takes to get a connection to the Internet, especially during busy periods. If too many people call the service at the same time, they will not all be able to get through at once, and some will be left listening to a 'busy' signal.

Ideally, you should always be able to get a connection the first time you try. Having to dial two or three times once in a while is not perfect but is still acceptable. Having to dial ten times is completely unacceptable – although some ISPs have attempted to offer this level of service to their customers. Smaller ISPs can suffer from the same kind of problem on a more modest scale.

The number of times you try to connect is directly related to the number of modems your ISP has installed at its headquarters, and also to the number of customers who are trying to use the service. This is usually called the 'modem to user ratio'. Five users per modem is a very respectable figure, and the average is usually about ten. Thirty is an unacceptably high number; if your ISP's modem to user ratio is as bad as this, you will certainly have problems trying to get through during busy periods.

To some extent this ratio also depends on the reliability of the modems. With thousands of modems, it is a near certainty that at any one time at least one of them will not be working. As more and more people call and start using the working modems, the chance of getting a faulty one increases. These kinds of problems can be even more annoying than busy signals because each failed call costs a small amount of money – usually 5p – whereas getting a busy signal costs you nothing.

Finally, you should also check if there are any known compatibility problems between the modem you use and the ones your ISP uses. Problems arise in the form of 'dropped lines' – connections which stop for no apparent reason – and connections which fail to complete. If you are having these difficulties, either your modem is not set up properly or your ISP is having trouble. In both cases the ISP should be able to sort out the problem.

Support

Support starts with your first phone call to the ISP, even if you are only enquiring about the service. If problems occur, you need to be sure that help is available. A handful of ISPs still expect an unrealistic level of technical expertise from their customers. You can eliminate these by making a short investigative phone call. Start by making it clear that you are a beginner and by asking some very basic technical questions. If the answers are far beyond your level of understanding, cross the ISP off your list (it will not be any better at helping you when real problems occur with the service). It is also important to check the times when technical support is available. Help that is provided only during office hours will be of no use if you intend to use your connection from home during evenings and weekends.

Some ISPs provide their own newsgroups, which their customers can use to support each other. These are ideal for slightly more experienced users who want support when attempting more advanced tasks, such as creating their own web pages. Newsgroups specific to an ISP will be more helpful than more general support newsgroups, because other contributors will be familiar with the ISP's individual technical quirks.

Other options include email support – although this assumes that someone on the other end will actually take the time to reply to your questions – and 'autoresponder' support, which is an email service for frequently asked questions (FAQs) that does not require any human intervention (see page 47). Again, the problem with all of these is assessing the level of technical expertise they are aimed at. It is one of the tragedies of the industry that very few support staff have much of an insight into the kind of frustration that beginners face when things go wrong. It is well worth taking the time to track down an ISP where staff show some appreciation of a non-technical person's point of view.

The other aspect of support is much more straightforward and can be summed up in one word – reliability. A good ISP can anticipate an increase in demand before it arises and will also have a number of backup facilities installed. If something goes wrong, or if new systems have to be installed to improve the service, you will not be left to suffer while the work is being done. Unfortunately, disasters do happen, and it is impossible for an ISP's staff to protect themselves and their customers from every possible problem. Backup systems, which duplicate vital components to improve reliability, do occasionally fail in unexpected ways. However, it is reasonable to expect that your email account will always be available, that email messages will never be lost and that you should be able to use the newsgroup service whenever you want to.

Not all ISPs can offer even this basic level of service. Newsgroups cause perennial problems because of the huge and ever-increasing amounts of information involved, and even the email system can be accident-prone. It is not unheard of for email to be 'bounced' when sent to a valid address because an ISP's systems were suffering from a glitch. This is an annoying fault, because the intended recipient gets no indication that a message meant for them never arrived.

Note that some 'free' ISPs charge exorbitant rates for technical support calls. This can be as much as £1 per minute. Remarkably, some of this may be spent listening to hold music. (The theory seems to be that beginners will need extra help, and so whatever profits are lost by offering a free service can, to some extent, be made up by charging them for this help.) It is obviously essential to be aware of any support charges before signing on the dotted line (or signing up electronically).

Free software

An ISP should give you 'click-and-go' software that does not require advanced technical skills, but the software offered by many often falls short of this ideal. The best ISPs do their utmost to hide the complexities of their software from you, while the worst ones provide software that makes the installation process seem like a technical nightmare.

Start by checking how much work you will need to do to get the service working. How much information do you need to type in? Is it obvious what should be typed where? Again, if you make it clear you are a complete beginner and the person at the customer services desk insists on using terms such as 'IP number' and 'nodename', then this ISP may not be the right one for you. Reassurances that the installation process is 'really very easy' should also be taken with a large pinch of salt if offered without supporting evidence.

Next, ask which software is available. At the very least you will be offered a web browser, usually Netscape Navigator or Communicator or Microsoft's Internet Explorer. This is very much the bare minimum needed to connect to the Internet. A more useful offer would include separate off-line email and newsreading software. (Facilities for newsgroups and email are included in web browsers, but these are very crude and clumsy compared with those available in dedicated newsgroup and email software.)

You can test certain software before you commit yourself to signing up with an ISP. Free versions or trial copies of the packages offered by most ISPs are given away on magazines' cover disks. However, these trials are not as useful as they might seem, because you will not be able to use the Internet properly without a connection. But you can at least have a go at installing the software before going on-line, and see how easy – or difficult – it is to get it working.

Remember that once you are on-line, you will be able to choose from the huge quantity of software that is available on the Internet. A start-up pack from an ISP should really be considered as a first step on to the Internet and not something that ties you to any particular software. Once on-line you will be able to find software to fit your needs.

Making a choice

Where once ISPs could be compared by asking their technical staff a number of questions, Internet access is fast becoming a commodity, and this approach is no longer as useful as it was. 'Sign-up CDs' are now available free for the asking from high street stores, on the covers of magazines, and attached to the inside back cover of Internet books. While free trials are helpful, it can be useful to stop and think before signing up for one. What exactly do you want to use the Internet for? What are your priorities? Questions like these can make it easier to decide among the many different ISPs and on-line services that are now available. Other aspects to consider include:

1. **Convenience and ease of use** For beginners and committed technophobes, an on-line service such as AOL is less likely to cause confusion and initial frustration than a 'proper' ISP.
2. **Technical sophistication** Someone who needs a full service and wants to find and use the most sophisticated software will most likely prefer an ISP instead.
3. **Access to specialised information** Banks, supermarkets, Which? Online, and others all provide – to a greater or lesser extent – access to interesting, and even potentially money-saving information.
4. **Communities of interest** If socialising, sharing friends and talking about hobbies and interests is important, then again on-line services such as AOL, and combined services such as Which? Online will be of particular interest.
5. **Relative performance** Internet magazine league tables will be very helpful here, and will make it clear which ISPs are able to offer

a reliable, speedy service. Performance is particularly important for those using paid-for ISPs; with these time is literally money. The criteria are less rigid for free ISPs, although busy people will still appreciate a speedy connection that does not keep them waiting.

6. **Support costs** How much does it cost to get help? Is it available 24 hours a day, seven days a week?

7. **Quality of the news service** This can typically only be gauged by trying it out. Signs that may give cause for concern include very slow copying of news information to your computer, groups that are clearly missing a large number of posts, or a very limited range of newsgroups. (Any fewer than 10,000 groups can be considered limited.)

8. **Consider the small print** Check for minimum contract periods, hidden sign-up fees, comments about 'passing your contact information on to interested parties', pricing schemes for paid-for services, and so on. AOL, for example, has been known to sign up new customers on its 'budget' tariff, which effectively means that after a small payment and some free time, they are then charged by the hour – even though the 'unlimited' service costs only slightly more per month, and is far more popular with established users. If it is a service which offers free telephone costs, will it be cut off after a certain period? (In one case an ISP offered a totally free connection for 24 hours a day – which cut off after ten minutes, rendering it useless for anything other than occasional email.)

9. **Might it be a scam?** Look out for ISPs that only advertise on the Web and have no postal address or phone number listed. A typical scam may claim a 24-hour completely free connection, but when the user fills in the electronic form he or she receives an email asking him or her to sign up another four friends before the scheme becomes available – which, the email claims, will happen eventually, once 'some technical difficulties have been sorted out'. (In fact this was simply an address-harvesting scam for a spammer. However, related schemes have been offered by genuine ISPs, which are using an illegal pyramid scheme to build a customer base.)

Beyond these considerations, the actual service offered by most ISPs is now very similar. It may also be worth noting any information about:

Web space 5Mb has become the minimum that is offered. In practice this should be plenty for a fairly complex home page. While more may

183

be welcome in theory, it is unlikely to be useful in practice unless you plan to include lots of detailed artwork on a site, or recorded music.

Unlimited mail addresses Some companies offer 'unlimited mail'. You get a mini 'domain name' of the form *@whateveryouwant. ispname.co.uk* and can then use anything in front of the '@' sign to create an almost infinite number of email addresses. Some (but not all) email software will be able to filter these, so they can be sent to different recipients. This is particularly useful for companies that run a network of computers. Other ISPs simply offer *whateveryouwant@ispname.co.uk* This is equivalent to a single email address, and is more suitable for individuals.

POP3 email This is now standard for almost all ISPs. It makes it possible to check your email from a connection made anywhere on the Internet. The older SMTP mail system could only be used with a direct connection to your ISP.

Appendix 2

Choosing hardware for the Internet

Choosing a computer

Computers come in two types – 'traditional' personal computers (PCs), which first became available in the early 1980s and have been improving steadily since then, and the much newer 'Network Computers' (NCs). At the time of writing (summer 1999), these look as if they are unlikely to have as much impact as their proponents had hoped. Examples to date have been too expensive to compete successfully with cheap personal computers. However, it is still possible the idea may come to fruition early next century.

Personal computers

You can use almost any personal computer (PC), although, of course, more powerful ones will give better results. The most important things to check are the availability of Internet software for your computer system and the speed at which it can handle incoming and outgoing information.

Any PC built after about 1993 which works with Windows 3.1, or a later version, or any Apple Macintosh that works with System 7, or a later version, will be able to use most of the latest Internet software. Users of more modern computers which can use Windows 95, 98 or NT on the PC, and System 7.5 onwards on the Mac will be able to use all the latest software, without exception.

If you have a personal computer other than those listed above, your use of the Internet will be limited. This is because your computer will not be able to read any type of information other than text; the full-colour graphics of the World Wide Web will be inaccessible, as will some of the special software needed to use an on-line service. What is

and is not possible for any particular computer is changing
continuously. For the latest information you should check one of the
relevant specialist magazines.

Network Computers

Today's personal computers are far too complicated and expensive for
many home users, and even business users have found them to be more
expensive than they at first seemed, because the cost of maintaining
them is much greater than the initial outlay.

Network Computers are an attempt to solve both these problems.
They are designed to be cheaper and easier to use than a personal
computer. Instead of working with software that has been installed
internally, NCs retrieve it from a network (the Internet, an intranet or
a more traditional business network). Because of this, NCs need only
enough working space to store the software while it is in use. Some
NCs are even simpler than this, and are a modern version of the old-
fashioned display and keyboard combinations that were used in large
centralised computer systems in the 1950s and 1960s. These NCs are
very simple indeed – all the work is done on a larger computer system
elsewhere, and they are used only to type in information and display
the results.

NCs come in a variety of shapes and sizes. Some are budget PCs
which – unlike existing PCs – cannot have new memory or other
extras added to them. This makes them simpler to design, build and
maintain. Others take a completely new approach, which is unrelated
to existing PC designs. These use the Java system (explained in
Appendix 5) to create a computer that is essentially a web browser in
a box.

Home users are unlikely to find NCs useful until the bandwidth
problem is solved. The existing telephone system is far too slow to
make the 'remote software' concept a practical option, because it takes
too long for the software to be copied over a telephone line. Cable and
satellite systems do not have this disadvantage, and the combination of
these with an NC system has obvious potential. By the early part of
the twenty-first century it is quite likely that the NC idea will be
successful and will probably combine telephone and TV services with
Internet access. In the meantime, a number of companies have
experimented with adding Internet and in some cases TV facilities to

products that have more in common with computer-game consoles than with home PCs. It is probably fair to say that the results of these experiments have been underwhelming.

If you are considering any of these systems, it would be wise to wait for this new potential market to stabilise and standardise. You should be wary of any new products that are not yet standardised across the whole industry, as they stand a good chance of becoming obsolete very quickly.

For business and corporate users, the low-maintenance approach of the NC concept has obvious attractions. But the usefulness of an NC relies upon the speed and dependability of its supporting network, and some companies are finding that maintenance costs are simply being transferred rather than reduced. There are also questions of security when information is centralised, and 'future proofing' – how well will the network cope with the new load if a company expands? Issues like these require the skills of an experienced network consultant. Although some parts of the computer trade are touting NCs as a solution for all kinds of problems, in practice they bring new ones of their own. These need to be assessed carefully when you are deciding whether or not an NC system is the best possible solution.

The Internet without a computer?

At the time of writing, most Internet users connect to it through a home or work computer. However, it is possible to connect other kinds of devices to the Internet, and still use some of the same services. (In fact in the long run it is likely that computers will become less and less prominent, and the Internet will become a pervasive part of everyday life. Cars will be connected to it, so will mobile phones, and perhaps even many domestic appliances.) Currently, there are three ways to use the Internet without a computer.

Set-top boxes have often been promoted as a replacement for a full computer, but so far no one has produced a system that is truly popular and lives up to the potential of the idea. This may change as bandwidth improves and both television and computer information can be sent to a home over the same connection. This may be of particular interest to users of satellite TV, as some schemes plan to combine satellite and Internet information in a convenient way.

In the meantime, it's perhaps best to avoid any set-top boxes that may appear until it is obvious that the market for them is stable and established, and that they aren't simply a short-lived technological cul-de-sac. Realistically, most set-top boxes are attempts to create a network computer, with all the caveats that that implies.

Mobile phones which offer built-in software for email and the Web – notably models from Nokia and Alcatel – are becoming more widely used. These are larger and heavier than conventional models, but include either a built-in mini-typewriter keyboard, or a 'virtual keyboard' that is used with the help of a large display. They are an excellent way to use the phone networks' SMS (Simple Message Service) which offers a simple, cheap alternative to email for mobile users who need to exchange short messages. They are not quite as convenient for true Internet use. Mobile connections are currently very slow (and hence expensive), and this makes web browsing problematic. This remains true even if all the illustrations are filtered out – an option available on some phones – and information is displayed as 'text only'. Nevertheless, they are a convenient way to be able to read and send short email messages away from the office. The inclusion of an address book and simple word-processing facilities makes them a viable replacement, for less demanding work, than a full-sized laptop computer and cellular modem.

Specialist telephones are simply conventional telephones with built-in Internet facilities. They typically include a small keyboard that can be hidden when not in use, and an unusually large display which can be used for reading and writing email messages. Otherwise they offer all the usual telephone services, including an answering machine, caller identification, memories for frequently called numbers, and so on. These may appear to be an ideal solution for the technophobic, or for anyone who doesn't want the expense and complication of a full computer.

An important point to check is the speed of any built-in modem. A version of a phone made by BT, for example, includes a 1,200bps modem when a 57,600bps model might have been expected. At these speeds, even email messages can add a sizeable amount to a phone bill. This phone transmits and receives information a shocking 48 times more slowly than a computer. While this may be adequate for someone who sends and receives a couple of messages a day, more intensive use will soon result in an inflated bill.

Links between computers and the Internet

Although most people use what is known as a modem link, this is in fact the slowest way to connect a computer to the Internet. Faster, more expensive options are available, although these will be beyond the means of most home users.

Choosing a modem

A modem (modulator-demodulator) is a unit that converts computer information into 'rasps and squeals' that can be sent over a telephone line to another computer. Modems for PCs are now relatively affordable, easy to install, even for non-experts, and available over the counter in computer stores. In fact many new computers are sold with a modem already built-in. But how can you tell whether a modem is any good? And if you already have a computer, how do you decide which modem to buy?

As with other computer components, the price of modems has come down dramatically since the middle of the 1990s. As a result, there is very little reason to settle for a modem that is not of very high quality. The main points you should check for are discussed below.

BT approval

When the Internet first started to become popular in 1994, 'illegal' modems – those that had not been tested and approved by BT – were widely available. Although it was illegal to use them on the UK telephone network, it was perfectly legal to buy and sell them. Some of these modems had minor compatibility problems, such as an inability to recognise a 'busy' signal. But they were also significantly cheaper than certified modems, and some people took the risk and ignored the legalities.

With the explosion of interest in on-line services, modems are much more of a commodity item now, and this shady practice is no longer necessary. Almost all modems are now fully BT-approved and marked with the green triangle symbol (as opposed to the red circle that indicates the absence of approval). It is still wise to check, just to make sure, because there is no reason why you should settle for a non-approved modem when an approved one with the same features at a similar price is available.

Internal/external modems

Internal modems are supplied as a circuit card, without a case, that needs to be fitted inside your computer. External modems sit outside the computer at the end of a special cable.

Unless you are very experienced you should *always choose an external modem*. They are slightly more expensive, but you will almost certainly save yourself hours of frustration when you try to install the modem and get it working. Internal modems are notoriously difficult to set up properly and require a combination of technical knowledge, persistence and – apparently at least – plain luck before you can get them to work. External modems are much more straightforward to set up.

When buying an external modem, check whether or not a certain type of adapter is included in the package. The connectors on the back of a Windows computer can have either 9 pins or 25. If you have an adapter you will be able to use either of these. It is likely that you will need an adapter, so you may save yourself time if you get one on the spot. These adapters cost a pound or two at most, and it can be worth asking for one to be included for free, just to close the sale. (If you have a Macintosh, make sure your modem includes a suitable cable to fit your Mac's 'serial connector' or 'USB connector' in the case of more recent models.)

Speed

Speed is the single most important factor to consider when you are buying a modem as it sets an upper limit on how quickly information can move between your computer and the Internet. This can make a significant difference to your phone bill. Slower modems are adequate for occasional use but leave you no room for expansion if you find your interest in the Internet starts to take off. Faster modems are, of course, more expensive, but prices are dropping steadily. The very fastest models cost between £100 and £200. Slower models are only rarely available.

Speed (bps)	Speed (kbps)	Code
2400	2.4	V.22bis
9600	9.6	V.32
14400	14.4	V.32bis
28800	28.8	V.34
33600	33.6	V.34+
57600	57.6*	V.90

* Modems that work at 57.6kbps are usually called 56k modems

A peculiarity of the modem market is that while more expensive models than those mentioned above are available, they do not go any faster and seem to offer few, if any, advantages over their cheaper siblings.

Until recently, a confusing system of code letters (the 'V' standard) was used to describe modem speeds, but in most advertising this has now been replaced with a straight measure of the speed in bits per second (bps) or thousands of bits per second (kbps.) The latter two are a direct indication of the speed at which the modem works: a 28.8kbps modem will move information twice as quickly as a 14.4kbps model, and a 57.6kbps model will move it twice as fast again. You will sometimes see this shortened form of the speed with a 'k' instead of the '.' – thus 33k6 means the same as 33.6kbps. (Note that for apparently random marketing reasons, modems that work at 57.6kbps are usually called '56k modems'.)

A 9600bps modem is adequate only for very occasional email, while a 14.4kbps is the absolute minimum needed for Internet use. More serious users need a faster modem: 33.6kbps has leap-frogged 28.8kbps as the standard speed, although in practice the maximum speed is impossible to reach on anything other than a crystal-clear telephone line. Many people find that 33.6kbps modems work only at the slightly slower speed of 31.2kbps. This depends on the quality of the modem and the telephone line and the modem's compatibility with the ISP's modem at the other end. When looking for a modem, read comparative reviews very carefully to see if this problem is mentioned.

The 57.6kbps speed suffers from similar problems. Modems can work at this speed only by stretching the limits of the UK telephone system and by relying on special techniques that bypass some of its shortcomings. These techniques work only one-way – from the Internet to your computer – so in practice these modems work at two speeds: 57.6kbps when receiving information, and the more usual 33.6kbps when sending it. Most people receive much more information than they send, so this is a relatively minor drawback. These very high-speed modems are even more susceptible to telephone line noise and interference than their slower predecessors, and in practice you will not usually get them to go any faster than about 44kbps.

Originally, 57.6 kbps modems used one of two standards – X2 from US Robotics or k56Flex from Motorola. These two standards were incompatible. In practice, this meant that buyers had to make sure that their modem used the same system as their ISP, otherwise connections would be made at slower speeds.

However, a new unified standard called V.90 was agreed at the start of 1998. To avoid compatibility problems you should make sure that any modem you buy adheres to this standard. Certain older modems can be upgraded easily. 'Flash' modems have special chips inside them to hold their operating software. These can be upgraded by copying and running special software created by the manufacturers from the Internet. For more details consult your modem dealer or the manufacturer's web site.

Extras and special deals

Many modems include free trial offer software for the major on-line services. While this should not sway your decision as to which modem to buy – these offers are freely available elsewhere – the free trials are a useful bonus to have.

Some modems are now being sold with Internet access. When you buy the modem, you also pay for a year's access to a service provider. These deals can seem appealing, if only because they save you a certain amount of research and shopping around. But you should never sign up for a deal like this without thoroughly checking the credentials and reputation of the service provider in the usual way (see Appendix 1).

Finally, it is well worth looking into the extra features that a modem may offer. All modems can send and receive fax messages – although remember that you will be able to send only a fax that has been created inside your computer. (If you want to send a map or hand-drawn diagram, you will need an extra piece of hardware called a scanner, which can copy an image from the outside world into your computer, or a digital camera, which can copy in photographs without requiring film or film processing.)

Some modems also include voicemail facilities, which transform the modem into an answering machine, complete with a pre-recorded message and the ability to store incoming messages as recordings inside your computer. This is a useful feature, especially now that the latest modems have the ability to remember a certain number of fax and voice messages even when the computer they are connected to is not turned on.

A second line?

It may be tempting to consider using a second telephone line for heavy Internet use. This is a much cheaper option than ISDN (see page 194) and in practical use the difference in connection speed is not as obvious as it might be. If you do decide to install a second line, watch out for an attempt by BT to install a 'DACS' box instead of giving you a truly independent line. A DACS box combines two telephone lines into one. While the effects are barely noticeable on ordinary telephone calls, Internet connection speeds are slashed dramatically. Even with a fast modem, these rarely rise above 30kbps. When challenged about this, BT sales staff often seem to resort to saying that telephone lines are only guaranteed for voice, and not Internet use, and that there is nothing that can be done. Some BT customers have proved this is not true, and calling the fault repair service, or writing a number of assertive letters, has often resulted in the connection of a true second line. As an extreme measure, some customers have also had DACS boxes removed by signing up for BT's ISDN service (which requires two separate lines) and then cancelling the order once the DACS box has been taken away. This is highly questionable behaviour which cannot be condoned in any way, and so is only mentioned here as interesting background information.

Portable modems

So that a modem can be used with a portable computer, the circuitry has been shrunk to a size that will fit into the wafer-thin PCMCIA cards used in portable computers. PCMCIA modems work in exactly the same way as their full-sized counterparts but they are significantly more expensive. From the point of view of installation and setting up, they are equivalent to external modems.

One point to check is whether the modem can be set to work ('homologised') with foreign phone systems – an important consideration for anyone who plans to spend a lot of time abroad. Also, check the sockets on the modem for any sign of weakness. If it is likely to get heavy use it is important to be sure that this part of the system will not fail at an inconvenient moment. If you are travelling abroad, remember that almost every country has a different-shaped telephone socket, so you will need suitable plug adapters.

Cellular modems (data cards)

While conventional modems use the existing telephone network, cellular modems use the cellular networks built for users of portable phones. These modems are still fairly expensive to buy and use but they do offer the advantage of truly wireless communication with the Internet. At the time of writing, the maximum speed available is 9600bps, which is slow enough to make call charges something of a worry for all but the richest of users. Some modems are starting to use a 'data compression' system which makes information take up less space before it is sent over the network. This can improve transmission speeds significantly, although it will not work with files that have already been compressed on a computer. In practice, this means that email, web and newsgroup access should be up to four times faster, but anyone intending to download software from the Internet will find it much quicker and cheaper to use a telephone modem.

Remember also that cellular calls are not known for being secure. The older analogue cellular networks can be monitored by anyone with simple and affordable equipment, which can be bought over the counter in many parts of the UK. Digital networks are more secure, but even so it is wise to encrypt all email, especially if it contains sensitive information.

When considering a cellular modem, check that your Internet service provider or on-line service provider is sure that it will work with its system. Some companies, such as Demon, have negotiated deals with certain cellular phone companies, so check also if there are any special offers available that combine the two services.

Faster options

The maximum speed the current telephone network is capable of is 57.6kbps, and unless BT or a consortium of cable TV companies invest in a national rewiring scheme to replace old-fashioned copper cables with high-speed fibre-optic links – something that seems extremely unlikely at the moment – Internet users will have to look at other ways to speed up their connections. Some options offer much better value for money than others.

ISDN

ISDN (Integrated Services Digital Network) is a digital-only connection to the existing telephone system. The cumbersome process by which modems convert information into sound (and back again at the receiving end) is bypassed completely. As a result, ISDN systems offer higher transfer speeds and can also create a connection much more quickly – typically within a second or so, as opposed to ten seconds for a conventional modem. Instead of modems, ISDN systems use 'terminal adapters' (TAs). These connect your computer directly to the exchange over the link.

Another advantage of ISDN is that it can use a clever system known as dial-back. With a dial-back connection, your ISP's computer will call your ISDN link whenever information is available but hang up before the call is completed. This costs the ISP nothing but lets your ISDN connection know who the call was from. Your side of the link will then immediately call back automatically to retrieve the information. Dial-back can simulate the permanent connection offered by a leased line (see page 198) at a fraction of the cost. Unfortunately, after experimenting with this option, most UK ISPs seem to have decided not to offer it to their customers, although this may change in the future.

If you are a professional Internet user, ISDN can save you money (although only if you use the Internet almost continually). It also has the potential for very fast fax transmissions using the latest generation of 'group 4' fax machines (existing models use the older and slower 'group 3' system), video conferencing and high-quality audio connections.

However, the savings are not as clear cut or as certain as they might be. In Japan and Germany, ISDN systems are available for the same price as conventional phone lines. In the UK, BT maintains a complex pricing scheme which gives you the choice of trading off an initial outlay against an annual call allowance in a number of different ways. Installation charges are extortionate, as are line-rental costs. Call charges are the same as those for conventional calls, although if you choose a payment scheme with a call allowance you will, in effect, be getting calls for free – or at least as a compensation for the huge increase in line rental.

Some cable TV companies will fit and run an ISDN line for much less than this, although most seem to charge broadly the same amounts as BT does. If you are considering ISDN, it is a good idea to check with your cable TV company to see what kind of deal it can offer you. Some also offer free off-peak telephone calls, which can save you money even if you have a modem. In either case, you may be able to arrange significant savings for yourself by asking a few simple questions.

ISDN hardware is more complex than the typical socket-in-the-wall most people are used to. There are actually three variants: ISDN2,

ISDN30 and BT's simplified version of ISDN, which is known as Home or Business Highway (see below).

ISDN2 offers two 64kbps channels (known, for no obvious reason, as type Bs) and a separate signalling channel which runs at 16kbps (known as a type D). The two faster lines can be used separately, with one carrying voice conversations, while the other is connected to the Internet, or they can be linked to give a total speed of 128kbps. (The signalling line is an 'overhead' line and does not contribute to the speed of the system.) It is vital to note that at this higher speed the call charges can start to mount up because the two lines are counted as separate calls running in parallel. ISDN2 is now only available to special order. It is of interest to companies that would like to consider integrating a telephone and computer network.

Even with a single line, ISDN2 is much faster than a modem connection. A 56kbps modem will only manage around 50kbps at the very most, and typical speeds are more likely to be around 44kbps. Because ISDN does not rely so much on line quality, the service offers a link that is guaranteed to work at 56kbps or faster. This can be very useful for those who do a lot of web browsing. Any increase in price can be offset by the faster speeds that are available.

ISDN30 offers 30 'B' channels and 1 fast 'D' channel. It can run at up to 2000kbps (2Mbps). It is usually supplied as a fibre-optic link and is much more expensive than ISDN2. ISDN30 was originally designed for businesses that need multiple telephone lines, and not as an Internet connection, so it is quite hard to run all 30 channels in parallel as a 2000kbps Internet link. Some companies, such as Cable and Wireless, will very occasionally fit an ISDN30 system for free in return for a guaranteed number of calls over the course of a year. It is sometimes possible to negotiate deals like this on any ISDN30 line, although some companies will be more receptive to this than others. An important consideration with ISDN is whether or not your ISP supports it. The smaller providers are unlikely to do so, as it requires a sizeable investment.

BT's Home and Business Highway products offer two lines. These can be used as two normal voice traffic lines, two ISDN Internet access lines (in tandem, if need be), or one of each. Where ISDN normally requires an adapter before it can be used with a conventional telephone, the Highway system includes two standard telephone sockets which can be used in the normal way. The only practical difference between the Home and Business versions of the scheme is the cost. Home Highway is offered at a fixed price, while Business Highway is sold as one of three separate price options. These offer a complex trade-off between an increased quarterly line rental (which can be up to £275 for Business Highway) and a certain amount of 'free' call credits. If all the credits are used, charges accumulate in the usual way, at the same cost as a standard telephone connection.

With so many hardware options, pricing schemes, questions about availability and also its future in the UK, the whole area of ISDN is a very complex one. Anyone considering an ISDN30 system for their business should think seriously about hiring a telecommunications consultant to help ease the process, because linking the switchboard with the business's computer network and from there to the rest of the world is not a job for the technically inexperienced. A reputable consultant should be able to oversee the process and can help to prevent expensive mistakes, for example leaving a 'trapdoor' open to the exchange which hackers can exploit easily to give themselves free telephone calls.

For home and small business users, the choice is even more complex. Home and Business Highway are undoubtedly convenient. But compared to the prices charged on the continent, they are also scandalously expensive. Deciding which price plan to choose can become very complicated. BT occasionally sweetens the deals it offers by halving the standard ISDN installation fee. But realistically, given the high costs, by the time ISDN has become a popular option it will already be technically out of date, superseded by much faster connection possibilities such as cable and satellite links.

ISDN hardware

Although the technology used is rather different, ISDN terminal adapters (TAs) are now being sold in much the same way as modems. The costs are comparable, and TAs are also available in internal and external varieties. The external option (as with traditional modems) is a better bet, as setting up and installation are simpler.

TAs are more demanding of computer hardware, and any computer built before about 1995 may have problems coping with the speed of the link, especially when two ISDN lines are running in parallel.

ISDN TAs are now beginning to be combined with more advanced options. An ISDN router can connect a small computer network to

ISDN, taking care of Internet connections for the people who use the network automatically. More expensive options make it possible to combine Internet and multi-line telephone access for an office in a single unit.

An interesting option offered by ISDN is the ability to assign individual numbers to specific items of equipment. Even though there may only be two lines available, equipment can be set up to respond to incoming falls for up to eight numbers. Note, however, that this service costs extra, and very few items of office equipment feature this facility.

Leased lines

If you run a medium-sized business and your staff need regular access to the Internet, an even faster and more expensive option is the leased line. A leased line is a permanent direct connection to the Internet. Mail appears in your mailbox as soon as it arrives, instead of being held at your ISP's mail computer until you dial in. You can also maintain your own private connection to the Usenet news service. The most important advantages of a leased line are:

- **speed** Your connection is permanently available. To some extent, you can 'queue jump' users of dial-up accounts. Leased lines can also be much faster than dial-up links – tens of times faster in some cases
- **the possibility of creating your own personal web site with your own computers** This is done instead of hiring time and space on someone else's system – typically an ISP's. Using your own computers saves you monthly rental charges and means you can make your web site as big as you would like it to be with no restrictions. It also means that you get exclusive use of your web server and do not have to share bandwidth with other users whose sites may 'steal' it from yours, making your own site slower.

Leased lines are very expensive. Prices start at around £3,000 for a 64kbps connection, for those who are prepared to shop around and find the best possible price (BT typically charges twice this). The cost increases to as much as anyone can bear to pay, depending on the speed of the link and the length of the line (a leased line must go from A to B, definite points). You get a fully professional level of service, with engineers who can be paged immediately whenever a fault develops, and often 24-hour access to support calls. At this price a leased line is obviously not something that most private individuals can consider. But medium-sized businesses will find it can save money compared with the cost of equipping hundreds of staff with modems and dial-up accounts. And, of course, all the computer equipment and information can be kept on-site, where it is easier to maintain and manage.

Apart from the physical cost of the line itself, it is important to be aware that a leased line has implications for the security of your system. Because your computer system is now permanently on-line, it is open to millions of Internet users. You have to take precautions to make sure that the system is as secure as it can be. (For more details about this see Chapter 8.) This means that installing a leased line is a major undertaking, and you should consider and cost out all the implications before deciding to install one.

A number of companies have recently started to offer 'pseudo-leased' lines, which use a telephone link via a modem that is left permanently connected. It offers the advantages of a leased line at much lower cost – typically less than £2,000 a year. Although these pseudo-leased lines are slower than ISDN – typical speeds are 33.6kbps – they can be cost-effective for anyone who uses the Internet professionally and would like to be able to set up a private web server for a relatively small outlay. In practice you will need to be doing a lot of business from your web site to make one of these links cost-effective.

Satellite links

High-speed Internet access is also available by satellite. This is not quite as complex as it sounds – in fact, it is no more difficult than installing a satellite TV system. Of course, this is easier in some parts of the UK than others. No one will think twice about yet another satellite dish in central London, while inhabitants of rural areas may find that they have to abide by planning laws, and perhaps run into resistance from neighbours, and this can make the installation of a satellite terminal problematic.

It is very likely that during the early part of the twenty-first century, the Internet will 'go wireless' and leave the telephone system behind completely. Proposals exist for a number of global satellite networks which will offer this service.

In the meantime, satellite access gives higher speeds than ISDN at a price that offers relatively good value. Two systems are available:

- **true two-way satellite links** are about half the cost of the cheapest leased line but give speeds of around 400kbps. This is very fast indeed and offers the kind of access most home users only dream of. Businesses may find this kind of access well worth considering. It provides some of the advantages of a leased line at a fraction of the cost
- Slower, but cheaper, access is also available by way of a **combined system from Hughes–Olivetti**, which works together with a conventional modem. The satellite dish can only receive information, and a modem link is still used to send email and web-page requests. This is not much of a limitation in practice, because most people need to receive a lot more information than they send. At just over £1,000 for the hardware, and with a variety of payment schemes that are based on the amount of information that is actually received, these systems are still expensive. But for many users they are likely to offer much better value for money than an ISDN link.

The disadvantages of satellite systems are their relative vulnerability to weather conditions and perhaps slower technical support, compared with that available with a leased-line system. Satellites are one-off installations that are supposed to work permanently, and if there is a problem it may be a while before an engineer can get to your site. This makes them less suitable for applications where reliability is very important. But for a company that wants to get large amounts of information from the Internet very quickly, they are worth considering.

If you are thinking seriously about a satellite system, it is important to have a demonstration first. Although 400kbps sounds fast, web pages may not appear any more quickly than they do over a 64kbps link. The bottleneck is at the other end – if a site is getting a lot of attention, it will not be able to supply information at a reasonable rate. This puts a practical limit on the speed at which information can be received and makes very high-speed systems less effective than they might otherwise be.

Cable modems

Some cable television companies are now experimenting with faster modems – in some cases as fast as 10Mbps, which is roughly 300 times faster than a 33.6kbps telephone modem. These use a system called ADSL and 'piggy back' on the existing TV channel system. They are designed to offer much faster access to the Internet than is currently possible.

There are rumours that ADSL connections may become available from sources other than the cable TV companies. (Note that the technology is sometimes also known in the computer press as xDSL.) At the time of writing, ADSL has been imminent for at least two years but – apart from a BT trial, and a commercial service which is only available from Kingston Communications in Hull – it shows no signs of appearing on a wide scale. However, this should change by the year 2000 at the very latest. This kind of very high-speed access will transform the way the Internet is used and make it possible to send live video information from place to place as easily as an email can be sent today. In areas where cable access is available at a reasonable price, these new networks are likely to render the existing telephone system redundant, and the high-speed links that result will help make the Internet a part of everyone's daily life.

Other developments

Digital TV broadcasts, which started in 1998, offer yet another prospective system. The BBC and the other broadcasting companies are experimenting with delivering email and web information using the 'space' available in Digital TV transmissions. This would work rather like today's Teletext transmissions, but would be much faster. It is far too early to tell whether or not these experiments will result in viable products.

Nortel, an electricity distribution company, has plans to pipe Internet information along mains wiring. Connections to homes would be fast and permanent and would require very little extra hardware – just a box to connect to the mains. Apart from one or two snags (such as the discovery that Internet information was being radiated by lamp posts) trials so far have proved promising.

The existing cellular phone network is being improved, and a new high-speed service for computer information is due to become available in 2002. This will offer speeds between 144kbps and 5Mbps. If successful, this mobile service has the potential to make fixed-outlet telephone connections – including ISDN – obsolete almost overnight. High-speed portable Internet access will become a fact of life, and the resulting changes will almost certainly revolutionise the way that the Internet is used.

Appendix 3

The Internet for business users

Some businesses use the Internet with a standard dial-up account. If only a handful of people are working in an office on a network, and they use the Internet for occasional email and perhaps for looking at the Web, a dial-up account is perfectly adequate.

However, business users can benefit from a number of other Internet-related services. These include intranets, customised email addresses, professional web design services, and so on. These are provided by a range of consultancies and other Internet-oriented businesses which cater for the more professional user.

Professional Internet facilities

Internet access can be enhanced with a number of optional extras. These are available from the larger ISPs and also from smaller specialist, business-friendly ISPs which advertise in the Internet press. It is possible to use either type of company for all of these facilities or to use one for one service and a different one for another.

Customised Internet addresses

Apart from a certain on-line cachet, personalised email and web addresses free you from dependence on any one ISP. If you or your company change ISPs – or even move to a different country – you can keep exactly the same address.

Two steps are involved in creating a customised email or web address. The first is to lay claim to the address itself. This is known as 'registering a domain name'. The second is to tell the computers on the Internet that this address is yours and that any information that accesses it should be directed to your computers. This is known as 'mail forwarding' for email and 'web forwarding' for the Web. If you have a permanent Internet connection (using a leased line or other system), this second stage will not usually be necessary. However, it is essential for anyone who connects to the Internet via an ISP or on-line service.

Domain names are relatively cheap, and you can claim one with very little effort. This process involves a one-off payment to a registration bureau – examples can be found in the more serious Internet press – and then a regular annual payment to whichever organisation administers your domain (the US Naming Committee for .com domains, the UK Naming Committee for .co.uk, .ltd.uk and .net.uk domains, and so on).

At the time of writing, a bureau may charge about £70 to deal with the paperwork, although charges seem to be falling. The administration fee payable to the US Naming Committee is $100, which covers two years – payable in advance – and then $50 per year after that. In return for the payment, you get exclusive rights on the Internet to your domain name.

There are two problems with the current domain name system. The first is that domain names need to be unique, and many of the more popular names are already in use. For example, if your company is called Ipswich Banana Merchandising, you will not be able to use the *ibm.com* domain because it has already been registered by IBM.

This is less of a problem in the UK, because you can often use the *.co.uk* extension instead of *.com* to create a unique name. However, the pace of registration is speeding up, and even with the latest set of possible extensions (see Glossary), it makes sense to register a domain name as soon as it becomes obvious that you will need it – and, if funds allow, preferably even sooner.

The second problem is a legal one. Some names are registered trade marks, and in some cases different companies in different countries may have a legitimate claim on the same name. At present, the law is unclear about how these should be handled. After some interesting legal wrangles, the US Naming Committee made it clear that no one would be allowed to register a name that was not in some way connected with his or her business or personal interests. You can no longer make a claim on *mcdonalds.com* or *mtv.com* in the hope that you will be able to make a profit by selling on the name – something that a few early net entrepreneurs attempted, with mixed results. However, it is less clear what will happen if you register a name in good faith, and are then sued a year or two later by a company that feels it has a prior claim. As with a lot of corporate law, the result seems to depend on which party can afford the better lawyers. Because of this, it is wise to check that your proposed name is not a trade mark in the UK, the USA, and preferably anywhere else in the world. Unfortunately, this kind of check will usually be too expensive or time-consuming to be practical, but if you are at all unsure about a name, it is worth doing this if you can, as it may save you a lot of legal difficulties later.

To confuse matters even further, a self-styled *ad hoc* committee of domain-name users has been pushing for a relaxation of the present tight rules about the forms that a domain name can take. In effect, they are trying to introduce a much wider selection of domain-name types (for example, *.firm*) than is currently available. These *ad hoc* domain names are not recognised by all of the Internet, and if you try to register one you will find that in some circumstances it will not work properly. However, the committee does have a point: the existing restrictions seem to be jealously maintained without a reasonable supporting rationale.

Note that most domain registration bureaux do not offer any legal services to help you make sense of these different considerations. Their job is to check that the domain name you want is free, and then fill in the paperwork to make sure that it is reserved in your name. They also set up their computers so that the rest of the Internet knows where to send information intended for your domain. But their responsibilities end at this point. If you want to avoid legal troubles, you will need to get professional advice from a suitably qualified law firm.

It is possible to check for domain names on-line. A number of registration bureaux offer on-line search facilities which can tell you in seconds whether or not a given name is already registered. It is wise to use these when selecting your name. Although some registration companies also offer a free postal or telephone checking service, running through a list of hundreds of names only to find that they are all taken already will probably try their patience. It is a better idea to do the searching yourself and then present them with a name that you know is available. In some cases you can even register on-line immediately and follow up the registration with a cheque or credit-card number to pay for the service. You can find these services advertised in the Internet press.

Legal considerations aside, you should consider a potential domain name's 'user friendliness'. The name will be printed on cards, and you and your employees will also have to give it over the telephone. It makes sense to have a name that is short, apt and easy to remember. Names that are ambiguous, very long or hard to spell should be avoided.

Mail forwarding

This service offers the email equivalent of a Post Office box. A company whose official domain name is, for example, *adomain.com* may really be using the mailbox supplied by an ordinary ISP. As soon as mail forwarding is set up, all mail sent to *adomain.com* will be forwarded to the registered domain. This service is typically offered by domain-name registration bureaux, whose computers will perform the forwarding operation for a small annual fee – typically less than £50 a year.

Email illustrates some of the most obvious advantages of a customised domain name: it is good for public relations and looks much more impressive and business-like than an address with an ordinary ISP, and it makes it easy to create an infinite number of personalised mail addresses. Although all forwarded mail is sent to the same address, it includes the original 'To:' information. As an example, consider:

the-boss@adomain.com
the-secretary@adomain.com
the-tea-person@adomain.com

Mail sent to these different individuals will all be forwarded to the same mailbox, but because the 'To:' information in the header is different, it is possible to separate it later and forward it to different people within the same company. Many of the most popular email software packages include features which can direct mail to the right person in this way. If the different mailboxes are protected with passwords, the email will remain private and secure. There are no limits on what goes before the '@' sign. You could create an absurd address such as: *this-is-a-ridiculously-long-address@adomain.com* and this will work as well as any other. This kind of flexibility keeps your options open for the future. Even if you suddenly find yourself with tens of thousands of employees, a single domain name will still fulfil all your needs.

You can also use your domain name to hide your address when sending email. You can do this by changing the 'From:' and 'Reply to:' settings in your software to a suitable address at your domain. Although your mail is still sent by your ISP, it will now appear as if it was sent directly from your domain name, and your correspondents will be able to reply to you at your official address in the usual way.

Web forwarding

Web forwarding is the Web's equivalent of email forwarding. You can leave your site on your ISP's web server, and then create an 'official' address for it which will route visitors to your ISP's web server automatically. As with mail forwarding, this hides your real address away and suggests that you can afford your own permanent Internet link. The difference in cost between a web forwarding and a web hosting service (see below) is often negligible. In most cases the latter is preferable.

Web hosting and mailboxes

These services stop you from being dependent on an ISP. Instead of using your ISP's computers for mail and web space, you use those of the bureau that maintains your domain name. Apart from – possibly – a more reliable service, the biggest advantage is that your web pages will be kept on a professional computer system, which may offer faster connections and extra features, such as a wider range of CGI (Common Gateway Interface) scripts (see page 231) and better visitor tracking.

Dial-up connections

Some domain registration bureaux also offer dial-up connections to complement their web servers and mailboxes. This breaks the final link between you and your ISP because, with such a service, the new company becomes your ISP and you can cancel your subscription to the old ISP altogether.

Data warehousing

A handful of companies – not necessarily ISPs – now offer a service called data warehousing. In effect they use their computers to back up your company's information over the Internet. This is believed to be quicker and more convenient than doing back ups in-house. It is also more secure, in that if your premises burn down you will still be able to retrieve your records from the data warehouse.

This service is not yet widely advertised, and is only suitable for business users with a reasonably fast permanent Internet connection. (It would take at least a couple of weeks to back up the information in a typical home PC using a modem link!) Clearly, the security aspects of such a service are crucial. While all warehouses encrypt the information they store (using a scheme similar to PGP), there may still be points along the connection between your office and the warehouse where a hacker could gain access. In short, these services are still experimental, and it is worth checking more conventional back-up systems for cost-effectiveness and security before opting for these newer possibilities.

Choosing a suitable package

If your business is small or medium-sized, it pays to shop around and weigh up the pros and cons of the offers made by the various companies. Many provide special business-package deals which include mail forwarding, web hosting and a selection of other services for an annual flat fee. These can seem appealing, but you need to ask yourself how these packages compare with the existing services offered by your ISP. If you do not expect enormous amounts of traffic at your web site and do not need any special security facilities, it makes sense to use the free web space offered by your ISP, together with a small extra payment for mail and web forwarding.

This is an area in which many companies are being conned. If you are paying only £5 a month to an ISP for a dial-up link with some free web space, it is not wise to swap to using a different ISP for a similar service costing ten times the amount just because it claims to specialise in 'business solutions'.

The difference in cost can be justified only if the 'business' ISP can offer a suitably professional level of service. In fact, when negotiating a contract for business use, you should be careful to specify an SLA (Service Level Agreement). This should include details such as the modem-to-user ratio, minimum bandwidth from the ISP to your computer and also to the rest of the Internet, and any other features that affect the speed and reliability of your connections. ISPs that are more used to dealing with the public than businesses will not be able to offer an SLA unless you order a leased line from them. Business-oriented ISPs should be more amenable to agreeing acceptable service levels in a contract, even for a straightforward dial-up link.

Once you have agreed a contract, it is worth checking regularly to see if the terms are being adhered to. If you try to visit your own web page and it takes ten minutes for the information to appear then you have the right to ask questions about the quality and commitment of the service you are paying for.

Apart from a good-quality service, business ISPs should also be able to offer more advanced facilities such as ISDN and leased lines (see Appendix 2), in addition to business-oriented payment terms with full VAT receipts. It is useful to check the cost of an ISDN connection to see how it compares with that of other ISPs. Some companies charge a hefty premium for ISDN access, while others charge exactly the same rate as they do for dial-up connections.

One final consideration, especially for anyone buying space on a web server, is security. If the ISP does not seem to have a properly maintained and managed security policy in place you should not sign up with it.

Given the international nature of the Internet, it is well worth bearing in mind that you can buy every part of the service from abroad, except for the basic dial-up link. If you do not own your web server you will find no particular advantage in limiting yourself to buying web hosting and other services from companies in the UK. Equivalent services can be significantly cheaper in the USA, and there will not necessarily be any practical disadvantages to keeping the information abroad. The only significant concern is that you will have to pay more for calls if something goes wrong and you need to complain.

Technical consultancies

Unlike the various business-oriented Internet facilities, which are used on a continuing basis, the services offered by technical consultancies tend to be one-off projects which are required when developing a business presence on the Internet.

LAN connections

A LAN (Local Area Network) connection is a special link to the Internet which is essential if your company already has a computer network of its own. Although individual computers on the LAN can be equipped with modems, it makes much better business and technical sense to integrate the company network as a whole with the Internet. A special computer called a 'bridge' or 'router' is used to do this. Companies that offer LAN connections will install routers and set up the associated software to make sure that internal and external email are seamlessly integrated. LAN connections often require the co-operation of your ISP, and you should discuss this with it before going ahead. LAN connections are also prone to the security flaws discussed in Chapter 8, and should be designed with security in mind.

Note that this level of sophistication is not required for very small businesses. Offices with around five people or less can give everyone access to the Internet by using modem-sharing software, which routes all Internet connections through a single modem. The software to do this is available as shareware or freeware on the Internet and can be set up by anyone with moderate technical skills. Although the speed of the connection this creates is too limited to give everyone in the office access to the Web at the same time, it is adequate for email and for allowing one or two people to browse simultaneously.

Intranets

Designing and installing an intranet is a major undertaking and something that only a few larger IT companies will be able to advise you about. The advantages of an intranet are: improved communication – for example, company-wide announcements can be made over the network – and easier workgroup management. The disadvantage is that more time is spent maintaining an intranet than a traditional network.

Web design consultancies

Many businesses are interested in being on the Web but do not have the time, the inclination or the skills needed to design their own pages. Since 1995 the web design market has undergone explosive growth as professional graphic designers and artists, beginners with a knowledge of HTML, and any number of others, have tried to make new careers for themselves as professional web designers.

HTML is relatively easy to use, and with a little help from some well-designed software, almost anyone should be able to create their own pages. But there is a big difference between creating an amateur home page and creating a professional site in a business setting. The latter requires a much better knowledge of how the Web works, how to use it for promotion, how to make the site accessible, informative, interesting and easy to use, and also some basic knowledge of graphic design. These are not skills that amateurs are likely to have.

Choosing a web designer or web design company can be nerve-racking because of the large range of possible candidates. This is a new industry, and some companies are start-ups that do not even have proper business premises. Others are spin-offs from existing large design companies that have all the impressive trimmings but do not necessarily have any practical experience of designing pages. Quotations for similar work can vary over a ridiculously wide range, and some designers are undoubtedly cashing in on the Web's popularity – although as more people experiment with HTML for themselves, the Web's mystique is starting to fade. To sort out the wheat from the chaff, it is helpful to find out about the following points:

- **Communication skills** The Web is all about communicating, and if a prospective designer cannot show that he or she understands what you need, you will probably not be happy with the end result. Unfortunately, some of the larger design houses have a reputation for arrogance and will attempt to force a grand vision on their clients whether or not it is appropriate. This is always unacceptable. You are not looking for a design that will impress other designers and win awards, but for a design that will reach the intended audience. Designers should show that they understand this well enough to know how to shape the site accordingly.
- **Previous work** A portfolio – which can be on-line – is essential. But, apart from examples of work, you should also ask about the success of the work. Was there an increase in business as a result of the site? Was the site successful? How was this success assessed? Is there anything that should have been done differently?
- **References** Reputable designers should not mind if you want to get in touch with previous clients. If you take up this option, do not

just ask about the success of the site but also about how easy it was to manage and finish the task and whether or not the designer was easy to work with.

- **Reliability** For a really big project, you can protect yourself to some extent by including a penalty clause for non-delivery in any contracts you negotiate, and also by breaking the design work down into clear stages. Another excellent idea is to have a contingency plan, perhaps in the form of one or more back-up companies that can step in at short notice. If a designer seems to be struggling, you should cut your losses and swap to someone more reliable as soon as you can.

- **Maintenance and documentation** You should always have access to the notes, the raw HTML files, and any other information that your designer has created while building your site. Where appropriate, a good way to save yourself money in the long term is to ask for a site that you can add information to yourself. Your designer can do this by creating a site that relies on a small number of templates which can be filled out with information by anyone at your company. High-maintenance sites, where every single page is designed from scratch, are very expensive and not usually necessary.

Appendix 4
The Web and how to use it

Using a browser

The best way to make sense of the information in this Appendix is to try out each step while sitting in front of a web browser connected to the Internet. Following the steps in practice rather than in theory will make them much easier to understand, and also easier to remember.

Note that this information is in no way a completely comprehensive guide. It aims instead to give complete beginners enough of a start to be able to use the Web efficiently.

Web browsers are very easy to use, and even complete beginners can pick up the basics within a few minutes. The information that follows is written for the Netscape Communicator browser, but with minor changes applies to all the widely used browser software. (Note that it assumes that you are familiar enough with your computer to understand how to 'click on' information with the mouse, and how the 'windows' that are visible work. If you are a complete beginner, you will need to find a book or other source of information which explains these first steps in using your computer.)

Typing in a URL by hand

Type a URL, for example from a magazine or this book, into the location box. To prevent a URL mish-mash, you'll need to clear the existing URL first. There is a very quick and easy way to do this. Just click on the existing URL with the mouse, and it becomes highlighted. When you start typing, the old URL will be cleared automatically. (This is a lot easier to do than it is to describe.)

URLs should always be typed in *exactly* as shown, with all the peculiar punctuation intact. Common mistakes include:

- Typing htp:// instead of http://
- Typing a single forward slash instead of two forward slashes
- Getting forward slashes confused with dots in the URL itself (for example typing *www.word.com.etc* instead of *www.word.com/etc*)
- Typing 'html' for a URL that ends 'htm' – and *vice versa*.

Some browsers allow you to the skip the 'http://' part of a URL. The only way to check if this is true for your browser is to experiment.

Sometimes, even if you don't make a mistake, a page may not appear. Web sites are occasionally 'down' (unavailable), or may be inaccessible at peak periods because the Internet is running too slowly. If this is the case, your web browser will eventually produce a message explaining that the web page couldn't be displayed.

Otherwise, at the bottom left of the browser window you will see numbers changing as the information that makes up the web page copies to your computer. Eventually these stop changing, and the page itself appears.

Following a link

Following a link is simpler than typing in a URL. Simply move the mouse pointer to an underlined word, and click on it. The new URL will appear in the location box, and the page at the end of the link will be loaded automatically. (Again, this is very much easier to do than it is to describe, as a few minutes of experimentation will show.)

Note that not all links appear as underlined words. Some appear as pictures, or other kinds of graphics. On many pages you will see a 'navbar' (navigation bar), usually at the left of the page. This lists the most important pages in a site, in much the same way that this book has a list of chapters and page numbers at the beginning. Clicking on any of the items in the bar will take you straight to that page. Instead of underlined words, navbars often use special effects, including animations.

If this seems confusing, you can usually tell whether or not something is a link by watching the mouse pointer as you move it over the page. Most of the time it looks like an arrow, but when it is over a link it changes into a pointing finger. Unfortunately this is not a completely hard and fast rule, though it does apply on the majority of web pages.

Using the 'forward' and 'back' buttons

If you follow a link, you can get back to the page you came from by clicking on the 'back' button. This simply returns you to the previous page. You can repeat this any number of times, and eventually you will get back to the very first page you started from.

The 'forward' button does the opposite, and moves you forward through a list of links you have visited already. If there is no 'forward' to go to – in others words, if the page you are looking at is unexplored territory for you – this button is 'greyed out', which means you cannot press it.

Some web pages have an extremely annoying feature that deletes the list of pages you have visited. This is equivalent to shutting a large door behind you, and means the 'back' button no longer works properly; instead of taking you back to the previous page, it returns you to the current one, no matter how many times you click on it. This is anti-social behaviour on the part of some web designers, but unfortunately it cannot be avoided. However, if you find yourself trying to escape a web page that has done this, there are some advanced options you can try which will almost certainly get you back to where you came from (see 'The link trail and history list' on page 216).

Using the 'stop' button

If you choose the wrong page by mistake, you can stop the browser in its tracks by clicking on the 'stop' button. This stops a web page copying to your computer even if it is only partially finished. This button is perfectly safe to use, although if a page hasn't been copied fully you will most likely see a blank page, or a page of semi-gibberish after you click on it. To get back to the previous page you can use the 'back' button in the usual way. If a page is taking a very long time to appear, it can be worth stopping it and then using the 'reload' button (see below) to see if it will appear more quickly the second time.

Using the 'refresh' button

If you stop a page by accident before it has appeared in full, or if a page becomes garbled, pressing 'reload' (sometimes called 'refresh') copies all the information to your computer again and the page reappears.

Using the 'Home' button

This takes you back to a starting URL, and is useful if you get completely lost on your travels. 'Home' is most often set up to be the home page of the ISP you use. Or, if you install a new version of Communicator, it is set to the Netscape home page. (The home URL can be changed by looking in 'Preferences'. You can also change whether the home URL page appears when you start Communicator, or a blank page, or the last page you visited. The latter is often the most useful option.)

More advanced tricks and tips

URLs in newsgroups and email

Many email and newsgroup packages can work with URLs automatically. If a URL is underlined, clicking on it with the mouse will often start your web browser and then the URL automatically appears in the location box.

Saving time with new browser windows

Some pages have long lists of interesting links, rather like an electronic index. Good examples include news pages such as those provided by the BBC and various other electronic news services, results from search-engine searches, and home pages that include lots of other new places to visit.

Newcomers to the Web tend to follow a link, read the new page, then backtrack to the starting page. This wastes time and money. The starting page takes time to reappear each time it is revisited, and while each page is being read, the Internet connection that's being used is most often idle.

A better approach is to use a browser's 'Open in new window' feature. This appears if you click on a link with the *right* mouse button instead of the left one (PCs only). If you use this feature, the index page stays visible, and a completely new copy of the browser appears that displays the page at the end of the link in the usual way. You can repeat this with as many links as you like, although if your computer has relatively little memory – for example only 32Mb – it may slow down dramatically if you try this too often. If you do this with many links at once, you can read one page while another is still appearing behind the scenes. When you have finished, remember to close all the new browser windows.

The link trail and history list

Whenever you visit a page, your browser makes a note of it – partly so that the 'forward' and 'back' buttons work properly, partly because it keeps a library of graphics and other information found in pages and it needs to know which items in this library are old enough to throw away. This library is called a cache, and is used to make recently visited pages appear more quickly.

If you follow a chain of links and then decide you need to backtrack a long way, you can keep clicking on the 'back' button to get back to your starting point. But this can be very time-consuming. A more efficient approach is to use the **link trail** feature in your browser. You can find this in Communicator and Internet Explorer by clicking on the 'back' button and holding the mouse button down. The list appears under the button. If you hold the mouse button down and move the pointer down through the list, it will select entries one by one. To go to a page, select the entry you want to visit and release the mouse button.

If you want to revisit a page you saw previously, but you didn't keep the details, the **history list** shows all the web pages currently in the cache. The list may look like a collection of gibberish, but in fact it's just a list of URLs that you have visited. If you click on one of the names at the far left, it will work like a link in the usual way and open a new browser window showing that page. Details of how to show the history list seem to vary depending on which version of the browser software you are using, but you can find the current details in the on-line help.

If you can't remember much about a site that you think may be in the history list, the menus along the top offer a search facility. So if you visited a site called 'The <something> museum of <something>' (but you can't remember any other details), you can find all the URLs that include the word 'museum'. You can also arrange the list in alphabetical order, time and date of first visit, time and date of last visit, and so on.

Parents who suspect their children are looking at adult material can use the list to see which sites have been visited. But note that computer-savvy teens will be knowledgeable enough to understand how the list works, and how to cover their tracks from it.

Using a keyword search engine

As with browsers, search engines differ in detail. The examples that follow refer to AltaVista, because it appears to be one of the more sophisticated and effective engines. However, all search engines use similar principles, and anyone who understands how these work should be able to use any search engine efficiently. But note that many search engines are cruder and simpler, so not all of the information below applies when trying to use them. If in doubt, check for instructions on the search engine itself.

In theory, using a search engine is very easy – simply type the word you are looking for into the marked box on the engine's web page, and click on the 'search' button. In practice, this most often produces too many 'hits' – links to pages that include the word you have typed – to be useful. Someone who is ill and looking for flu remedies, for example, will find more than 150,000 'hits' if they simply look for the word 'flu'. Because the search engine is completely literal minded, it will include not just information about coughs and sneezes, but about other completely unrelated topics, such as 'Fiat Lancia Unlimited' (a motoring club in the USA).

There are a number of ways to make a search more manageable. Some engines now include a system which attempts to make searches based on English sentences. Despite appearances, their understanding of English is minimal, but as a first step, typing 'Where can I find information about flu remedies' should produce a more focused collection of results.

While AltaVista may not be particularly intelligent, it has been programmed to notice words that many people look for and offer other search options to make it easier to find specific related information. It does this in two ways. First, it provides a list of 'related searches' that appear around the word that you typed in. For example, if you simply type in 'flu', you will see 'flu symptoms', 'flu vaccines', 'yuppie flu' and so on appear here. If you click on one of these, the new words are copied to the search box and a new search is carried out. So, if you click on 'flu symptoms', AltaVista conducts a new search on 'flu symptoms' instead of just 'flu'. While useful, it is likely that you will still get an overwhelming response if you do this, but it may be a little more focused on what you are looking for.

The other option is the 'AltaVista knows the answers to these questions' information that appears at the bottom of the page. This literally means what it says – it is a list of commonly asked questions for which the engine has produced a catalogue of relevant pages. Sometimes one or two questions appear here, and you can click on them to find pages that may answer them. Here, AltaVista claims to know 'What are common home remedies used to ameliorate colds and flu?'. Clicking on the 'answer' button will take you to a page that tells you about vitamin C and zinc self-treatments. If you click on the 'more answers' button instead, AltaVista takes you to another page of related questions. These offer a broader set of background information. For example, clicking on 'Where can I learn about vitamins, supplements, and herbs for influenza?' will lead to another page of related information, which looks more closely at dietary supplements. (As an aside, if you click on the arrow at the right of the box that says 'influenza', you will be able to choose from a large list of other illnesses.)

AltaVista does its best to take users straight to the pages it thinks include the most important information or facts. Realistically though, there are likely to be hundreds of other pages of related information on-line, and to find them you need to know more about how to narrow down a search.

How computers think

Before going further, it helps to understand how search engines organise information for themselves. As far as the search engine is concerned, the meaning of the words in a search is irrelevant – it simply checks whether or not the words appear in a web page, and produces a list of links on that basis. To narrow down the selection of links that appear, the engine can be asked to combine words in different ways.

The four main kinds of combinations are:

A and B   Only lists pages that include both A and B
A or B   Lists pages that include either A or B
A not B   Lists pages that include A, but not B
'A B'   Lists pages that include the phrase 'A B'

This may seem abstract, but a little practice shows how these different options can be used. For example:

flu AND vitamin   Lists pages that are likely to contain information about vitamin supplements and flu

flu OR ME   Lists pages that discuss flu and its relationship to Chronic Fatigue Syndrome (also known as ME)

flu NOT colds   Lists pages that mention flu, but ignore the ones that also mention 'colds'

'flu remedy'   Lists all pages that include the phrase 'flu remedy'

Alta Vista also uses the '+' and '-' symbols as a shorthand for some of these options. These work in a related but slightly different way: '+' means 'include'; '-' means 'exclude'.

A B   (The words A and B typed into the search space with no other information) This is equivalent to A or B

+A B   List pages that include A, and possibly B too, but A gets preference

+A +B   Equivalent to A and B

A –B   Equivalent to A not B

These can be combined in various ways. Often it takes two or three attempts to narrow down a search as far as possible. For example, starting a search with

```
'flu remedy'
```

will get a long list of sites that mention flu remedies. However, sometimes the same sites will be listed many times, cluttering up the results. Aggressive marketers, for example, often use various tricks to persuade search engines to move their sites to the front of any listing. If the flu remedy search returns a large number of hits on a site called 'Dubious Medicines', with a URL of *www.dubiousmedicines.com* it is possible to get rid of these by specifying a new search on

```
'flu remedy' -dubiousmedicines
```

This will return a cleaner listing, with all mentions of the Dubious Medicines web site removed. At this point the search can be narrowed down even further. If the herbal remedy Echinacea looks interesting, sites that refer to it can be found with a new search on

```
+'flu remedy' -dubiousmedicines +echinacea
```

And so on. The easiest way to make sense of these different options is to practice with them.

Advanced options

The advanced search options appear as a link in the main keyword box. This leads to a new page which can be used to create a more complex set of search options. These options can further narrow down the pages displayed according to date – just type the earliest and/or latest pages you want to see in the 'before' and 'after' boxes. Date searches are useful if you only want the most recent information available on a topic (for example 'After 2/Dec/99') or, less usefully, the oldest information if you are looking for historical records on the Web.

Advanced searches can also use more complex selection options. These are known technically as 'Boolean Operators', which simply means some combination of the words AND, NOT, OR, and NEAR. AND, OR and NOT work as above, but use different symbols here. NEAR works differently.

In words...	In symbols...	Result
A AND B	A &B	Lists pages that include both A and B
A OR B	A |B	Lists pages that include A or B (or both)
A AND NOT B	A &!B	Lists pages that include A, but not B. (Somewhat irrationally, this always has to be typed in as 'AND NOT' or '&!'. 'Not' and '!' on their own do not work.)
A NEAR B	A ~B	Lists pages that feature the word A close to the word B.

Again, these can be combined in various ways. For example

```
Flu AND vitamins AND NOT 'herbal tea'
```

Or in symbols

```
Flu &vitamins &!'herbal tea'
```

Other languages?

AltaVista can filter searches by language. Most web pages are in English, so for English speakers this option is usually unnecessary. If you are specifically looking for foreign-language web sites, then simply select the language you want using the box that appears that in the main search area. Alternatively, if you are researching a subject with many foreign-language contributions that you can't read, use this box to select 'English' to remove them from the search.

Looking for photographs

Originally, search engines could look only for the text of web pages. But it is now possible to look for photographs, drawings, and other kinds of non-text information. One way to do this is to type

```
photos of the flu virus
```

in the search box in the usual way. Alternatively, you can use the 'AV Photo & Media' search option, which brings up a special search box that lets you specify what you are looking for. This option is still experimental to some extent, although eventually it is likely that the Web will contain almost as much information in the form of music and video as it currently does text.

Note that most images on the Web have copyright restrictions. You do not have the right to use them in your own web site, or in any other project, without the owner's permission.

How good are search engines?

According to some estimates, search engines index less than 20 per cent of the available web pages. Short of randomly following links, which is an impractical option, there is unfortunately no way to find these other pages. Unless someone sends you the URL personally in an email, or it is posted in a newsgroup article or on a mailing list, you will never know about these pages. Fortunately there is so much information available on the Web already that this is unlikely to be a major inconvenience.

Note also that the different search engines have different search strategies. Some will find pages that are missed by others, and so it can sometimes be worth searching using a number of search engines if you want to broaden the range of information you can access.

Designing your own web pages

Creating your own web site is a relatively straightforward process – so straightforward that even relative computerphobes have been able to produce an interesting web site. An outline of the process is given below:

1. **Find a home for your site** Most ISPs now include some web space free with their accounts. Alternatively, you can use one of the 'electronic homesteading' services such as a Geocities or Tripod. (But note that while these are free, they are often rather slow. And unlike most ISPs, they forcibly add advertising to your site.)
2. **Decide what you would like your pages to say** Some people go as far as to sketch out a map of their site showing how links connect the different pages together. For simple sites with only a few pages, this is unlikely to be necessary.
3. **Design the pages** The easiest way to do this is to use the on-line web-design facilities offered by a handful of ISPs and on-line services. AOL users, for example, can create their own pages simply by filling in an electronic form. This produces a page that lacks any real sophistication, but is still enough to satisfy those who don't want to spend more time on a more complex set of pages. The next easiest approach is to buy some commercial web-design software, preferably of the What You See Is What You Get (WYSIWYG) variety. Popular commercial packages include Adobe's Pagemill and Microsoft's FrontPage (although some people find the latter unnecessarily complex for a simple site). Apart from the web-design software itself, these include a built-in web server. This is a piece of software that makes it possible for you to try out your web site in full, just as if it were already copied to your ISP's computers and

visible to the rest of the Internet. If your computer is connected to a network, others on the network will be able to see your pages as well.

For those on a tight budget, web-design tools are often given away free with computer magazines. These are sometimes just trial versions with a limited life. But full-scale editing systems have on occasion been made available for free in this way. The Internet itself also offers a huge range of suitable free, or very low-cost software. AOL users can download a package called AOLPress, which is very easy to use indeed, and can, with a little effort, be persuaded to work with other ISPs. Many integrated office software packages, such as Microsoft Office 2000, now include web editing and design features, although these are typically rather clumsier and less flexible than those available in a stand-alone editor. Popular web browsers also include simple web-editing features, although these are often rather crude.

As a last resort you can design simple pages using a basic text editor, although this is only a practical option for those who are very patient or reasonably technically minded. The 'language' used by web pages is known as HTML. This specifies all the codes and details that define how a web page appears. Reference information that explains how HTML works, how to use it, and how to take advantage of its advanced features, is available on-line (try searching for 'HTML reference'). Computer bookstores also stock a large number of web-design reference titles, although these are often quite expensive.

4. **Copy the pages to a web server** When your pages are finished, copy them to your ISP's or on-line service's web-serving computers. The best web-design software does this for you automatically. Alternatively, you can use FTP to copy the pages yourself. (Exact details of how to do this, including any passwords that may be required, will be available from your ISP.) Note that some design software allows you to make changes to your pages once they have been copied. However, this facility should be used with care. Always keep a safety copy of the whole of your web site, including any recent changes. If something goes wrong you will not then have to recreate the whole site from scratch, or worry about remembering what it was that you changed recently.

Once all the pages have been copied from your computer to the ISP, they start working automatically. Visitors will see them appear on the Web in the usual way. You can then start including the URL for them in your email and newsgroup postings.

Information to include on your site

Some ISPs have limits on commercial sites, so check for these before you start advertising a small business. Otherwise, providing you do not break libel or decency laws with too much enthusiasm, your site is yours to do with as you like. Popular information includes:

- simple biographies and photo albums of family members, including pets
- lists of favourite music, books, films, and TV programmes
- information about hobbies and crafts
- details of interesting travel or holidays, with photographs
- home-made artwork, fiction, writing or music (which may even be offered for sale)
- information about any spiritual or religious interests
- information about any causes or organisations that are supported
- magazine-style articles about interesting topics
- a 'guest book' in which visitors can leave their comments
- contact details (A postal address and phone number are strictly optional, however. Those with more controversial pages, or who value their privacy, may wish to leave them out, or perhaps use a PO Box.)
- interesting links, which can add to any or all of the above (for example links to friends' sites, to supported organisations, and so on).

In practice, home-made sites seem to fall into two categories. True home pages are mostly biographical, and are limited to family and personal details. Magazine-style pages concentrate on one or more specialised interests and enthusiasms of the designer. The latter are often more complex. (Surreal, satirical, or quirky topics and editorial styles are particularly popular on-line.) While some can take on a life of their own, becoming a major focus on the Internet for people with an interest in similar issues, you should be aware that attempting to create a site like this can take very much more work than a simpler, more autobiographical collection of pages.

Elements of web design

With a good web-design package, creating a web site is very straightforward. Web pages typically include a combination of the following elements:

Text is typed in by the designer, or prepared in a word processor and copied into place. It can be made to appear in different sizes, colours, and positions on the page. More advanced design software can make it appear in a variety of different lettering styles, known as fonts. While this can look impressive, it is something of a special effect, and is an unnecessary complication for a beginner's first pages.

Photographs are available from a number of sources. They can be copied into a computer using a hardware extra called a scanner, which can convert a photograph, or any other kind of picture, into an electronic image which can then be modified using an 'image editor' – a kind of electronic darkroom, with a range of sophisticated tools for working with images electronically. Scanners now cost less than £100 and are very easy to use. Good image-editing software is also very affordable, for example on the PC a package called Paint Shop Pro costs around £50. Apart from tidying up photographs by correcting brightness, contrast, and colour balance, it is also possible to 'cut out' the most interesting part of a photograph electronically. This makes it easy to cut out someone's face from a group shot, for example. Even the simplest image-editing software can add a huge variety of special effects. Once a photo has been prepared, it can then be 'imported' into a web design, and positioned on a web page.

Graphics typically include cartoon-like illustrations, drawings of buttons, arrows, and so on, or purely abstract decorative designs, and can be bought in bulk from major computer stores. Or they can be copied from other web pages. (This is an automatic process. When you view a web page, all the information appears in your web browser's 'cache directory'. Graphics and other information can be copied out of this directory for use in your own pages.) Using graphics from other sites may, on rare occasions, cause copyright problems. However, some graphic elements (such as the 'rainbow bar' – a small rainbow-coloured line) are used on so many pages that they appear to be public domain and can be used freely by anyone. Some web sites specialise in offering graphics to web designers for free, or at a very small cost. To find these, use a search engine to look for 'web graphics'. Graphics can also be home-made, again using image-editing software. Unlike photographs, however, they can only be created successfully by those with some artistic talent.

Background textures are simply standard web graphics used as a background. Unlike other photographs and graphics that appear on a page, these are *tiled* – in other words, they are copied repeatedly in the background, to make a pattern. You can use any graphic or photograph as a background texture. Very colourful or complex designs, however, tend to clash with text, and large images increase the time it takes the page to appear, and can sometimes look lumpy. The most successful backgrounds are either quite dark (and suitable for light text), quite light (and hence suitable for dark text), or concentrated on a single colour (using a contrasting colour for any text on the page then makes it easy to read). Abstract designs often look attractive as web page backgrounds. As with other web graphics, these can be bought in bulk or – copyright permitting – copied from other web pages. They are usually modified so that they provide a seamless texture without edges when tiled, and good image-editing software can smooth out the edges of an image to make this possible. It's perfectly acceptable to use a single colour for a background, instead of a graphic, and many web pages still use the default shade of grey as a background for plain black text.

Links can be created on any word, phrase or image. In most design software, this is very easy, and can be done by highlighting the word, phrase or image with the mouse, selecting a 'create link' option, and then typing in the URL the link leads to.

With good design software, combining these elements into a page design is simply a case of telling the software where you would like each element to appear – for example, you can place some large text in the middle at the top of the page to make a heading, insert a photograph underneath it, add more text in a smaller size underneath the photograph, set up a short phrase in this text so that it acts as a link, and so on, until the design is complete. Once your page layouts are finished, they are converted to HTML. The HTML is a kind of 'recipe' that defines what appears on the pages.

Note that while all the text of a site is included in the HTML, photographs and graphics are not. When you copy your pages to your ISP's web computers, the latter also have to be copied in full to make sure that your page appears exactly as you designed it.

All the most popular design software includes tutorials which explain how to get the best from it, and shows beginners exactly how to create their site in detail. Some also offer 'wizards' – automated design tools – which aim to simplify the design process as much as possible by providing a range of standard pre-prepared site designs which can be filled in with suitable text and images.

While it can help to know the details of HTML, this isn't usually essential at this basic level. It can, however, become useful for those who want to add more sophisticated features to their web pages.

Frills and extras

With strong content, interesting information and a touch of artistic creativity, the basic elements listed above are enough to create a successful set of pages. However, many sites now include a number of special effects and extras which attempt to make them even more interesting.

Animated GIFs are animated graphics. They show a stream of stills, rather like the flick-books that children sometimes play with. As with other graphics, these can be bought, copied from other web sites, or made by those with the patience and the skill to do a convincing job. (Many image-editing packages now include tools for creating these animations.)

MIDI files control the music synthesiser that is now built into most home computers. They are rather like the electronic equivalent of a piano roll for a piano player, only the range of sounds and musical effects they can make is much wider. MIDI files can be made at home with a MIDI sequencer, although getting good results relies on a fair amount of musical ability. Or they can be copied from other web sites, though this is very likely to cause copyright problems. MIDI versions of popular music are widely available, and record companies have been known to cause legal problems for anyone found using these on a web site.

Java and Javascript offer very advanced special effects. These systems make it possible for small computer programs to create customised animations and other sophisticated special effects. A popular example is a 'water reflection' effect, which can be combined with a graphic to make it look as if it is being reflected in a rippling pool. 'Roll-overs' are buttons that become animated (for example, by 'lighting up') when the mouse pointer is positioned over them. The programs that make effects like these possible are available in two forms. Self-contained units (called Java applets – or simply applets for short) can be included in a page in much the same way as graphics or photographs. Or, as Javascript 'code', they can be copied into the HTML that makes up the page. Creating these special effects from scratch requires professional-level programming skills, and is beyond the reach of all but the most dedicated and persistent beginners. But pre-written examples are available on-line, and these can be used even without an understanding of how they work. Even so, they require some basic knowledge of HTML to be included in a page. More dedicated web designers can also create them using various professional web-design tools. While capable of extremely impressive results, these are inevitably rather expensive (for example Macromedia's Dreamweaver costs around £300).

Hit counters display a box that shows the number of times a page has been visited. Technically, these are actually an example of a CGI script (see pages 231–2), but in practice they can be produced with a few short lines of HTML that can be copied into an existing page design.

Guest books can be added in the same way. Examples of both abound on the Internet, and are widely available for free, although a basic understanding of HTML is required to include them in a page successfully.

Frames can divide up a web page into different areas. This makes it possible to include a set of navigation buttons on the left of the screen, and an 'active area' which changes depending on which part of the site is being viewed. For most applications, frames are simply gimmicky and unnecessary. They cannot be viewed properly by anyone using a handheld computer, or a very old web browser.

Some designers fill up their pages with every possible frill, including huge photos, animations, special effects, and music. This inevitably results in pages which take a long time to appear on someone's computer screen. Apart from being anti-social in the UK where net connection time is paid for by the minute, it also limits the number of people who will visit the site. Some will simply hit the 'Stop' button on their browser as soon as they lose patience with the long wait. Others who may be using older computers, older browser software, or a mobile Internet link, will not be able to see the page in its entirety at all.

Unless there are good reasons for adding frills, it is often possible to make a site look more interesting by putting more time into the basic design. As a rule of thumb, it is the content and not the decoration that makes a page interesting. The stronger the former is, the more likely the site is to attract visitors.

Professional-level frills and extras

Web pages can be further enhanced with a variety of even more complex extras. All of these require some knowledge of computer programming, and are typically used only by professional web designers who are creating large, complex web sites for businesses and companies. As such, they are mainly included here for completeness and for reference, and beginners may wish to skip this section completely.

ActiveX

ActiveX is Microsoft's answer to Java. ActiveX offers very similar features, but to date – despite Microsoft's efforts – practical demonstrations of it remain tied rather closely to Microsoft's Windows system. As a result, ActiveX lacks Java's universality. Microsoft is very influential in the personal computer trade and in the past has often been able to impose its wishes on the market. However, the future of ActiveX's relationship with the Internet remains uncertain. Many Internet users do not use Microsoft's Windows, and unless ActiveX can match Java's ability to work on any machine it may remain something of a side interest for the Internet.

Dynamic HTML

ActiveX, Java and Javascript are all facilities that are sometimes grouped together under the heading of Dynamic HTML (DHTML). DHTML is still something of a hotchpotch of ideas. Apart from animation options, DHTML also includes various page layout features which bring web design closer to the facilities offered by desktop publishing. For example, it becomes possible to use text styles which have more character than the standard Times and Helvetica fonts traditionally used on the Web.

DHTML's big drawback is that these options – and the others, which are too involved to list in detail here – work differently in the current Microsoft and Netscape browsers. To create DHTML pages that work as they should with either browser, it is necessary to write two sets of HTML, one specifically for each browser, or resort to a range of complex and confusing programming tricks which persuade the HTML to work properly with both.

These subtleties put much DHTML beyond the reach of beginners. Amateur web designers who want the sophistication of DHTML can purchase professional web-design software, which is now starting to offer WYSIWYG DHTML facilities. At £500 such software remains expensive, although adventurous business users who want to create their own professional-looking sites may find it a more prudent investment than paying out significantly greater sums to a web design company.

CGI

In the same way that Java is a computer language that was originally designed to add extra features to web browsers, the Common Gateway Interface (CGI) was designed to add features to web servers. CGI programs are known as 'scripts' and make it possible for web servers to perform a variety of useful tasks with web-related information. Examples include search facilities for a site, on-line registration forms, counters that show the number of times that a site has been visited, and so on.

The biggest difference between CGI and Java is that Java software is copied to your computer before it does anything, whereas CGI software stays on your ISP's web server. Because CGI is a very powerful tool and has a much higher security clearance than most software, many ISPs are reluctant to allow full public access to CGI facilities on their machines. For example, Demon Internet offers a number of pre-written CGI scripts to its customers, which they can use in their own web page designs. Other scripts are banned. This makes sure that knowledgeable customers cannot 'beat the system' and change someone else's pages without permission, take complete control of the web server, or perhaps intercept someone else's mail. For professional users who need CGI facilities, Demon offers a different server, which is available at extra cost.

CGI programming is a job for professionals. If you have an aptitude for computers, the language is not hard to learn, but using it properly

– and avoiding disasters, especially of the kind that can compromise a system's security – requires a high level of skill. For most web publishers it is easiest to use 'off-the-shelf' scripts, such as those offered by Demon and other ISPs. These come with instructions, so you can use them without a detailed knowledge of how they work.

Perl

Perl is another computer language, which is designed to extract and process information from large amounts of text. A simple example would be searching for a certain word in the text of an email or showing the differences between two messages. Perl is frequently mentioned in the context of web-page design because it is often used to write CGI scripts. Again, this is a language for computer experts, and beginners will not usually need to know how it works – although knowing what the name means can sometimes be useful.

FrontPage Extensions

These are used with Microsoft's FrontPage web-design software, which includes a number of CGI-like features that work using Microsoft's own proprietary system. As with ActiveX, these extensions work only with other Microsoft products. This means they lack the universality of CGI and Perl, which will work with any web-related computer systems. However, they are easy to install on a web server, and many professional web-server companies offer them.

Ecommerce?

This popular buzz word simply means using web pages to advertise a business, and perhaps even to take orders for it, as well as automatically maintaining an electronic catalogue on-line. You can use any or all of the design elements and extras listed previously to do this. Some companies (such as Actinic, which produces a product called 'Catalog') offer 'all-in-one' software packages that attempt to make this as easy and cheap as possible. Others, such as VInet, include ecommerce facilities which can be hired on-line. In return for a monthly fee and some initial setting up on your part, they offer a pre-packaged on-line selling service.

Ecommerce systems can range from the very simple, where customers contact you by email to place an order, to the very complicated, where credit orders are processed on-line automatically, product catalogues are maintained electronically, regular promotions and special offers are targeted at certain groups of customers and sent out by email, and so on. Full details are beyond the scope of this book. It is worth pointing out, however, that for certain kinds of businesses, even a simple ecommerce web site can add substantially to turnover. (For more details see the *Which? Guide to Computers for Small Businesses* which discusses ecommerce, and other ways of turning a web site into a money-making business, in detail.)

Promoting your pages

When you have finished designing your pages and have made them available on-line, you may want to promote them. One important way to do this is to let the various search engines know where to find them. This makes sure that if someone searches for a word mentioned in your site, it will be listed by the search engine. In theory, they search the entire Web, but in practice they follow only links from other pages. If no one includes links to your pages, they will remain invisible and will not be included in any listings.

You can make sure your pages are listed properly in two ways. The first is to use the on-line forms, which some of the search engines provide, to submit details about your pages manually. On Yahoo!, for example, you can specify which categories and sub-categories you would like your pages to appear in. A submission service – Submit It! at *www.submit-it.com* – offers a free service which will submit your site to all the major search engines on your behalf.

The other way to determine how your pages are listed is to use 'meta tags'. Normally, when a search engine visits a web site it notes the first few lines of text it finds there. This text appears whenever the site turns up in a search, and is often cut off at random. For example:

```
'Welcome to our home page! This is the home page of' ...
```

Clearly, there are situations in which this can be less than informative. *Meta tags* solve this problem by telling the search engine two things: the first is the text that you would like to appear when your site is listed; the second is a list of relevant keywords that apply to your site, which will make it appear in a listing whenever anyone searches for them.

For example, adding:

```
<META name "description"
content "We specialise in breeding pink parrots in West
Yorkshire.">
<META name "keywords"
content "pets, breeding, parrot, West Yorkshire">
```

to your site will make sure that when someone looks for information about pets, breeding, pink parrots, or West Yorkshire on a search engine they will see the following:

```
Pink Parrots.
We specialise in breeding pink parrots in West Yorkshire.
http://pink.parrot.co.uk - size 3k - 29 Feb 97
```

Web rings

Another way to make sure your site is noticed is to join a Web ring. These are groups of sites with a common theme that are linked to each other. Visitors can link through all the sites in turn or jump to any site in the ring. For more details about the Web ring system, including a list of the tens of thousands of rings already in existence, see the Web ring site at *www.webring.com* A similar scheme is available at Link Exchange (*www.linkexchange.com*). This allows participants – who currently number in the tens of thousands – to advertise each other's sites with free banner ads that appear on every page. As with Web rings, the scheme is simple to use and can be a highly effective way to generate interest in your site.

Appendix 6

Information for experts

This appendix is an introduction to some of the more advanced features of the Internet. The information that follows is intended for anyone who feels they have a basic working knowledge and would like to get more from their hardware and software. Some of these techniques are 'trade secrets' used by established Internet users. Others are included here for reference, to explain some of the more intimidating jargon that is used or simply for the sake of completeness.

How the Internet really works

The Internet was originally designed as a computer network that could survive a nuclear strike. Its most distinctive feature is its lack of centralised control. Instead of one big computer that controls everything, the Internet is a rather ramshackle network of all kinds of different computers. It only works at all because everyone who uses it agrees to use the same technology.

Once you start using the Internet, you will notice that information seems to travel across it in fits and starts. In fact, information travels in 'packets' – small chunks of information that act independently of each other. Packets can go across the Internet via any available route. The real world equivalent would be a newspaper delivery service that sends one page via the next street, another via the next town, another through a different country and another to the moon and back, before finally reassembling the newspaper and pushing it through your letterbox. This may seem wasteful but it allows the Internet to deal with problems intelligently. If one computer fails, packets are sent over a route that avoids it. This switching process happens instantly, and no information is lost.

The Internet's other great strength is that the system that controls packets – called TCP/IP (Transmission Control Protocol/Internet Protocol) – works in exactly the same way on every computer. TCP/IP is powerful enough to do the job of creating packets and reassembling them when they arrive – even if they arrive out of sequence – but simple and undemanding enough to work on small personal computers as well as large scientific and commercial ones.

Personal computers use a small piece of software called a 'TCP/IP stack' to do this job. (This is supplied with some Internet software, but in many cases it is included with your computer when you buy it.) This provides the 'pipe' that makes information flow in both directions between the personal computer and the Internet. If the stack is not working, the Internet connection will be dead. When you buy a connection from an ISP, what you are really paying for is the technology needed to link this 'pipe' to the ISP's own network, which has a permanent direct connection to the Internet. All the software you use relies on the stack being in place and working correctly.

On personal computers that use Microsoft Windows, the TCP/IP stack is often known as 'Winsock' – short for Windows Socket. Sometimes, when Internet software does not work properly, you will see a message that refers to a problem with the Winsock. Setting up Winsock from scratch is not a job for beginners. Windows 95 and 98 have their own version, which – to some extent – sets itself up automatically. Unfortunately, Winsocks for older versions of Windows have to be set up by hand. Some Internet software packages install a Winsock of their own, which again – in theory – sets itself up automatically. This works just as well, providing you do not already have software from an existing ISP installed on your computer. If you do, the two Winsocks may conflict with each other, and the connection will not work. Unravelling this problem is again a job for an expert – yet another reason why it is important to check an ISP's technical support before subscribing.

On-line services do not generally use the Winsock system. Instead, they use either proprietary software of their own, which works differently, or a unique Winsock which works only with their software. It is sometimes possible to replace the unique Winsock with a 'proper' Winsock, allowing you to use standard Internet software instead of the software supplied by the on-line service. The browsers offered by some services are not as good as the 'standard' Netscape or Microsoft browsers that the rest of the Internet uses. By installing a suitable Winsock, you will be able to use one of these standard browsers, while at the same time keeping all the facilities of the existing software offered by the on-line service. You may need to do a little research to find out if this is possible, and if so, how to do it in practice. You will usually be able to find help in one of the computer forums specific to the service.

Servers, clients and hosts

On the Internet, computers and their software are often divided into three categories. A **'server'** is a computer system that offers access to a particular service or facility, usually on the Internet. A mail server collects and stores all the mail that arrives addressed to an ISP's customers, and a news server does the same for news. A web server 'serves up' web pages on the Web so that they can be read by anyone. A news server 'serves up' copies of newsgroup postings, and so on.

Although servers are usually big, fast and powerful computers that can handle thousands of requests for information every minute, it is possible to install server software on any computer. One common situation in which this is necessary is when someone is developing a web site on a home PC. Pages can be viewed with a browser while they are being developed, but without a 'personal web server' installed on the home computer none of the links between pages in the site will work. This makes it hard to check that the links are working properly. With a server, all the links within the site will work correctly because it will be able to 'serve up' the relevant pages when asked. This means that you can test the site in private at home before making it public by copying it to an ISP's web server.

'Clients' are computer systems that copy information from a server to you and display it in a form that you can use. An email client connects to the mail server, finds your messages out of the thousands of others that are stored there, copies them to your computer and organises and displays them for you so you can read and reply to them. In practice, most Internet software used on home computers is client software, even though it is not always labelled as such.

The client/server idea is an important one and may have a big effect on the way that the Internet develops in future. One proposal is the 'thin client' – a computer system that is not much more than a screen and keyboard, with some memory, a processor chip to do the work and perhaps a hard disk. The thin client concept attempts to move the maintenance usually associated with personal computers – especially the frustration which software installation can sometimes cause – over to a big general-purpose server computer. Instead of installing the same software on many machines, it needs to be done once only. In theory, this thin-client computer should then be much easier to use. ('Thin client' is really another name for 'Network Computer', discussed in Appendix 2.)

You will sometimes see the words 'server-side' and 'client-side'. These are industry jargon for 'used by servers' and 'used by clients'. For example, server-side software is simply software that can be used on a server.

'Hosts' are more or less the same as servers. A host computer is one that hosts some action or exchange of information. In most contexts the word simply means 'the computer at the other end of the link'.

How the Web really works

When you select a page from a link or a URL, the first thing the browser has to do is to find the page's position on the Internet. This means finding the location of the computer system that 'hosts' the page, which is why the remote computer is often known as the 'host'.

To do this, it passes the address you have selected to one or more 'domain nameserver' (DNS) computers. These maintain a kind of 'telephone directory' and convert the name – which is written in words for the sole convenience of humans – into a list of numbers, which is the 'true' Internet address. You will sometimes see addresses listed as these numbers, and you can type these in in the usual way. But it is more common to use words in a URL because they are easier to remember and more informative.

If the nameserver cannot find the address in its directory and cannot get the information from any of the other nameservers on the Internet, it sends a message back to the browser explaining that it cannot fulfil the request. The browser passes this message on to you, and you will see a cryptic error message that says something like: 'The remote server does not have a DNS entry'.

Otherwise, the nameserver passes the address to the browser, which then attempts to create a connection. If you look at the bottom left-hand corner of your browser while all this is happening, you will see a message that says something like: 'Connect: looking up host'. This tells you that the browser is still trying to find the address. Once it has found it, this changes to: 'Connect: contacting host'.

When this appears, the browser is attempting to create a connection between your computer and the remote one. This involves making contact and then negotiating a connection, so that the remote computer knows that it needs to give your computer some attention. The process sometimes stalls at this point, either because of heavy traffic across the Internet or because the remote computer is too busy to respond. Occasionally it is because it has been switched off and is not working. If this is the case, the browser keeps trying for a few minutes and then gives up, showing a message that says something like: 'Could not contact host'. It is sometimes worth trying again if this happens, although it is usually a better idea to give up and try later, when traffic is not so heavy. Even if you do get a connection after an error like this, the chances are that it will be too slow to be useable.

Once the two computers have agreed to connect to each other, the raw HTML on the web host is copied to your computer, together with any images and other information that is needed to display the page. This happens in spurts. While it is happening, your browser is attempting to display the page – or at least as much of it as it can. You can follow this process by looking at the status line at the bottom left-hand corner. The amount of information needed to show each part of the page is shown as a percentage. The browser and host try to copy all the parts at once, which is why this percentage seems to switch at random – each percentage refers to a particular part. Unfortunately, you cannot check how many parts are involved or see the percentages for all of them at the same time.

Eventually, all the information arrives on your machine and the page is shown with the text and images. If you click on a link, the process starts again with a different page. However, if you then click on the 'back' button, the original page appears immediately. The browser is clever enough to 'cache' a copy of the information inside your computer – this means it keeps a copy for its own use, so it does not have to wait while the information is transferred again.

Making sense of addresses

A common mistake made by beginners is to assume that Internet addresses are written in English, and therefore all the normal rules about grammar, capitalisation and punctuation apply.

This is not true. Addresses are always typed in lower case. The only exceptions to this rule are the addresses used internally by certain on-line services, although once these are converted into Internet addresses, they also always appear in lowercase.

Addresses should always be typed in exactly as shown, with no extra spaces and with all the punctuation intact. It is easy for beginners to get this wrong and to miss details such as the difference between the backslash '\' and the forward slash '/' characters. If you are trying to use an address and it is not working properly, check your typing before trying anything else. Even experienced users sometimes misspell names – although using the address book feature (see page 43), available in most email software, can help minimise this.

Although Internet addresses may seem like a random jumble of letters and punctuation, they have a definite logic of their own. Knowing how they work can make it easier to spot errors, to find useful information about someone on-line and even to correct mistakes in addresses that are printed in magazines and other publications.

Email addresses

These have two parts: a 'public' part, which makes sure the information is sent to the right computer system on the Internet; and a 'private' part, which tells the computer system whose desk or computer terminal to send it to. For users of ISPs, the public part is the address of their ISP, and the private part is their own personal mailbox. In all cases, for all addresses on the Internet, these are separated by the '@' sign, pronounced 'at'.

In essence, all email addresses are simply *name-'at'-location*, where the location is the name of a computer system. The location – which is known in the industry as a 'domain name' (see Appendix 3) – has to be unique, because otherwise the Internet would be unable to work out which computer to send the mail to. Apart from the name of an organisation, domain names also include information about the type of organisation that uses the domain and the country it is based in. These appear as short codes separated from the main name by dots. A typical domain name is *intelligent.co.uk*. The first word, 'intelligent', is the short form of a company called Intelligent Realtime Information Systems. The full name would be too long, so it has been shortened to make it more convenient; this is standard practice among companies on the Internet – either a single descriptive word is used for this part of the address, or a long name is shortened to its initials. The next part, '.co', is short for 'company' and indicates that this is a commercial address. Finally, '.uk' is the country code and shows that the company is based in the UK. If it was based in Australia, this part of the address would be '.au', if in Belgium '.be', and so on. The full list of country codes is included in the Glossary. The full list of organisation codes is much shorter. Most are used internationally, but some are relevant only to particular countries.

While the rules about what can go after the '@' sign are quite strict, anything at all can go before it. Any restrictions on this part of the address are up to each domain. For example, someone using AOL has to limit his or her name to ten characters without spaces, anyone using Which? Online will have an address that looks like *firstname.secondname@which.net//* unless he or she specifies otherwise, and someone who uses CompuServe may have an address that consists of two long numbers: *1234.5678@compuserve.com*

Address conversions

Email sent between users of the same on-line service follows different rules. Because the email remains within the same organisation there is no need for a domain name. There are no '@' signs, and the address follows the service's own conventions. Some people include this internal form of their address on their business cards and letterheads. If you are not a member of the same service and try to send email to this internal address, it will not get through. So it is useful to know how to convert internal addresses into working Internet-style addresses:

- **CompuServe** Old-style CompuServe addresses look like this: *1234,56789*. The number of digits in each section can vary. Note that a comma is used instead of a full-stop. To convert this to an Internet address you replace the comma with a full stop and then add *@compuserve.com* – thus: *1234.56789@compuserve.com*. CompuServe has now changed its address system and allows words instead of numbers. To convert these newer addresses, similar rules apply. As long as you add '@compuserve.com' to the end and make sure that any words in the first part are separated by full stops, your email should get through.

- **AOL** These addresses can be any combination of letters and spaces. Letters can be in upper or lower case. To convert this to an Internet address that works you need to strip out any spaces, change all the letters to lowercase, and add *@aol.com* So, for example, *Sorcha V* becomes *sorchav@aol.com*
- **Other services** Similar rules apply for all the other services. Usually, all you need to do is add *@servicename.com* to the end of the address, where 'servicename' is the name of the service. This rule has one or two exceptions. A handful of Internet addresses use a different addressing system called X400. X400 addresses are long and extremely complicated and include lots of '/' and '=' characters. The conversion process is equally complex and can sometimes even confuse experienced professionals. If someone is using an X400 system, the easiest way to work out that person's address is to ask him or her to send you an email, so that you can use the 'reply' option in your email software. If you have tried all these methods and nothing seems to be working, as a last resort you can either email or call the postmaster at the service to see if someone there can help you with the conversion.

Finding an email address

The easiest way to get an email address is to get someone to mail you first, but, of course, this is not always possible. If not, try the following:

- **ask for it** For addresses of people in the UK, it is easier to ask for an address in person or over the telephone than it is to get it any other way. This is not so true of addresses abroad, especially those that are in very different time zones.
- **consult a paper directory** Bookshops now sell Internet directories, and some of these include interesting and useful email addresses. This technique can work well if you want a commercial email address or one belonging to one of the less net-shy celebrities.
- **consult an on-line directory** The InterNIC directory and database at *ds.internic.net/ds/dspg01.html* is a 'directory of directories' that lists all the widely used public access on-line directories. These are useful for commercial or educational email contacts, but may not include information about anyone outside these kinds of organisations.
- **consult an on-line archive** Doing a web search on someone's surname can turn up some surprisingly useful leads, as can searching

through the Usenet archives. If someone has posted to Usenet, his or her email address will appear there. Obviously, this approach works best for people with unusual surnames, although adding a first name can narrow the search down significantly. On the Web, someone's name may appear if he or she contributes to any of the mailing lists that are archived there.

- **Mail 'postmaster@...'** If you know the name of the organisation where the person has an email account, you can mail the postmaster, who will often send the full address by return.

- **Try 'finger@...'** Most of the large Internet service providers and many universities and other institutions have machines that can be fingered to see who is connected (see pages 118–9). If a name looks likely from the long list you get back, you can Finger that name in turn and see if it is who you think it is. Some universities offer search facilities which can be accessed with the Finger command. If you finger a name you will receive a 'best match' and perhaps more information on possible leads and other contacts. On IRC, the '/who' and '/whois' commands give people's nicknames and often provide a clue to their email address. Again, Finger can be used to get more information about these. Some people, notably famous academics and other celebrities, like to keep their email addresses very private. You will not have much luck getting hold of these.

Making sense of headers

You will often see 'headers' referred to in newsgroup postings. Headers are extra lines of information that arrive with each email and newsgroup message. They are rather like envelopes and contain the Internet's equivalent of address and postmark information. Normally headers are hidden – they are not very interesting and tend to clutter up your screen. But there are times when it is useful to be able to read them and pick out the useful information they contain.

To do this you need to get your software to show header information. Most software has a menu option somewhere that says 'show headers'. If you select this option when looking at a message – either email or news – a number of lines of gibberish should appear above the text of the message. (To get rid of the headers you will usually need to select this option again – otherwise they will appear for every message you look at.) If your software does not have such an option, look for 'headers' in the on-line help facility or the paper manual. If all else fails, try calling the relevant technical support number for an explanation of what you need to do.

Headers are arranged in lines, each of which tells you something about the message. The most common entries for email messages are:

To: This is usually your email address. If the email was sent to more than one person, their addresses will also appear here.

From: This is the email address of the sender.

Sender: Again, the email address of the sender.

Return-path: This is also the email address of the sender. However, sometimes this and the 'From:' line are different. This might be due to a number of reasons: some organisations have a single incoming address but multiple outgoing addresses; occasionally, the person's software is not set up properly; the sender could be trying to anonymise the email (see Chapter 8) or make it look as if it is from someone else by deliberately changing one of these settings in his or her software. To decide which applies, you will need to use your judgement and consider the context.

Subject: The subject of the message.

Date: The date and time. The time is the local time that applies when the message was sent, and includes a local time zone – for example, email sent in the UK will have 'BST' when British Summer Time applies. Sometimes the time is also the Greenwich Mean Time equivalent of local time.

Precedence: A priority measure set by the sender's ISP. This is usually set to 'bulk', which means the message gets no special treatment.

Message-id: This is another header set by the sender's ISP. It is the code number left in the log of the ISP's email server as the message passes through its system.

Received: There is usually a string of these lines. They should be read from the bottom upwards. They list the different computer systems that the email passed through on its way to you. Included in each line is:

- time and date of arrival of the message
- the message-id on that particular computer

- the make, version number and/or operating system of the email control server used by that computer (this is optional).

Newsgroup messages include many of the same lines but also have the following:

Newsgroups: This is a list of the newsgroups the message was posted to.

Organisation: The name of the poster's organisation (often a joke name if the poster is not at work).

References: A long list of news message-ids which refer to related messages in the same thread. Unfortunately, these are different for every news server, which makes them unhelpful.

Path: The newsgroup system's equivalent of the 'Received:' lines. This is a summary of the computers that the message passed through on its way to you. Starting from the computer that sent the message at the end of the line and working backwards, it is possible to trace the route the message took. Each step is separated by a bang '!' character.

NNTP-Posting-Host: The name of the ISP's newsgroup server. When present, this tells you explicitly which ISP was used to send the message.

Both email and newsgroup messages can include any number of lines that start with 'X-'. These include extra information supplied by the sender's software. Examples include:

X-newsreader: Tells you which newsreader software the sender is using.

X-mailer: Tells you which email software they are using.

X-noarchive: Tells the Deja News archive service whether or not to ignore the message.

This may seem like a lot of very dull information to wade through for no good reason – and for most messages it is exactly that. But this information can be useful in two types of situation: dealing with 'spam' and junk mail, and checking for forged email.

As mentioned in Chapter 6, it is possible to complain about spam and junk mail by sending a message to the postmaster – the administrator – of the ISP that the offender posted from. However, some 'spammers' and junk mailers attempt to disguise their tracks by using false addresses.

By checking the headers it is possible to guess which ISP the poster is using. This information will appear in the 'Received:' lines in an email and the 'Path:' line in a newsgroup message. (Some offenders are inept enough to leave this information in the 'From:' line as well.) To find the source, read the lowest 'Received:' line or the rightmost couple of 'Path:' entries. With experience, you will be able to recognise an ISP's name among these. You can then compose a message to the postmaster at that ISP, even though an attempt has been made to hide this information from you.

Note that headers, especially email headers, contain computer names rather than domain names. For example, one of Demon Internet's email computers is called *punt2.demon.net* You probably will not get a response if you send a message to the *postmaster@punt2.demon.net* because this is an 'administrative' computer that works behind the scenes, rather than an official address. But if you leave out the computer name and make an educated guess at the domain name – in this case 'demon.net' – you will be able to work out an address that will get your complaint to the right person.

Forged email can be spotted in a similar way. If the person's return address or 'From:' line does not match the computer or domain name listed in the original 'Received:' line, either the email is forged or the sender has used a mail-forwarding service (see pages 205–6). You should be able to decide which is the case, depending on the context. To find the source of junk mail, you can follow a similar process of elimination to work out the address of the ISP being used.

Making sense of URLs (Uniform Resource Locators)

The word 'Uniform' in 'Uniform Resource Locator' is something of a mystery to many net users. Most people associate URLs with the letters 'http://' and assume that URLs always follow the same format.

In fact, web browsers can read and make sense of other kinds of information. The 'http://' part of an address will be changed accordingly. From a technical point of view, one of the clever things about the Web is that it ties all kinds of addresses into a single uniform format that can be accessed with a single piece of software. This is the source of the 'uniform' description. The most common kinds of addresses are:

http://	'Hypertext Transfer Protocol', or a web site
https://	'Hypertext Transfer Protocol, secure' or a web site with security features. Credit-card numbers should be safer here
gopher://	a Gopher site
file://	a file (usually of HTML information) on the user's own computer. (Note that this is always followed by another forward slash. This refers to the first part of the address – or path, as it is known – of the information on the user's hard disk)
localhost://	information from a local web server – typically on a user's own computer
ftp://	File Transfer Protocol – an FTP site.

Knowing this information enables you to get more from your browser. If, for example, you come across a Gopher address you can use the 'gopher://' prefix to view the information with your web browser instead of finding and installing special software.

If you try a URL and it does not seem to work, you can sometimes still find a way to view the information by doing some exploring. A useful trick is to leave out the rightmost parts of the URL one by one until the browser responds. A part is defined as anything after a slash '/'. For example, you would start by trying: *http://www.somename.some-extension/someword/etc1* and then *http://www.somename.some-extension/someword* and finally *http://www.somename.some-extension*, which is as far as the process will go ('http://' will not work as a URL – there have to be at least two words separated by dots after it). This trick works because URLs with lots of parts actually take you straight into the middle of a site. As you backtrack you will sometimes find you get closer and closer to a 'welcome' page which introduces the site. Often this welcome site lists all the options available – perhaps including the information you are looking for. This technique is not infallible and should be used only as a last resort, but it is worth trying if you have problems.

When using an ISP's web server, your address will look like this: *http://www.(your isp's web address)/(your user name).htm*

Making sense of killfiles

Killfiles (see page 89) work by downloading newsgroup headers, scanning them to look for certain information and then marking the articles that fail the tests. Some software does this with a 'mark as read' option, which copies the article to your computer, but makes it look as if you have read it already. This is not as effective as the 'skip' or 'delete' option, which saves time and money because the offending article is never copied to your computer in the first place.

Killfile scans can be set up in two ways. The simplest way is to list all the offending authors and subjects. The more complicated approach is to killfile by creating a set of rules which attempt to pick out unwanted postings. Not all software gives you both options.

To use the second approach you need to understand the meanings of certain symbols. The most useful are:

'*' This is a 'catch-all' symbol. For example 'new*' would kill all information that started with 'new'.
'|' This means 'or'. So 'new | old' would kill all information that mentioned the words 'new' or 'old'. By combining these symbols with the relevant words, it is possible to kill a wide range of messages with a single killfile entry. Thus:

```
subject: (((fast | free | get | mak* | legal | quick | easy) &
(cash* | money* | dollar* |$10*| ($ |$50*))) | ($$|$$$*) |
make$* | $$cash* | ca$h* | $mo* | fastcash* | fastmoney* |
(DOLLAR* & week*))
```

will kill most 'get-rich-quick' scams.

Other useful tricks include killing all messages from authors using a certain ISP – *author: (isp's domain name goes here)* – and anything that asks you to call a free number in the USA – *subject: (1-800*)*.

If your software has the facility, it is also useful to killfile all articles that have been cross posted (see page 88) to more than one newsgroup. You run the risk of missing something interesting this way but you are more likely to save yourself the trouble of reading through a lot of annoying postings. You can also set up some software so that a killfile entry is temporary or specific to a certain newsgroup. Killfiling takes quite a bit of time, so it is useful – as well as cheaper – to keep your criteria as short and as simple as possible. A list of useful killfile criteria posted on Usenet includes the following:

- all posts by people who do not use a real name
- all get-rich-quick scams
- all advertisements
- anything with 'sex', 'nude' or 'teen' in the subject line
- any argumentative subject line, for example, 'You are all idiots'
- any subject that has more than one thread
- anything that has been cross posted
- posts with more than two paragraphs of quotes.

Initially, you may need to set up some of these by hand after encountering an offensive article or thread, but from then on all articles in that thread will no longer appear. Following this advice will make your experience of Usenet much more pleasant than it might otherwise be.

Finding or starting a mailing list

The easiest way to find a list is to search the newsgroup archives and the Web for a word that describes your interest and add the words 'mailing list' to it. New mailing lists are always announced in newsgroups, and a news archive search will reveal the relevant article/s. Similarly, back issues of some lists are published on the Web.

If this approach does not produce anything, the next step is to find a newsgroup related to the subject matter. This will either have an FAQ, which contains the appropriate details, or the newsgroup's members will know of a suitable list. As a last resort, it can be worth trying to search through the Liszt list directory (*www.liszt.com*) This is an automatic search system that scans the Internet looking for mailing lists. In its current incarnation it does not seem to be particularly reliable, and many lists which should be included appear to be missing. But it can be a good source of leads, and if all else fails you can always email the maintainer of a list dedicated to a related subject to see if he or she knows of one that is closer to what you have in mind. Some lists occasionally list other relevant lists. Finally, do remember that news of mailing lists is often passed by word of mouth. Friends who share your interests may know of something suitable.

If all else fails, it is possible that no such list exists. At this point you have the option of starting one yourself. This is fairly straightforward.

Some ISPs offer the facilities for you to do this, and may even help you get started. Alternatively, consider a dedicated list web site, such as OneList at *www.onelist.com*, which specialises in easy-to-use facilities for anyone who would like a list of their own. Starting a list implies that you have volunteered for the job of moderator, and, of course, this is not a role that everyone will feel comfortable with. But if you feel confident that you can keep a group of people in order and 'on-topic' without being too heavy-handed or getting drawn into unnecessary personal conflicts, then creating and maintaining a list can be a very satisfying exercise.

To offer a mailing list service, your ISP needs to have a list server running one of the popular list-maintenance systems – either Majordomo or ListServ. If it does not have this facility and is unwilling to install it, you will have to look elsewhere. If it does, you will need to set up your list by following the instructions your ISP sends you. This is only slightly harder than setting up an email account and much more straightforward than creating a web site. The next step is to advertise the list. You can do this on your web page, if you have one, but by far the best approach is to announce the list in one or more relevant newsgroups. The rest of your job will be maintenance – you will sometimes need to add and remove people from the list by hand if they forget how to leave or join the list or if they step out of line, but otherwise the software does most of the maintenance for you.

Some lists do occasionally lie moribund for days or weeks on end, but most come to life immediately. If after a while you find the list is taking up too much of your time, you will usually be able to find a volunteer who will take on the job of moderating it. Like newsgroups, once a certain number of enthusiastic posters has appeared, a list can become self-sustaining and will carry on indefinitely.

HTML basics

Although at first sight it can seem rather daunting, HTML is really very straightforward. In fact, it is possible to create a simple page very quickly. The language has two parts: 'keywords', which are special words or letters that have a specific function, and 'content', which is the text and other information that you are publishing. Keywords appear within angle brackets '<>' and are always used in matched pairs. The second word in the pair is the same as the first but with a '/' character added in front. Anything between these two keywords will be influenced by them in some way. Note that quite a lot of other information may be separating the first word in the pair from the second. Keywords will not appear when you look at the page with a browser – they are simply there to tell the browser how to display the content but remain 'invisible' otherwise. It is easiest to understand this with an example. On web pages, text is arranged in paragraphs. The start of a paragraph is marked with the keyword <p>, and the end with </p>. This is repeated for the next paragraph, and so on, for example:

```
<p>Here is a short line of text</p>
<p>Here is some more text, which will appear on a new line.
Without the paragraph markers it would be added to the end of
the previous line, even though you typed it on a new line.</p>
```

Keywords are really just a novel and elaborate form of punctuation. For example, text between the <b> and </b> markers will appear in **bold** type, while <i> and </i> set *italic* type. More complex keywords such as <A> and </A> specify that the text between them is a URL (address) or a link. The actual address appears within the angle brackets following the 'A', and this is followed by a line of text that appears underlined on the screen. This makes it possible to create links that say things like:

```
And you can see my other page here.
```

Clicking on 'here' will take you to a different page. Below is a short example of a complete page which demonstrates how this works:

```
<HTML>
<HEAD>
<TITLE>This is a page of HTML</TITLE>
</HEAD>

<P><B>Welcome to my home page!</B></P>
<P>This is a link to my email address:
<A HREF="mailto:somewhere@someaddress.com">My email
address.
</A>
</P>
```

```
<P> This is a link to my web site:
<A HREF="http://www.somesite.sometype/">My web site
</A>
</P>
</HTML>
```

It does not matter how the information is laid out, so it is more likely that the page would appear like this:

```
<HTML>
<HEAD>
<TITLE>This is a page of HTML</TITLE>
</HEAD>
<P>Welcome to my home page!</P>
<P> This is a link to my email address: <A
HREF="mailto:somewhere@someaddress.com">My email
address</A></P>
<P>This is a link to my web site: <A
HREF="http://www.somesite.sometype/">My web site</A></P>
</HTML>
```

Although it is no longer clear where the pairs of keywords are, a web browser will still display all the content correctly. In fact, you could squeeze all the information into a single long, completely incomprehensible line, although this would be a bad idea if you ever wanted to make any changes.

The Year 2000 date-change problem

Is the Internet ready for the Year 2000? The answer seems to be 'it depends'. The Y2K problem – or the Millennium Bug, as it has become known – highlights the complexity of the Internet and how the many different components have to work smoothly to get information from place to place.

Basic services

Email and news have an open-ended approach to date information, and hence are inherently robust. The relevant details are stored as text (e.g., 4 April 1999 08:52:22 GMT), and it is up to the client software to make sure these are created and maintained correctly.

Client software

Most recent packages are Y2K-compliant. For those that are not, any problems that result are irksome rather than fatal. For example, date-sorting facilities, if available, will put new messages at the beginning of a list instead of at the bottom. Or a newsreader may get confused about whether or not to expire messages. To minimise these kinds of inconveniences it is a good idea to update software to the very latest Y2K-compatible versions some time towards the end of 1999. Manufacturers will be keen to make the most of the marketing opportunities offered by the Y2K problem, and suitable packages will be widely advertised.

Server software

Most users are at the mercy of the systems created and operated by their ISPs and by other servers on the Net. Most of these will be Y2K-compliant, but a minority may not. What this means in practice remains to be seen. Email and Web services are unlikely to stop working, but some servers may drop off the network, causing congestion and a slower service across the whole of the Internet. Although nothing can be done about servers to which you have no access, it is well worth checking with your ISP beforehand to see if its services are Y2K-ready. This also applies if you are buying Web hosting and domain name mapping services from a company.

Telephone lines and other related services

BT, Cable and Wireless and other smaller telecom and cable companies have active Y2K teams which are attempting to minimise any problems for their customers. It is too early to tell whether or not they have the skills and resources to make the transition completely painless and trouble-free. Again, check with your telephone company nearer the date to see what the state of play is, and whether or not disruption is likely. This is especially important if your business is renting a leased line, and your revenue depends on having this facility in place.

Setting up a dial-up connection in Windows 95/98

Normally, when you start the sign-up process supplied on an ISP's CD (whether a trial or a full version), two things happen. The first is that some software is copied and installed in your computer. The second is that the installation creates a 'Dial-up networking' icon, which typically appears on your desktop as a small picture of a telephone. When you want to connect to the Internet, you simply double click on this, and the computer dials in via the modem, and the connection is made.

If you are happy with the software you are already using, or if you want to try a free ISP without using any of the special software provided, you can create your own dial-up networking connections very easily. Creating a connection to any ISP will let you copy incoming email to your computer, and look at web sites. (Note, however, that for technical reasons you will only be able to *send* email and read newsgroups from your original ISP.)

To create a connection, you will need:

- The telephone number of the ISP
- A 'login name' or 'user name'
- The password for that name.

Details about how to obtain these items of information without using an ISP's own sign-up procedures (which will most probably add unwanted extra software to your computer) are widely available on-line. If you do a web search on '<ISPname> signup' – for example 'Freeserve signup' – you will usually find the steps you need to follow. Alternatively, this information, or a URL for a web site that lists it, is sometimes posted on the *uk.telecom* newsgroup.

Once you have the details, follow these steps:

1. Close all open windows. Open the 'My computer' folder, by double-clicking on the 'My computer' icon on your desktop.
2. Double-click on the 'Dial-up networking' folder that appears. (If you are using a very old version of Windows 95, you will need to upgrade to Windows 98 before this appears.)
3. Double-click on 'Make new connection'.
4. Select a modem (which will usually be the one you use anyway) and type in a name for the connection.

5. Click on 'Next', and type in the telephone number of the new ISP.
6. Click OK.
7. Open Wordpad or Notepad or some other word processor.
8. Type in the listing which appears in the box below exactly as shown, substituting your user (login) name where <user name> appears, and your password where <password> appears. (Do not type in the angle brackets, but do type the quote marks. The '^' symbol usually appears above the '6' key at the top of the keyboard.) Save the file as plain text, with the extension '.scp'

```
proc main
delay 1
waitfor "ogin:"
transmit "<user name>"
transmit "^M"
delay 1
waitfor "assword:"
transmit "<password>"
transmit "^M"
delay 1
endproc
```

9. When the new telephone icon appears on the desktop, click on it with the right mouse button.
10. Select 'Properties'. Check the phone number box.
11. Click on the 'Server types' tab and make sure that only 'TCP/IP' is ticked, and that 'Require an unencrypted password' is *not* ticked.
12. Click on the 'Scripting' tab, and select the '.scp' file you created earlier.
13. Click OK and check the connection is made correctly by double-clicking on it.
14. If a window with the login process appears, but sticks with the word 'Protocol' showing, add the two lines:

```
waitfor "otocol"
transmit "PPP^M"
```

before 'endproc'

15. If the window disappears, but you see a message saying that the computer couldn't complete the connection, check the user name and password. If these are correct, return to step 11, click on the 'TCP/IP' button, and select 'Server assigned IP address', 'Server assigned name server addresses', and 'Use default gateway on remote network'.
16. If this also fails, call technical support for further help.

Further information

This section includes a summary of the various resources available on the Internet. It is not in any way comprehensive – a full survey would fill a whole bookshelf – but it does provide some useful starting points for further exploration.

Unusual Internet facilities

This is a selection of some of the more unusual options and facilities that the Internet offers. Some are experimental and are included because they are a taste of what the Internet may offer in the future.

Video conferencing

You can find out more about CU–SeeMe and try a free version of the software at *www.cu-seeme.com* The company also has a UK distributor which can be emailed at *sullivand@e92plus.co.uk* Tiny video cameras and suitable software are made by Logitech at *www.quickcam.com*

WebPhones

There are a variety of WebPhone options. WebPhone software is beginning to be standardised to the ITU (International Telephony Union) H.323 standard. Any WebPhone that uses this system should work with any other. Free trial versions of suitable software are available from Intel and IBM. You can find details of the latest products by doing a web search on 'web phone' or following the details regularly announced in the Internet press.

MUDs

Some MUDs are on the Web, but most require Telnet access. A comprehensive list of MUD-related resources, including lists of MUDs, details of what MUDs are and how they work, FAQs, links to relevant newsgroups, and so on, is available at *www.godlike.com/muds*

Fax/email gateways

A rather technical description of this service is available at *www.tpc.int* This explains which kinds of attachments are and are not allowed with emailed faxes.

Privacy resources

Privacy resources are used to make up for the Internet's security flaws, to keep private information away from accidental or deliberate public scrutiny.

Anonymous remailers

A list of links and information about remailer-related facilities is at *www.cs.berkeley.edu/~raph/remailer-list.html* The site seems fairly technical at first glance, but some of the linked articles are written at a level more suitable for beginners.

Anonymisers

The anonymiser site at *www.anonymizer.com* lets you view web pages anonymously.

PGP

PGP has its own newsgroups – *alt.security.pgp* and *comp.security.pgp* – and these have their own FAQs. A copy of the *alt.security.pgp* FAQ is available at *www.rivertown.net:8080/pgpfaq.html* Both cryptography and PGP require a reasonable level of computer literacy, so you may find you need to do some background research before you can start using the system for yourself. There is a non-commercial PGP home page at *www.pgpi.com* and a commercial page at *www.pgp.com* The latter includes free trials of the older version of PGP called PGPmail, as well as news of commercial versions which can work with most popular email packages.

Resources for business opportunities (and how to vet them)

The Financial Services Authority (formerly the Securities and Investments Board – SIB) site at *www.fsa.gov.uk* includes information on how to distinguish between scams and genuine investment opportunities. FraudNews (*www.silverquick.com/fraudnews.htm*), the Fraud Information Centre (*www.fraud.org*) and Scambusters (*www.scambusters.com*) are good sources of information about the latest scams and con tricks. In addition, the newsgroup *uk.finance* is well worth reading.

Software resources

Software on the Internet appears in three forms: commercial software, which you need to pay for immediately; shareware, which is offered on a 'try before you buy' basis; and beta software, which is offered for free in an unfinished and possibly accident-prone state, and which you use at your own risk. Some software is also available for restricted use – typically, if you use the software commercially you are expected to pay for it but if you use it at home for your own non-commercial use it is free. Most software states clearly which category it falls into. Shareware demands a certain amount of honesty, and if you do find yourself using a piece of shareware regularly you should pay for it. Some shareware authors rely on these 'voluntary' payments to make a living, and the existence of shareware is a resource that benefits everyone.

Browsers

The two most popular browsers are Netscape's Communicator and Microsoft's Internet Explorer version 4. Older versions of both are still widely used and are still being offered by some ISPs as part of their start-up software kits. Communicator was originally known as Navigator, while the different versions of Internet Explorer are described with a number (e.g. 2.0, 3.01, and so on).

Because these browsers are free, it is well worth using the latest versions. They can be downloaded using FTP but they tend to be rather large for this; a full download can take a few hours using a fast modem. Fortunately, they are often given away on the cover disks of the various Internet magazines. The big problem with both browsers is that they are too cumbersome to work on older computers.

In 1998 a new browser called Opera started to become popular. Opera requires much less in the way of computer resources than Communicator or Explorer. It can be downloaded very quickly – typically in less than 15 minutes, even with a slow modem – and it displays pages significantly faster than the more established browsers do. Its disadvantage is that it is shareware, offered on a 30-day free trial basis. It also does not include all the very latest and most complex browser features. On the other hand, it can be used successfully on old 386 computers with 8Mb of memory, which makes it an excellent choice for those who either cannot afford or do not want to keep upgrading their computer hardware.

For more information about these browsers see the relevant web pages at:

www.netscape.com
www.microsoft.com/ie/default.asp
opera.nta.no/index.html

Plug-ins

The latest list of Navigator plug-ins is available at *home.netscape.com/plugins/index.html* The list is very long and increasing all the time. As a rough guide, it is not usually worth getting a plug-in until you come across a site that demands it. Some plug-ins are very obscure, and you will not need them at all unless you work in a specialised technical field. The most popular ones – Shockwave, RealPlayer and VRML – are widely available. At the time of writing it was not possible to find a corresponding list of plug-ins for Internet Explorer. Some plug-ins will work with both browsers, but there are technical differences between Navigator and Explorer which make these plug-ins the exception rather than the rule.

Other software

Many excellent collections of software are available on the Internet. Tucows at *www.tucows.com* is a very comprehensive list of sites that offer

Internet-specific software of every conceivable kind, arranged by category and rated for quality. Software is available for PC compatibles that use Windows, and for the Apple Macintosh and its clones. Tucows has over 200 mirror sites around the world. When downloading software, use the mirror site that seems to be the fastest, even if it is not necessarily the closest to you geographically.

A similar list of software is offered by download.com at *www.download.com* for both PC and Apple Macintosh computers, together with newsgroups and links to a variety of other useful Internet software and information sources presented in a magazine-like format. When choosing newsgroup and email software make sure that it works off-line. A number of ISPs and other services offer on-line email, which is needlessly expensive. Off-line software is much cheaper, and well worth copying from the Internet.

Search systems

Use these search systems to find information about anything and everything on the Web.

Search engines

The most popular engines are:

AltaVista	*www.altavista.com*
Hotbot	*www.hotbot.com*
Lycos	*www.lycos.com*
Webcrawler	*www.webcrawler.com*
Yahoo!	*www.yahoo.com*

Meta search engines

Instead of searching with one engine, these set up a search using many engines simultaneously, and then collate and present the results for you. They offer a handy way to check lots of engines at once. For a list of these see *www.yahoo.com/computers_and_internet/internet/world_wide_web/searching_the_web/all_in_one_search_pages*

Mailing lists

The Liszt list of mailing lists at *www.liszt.com* is an attempt to create a complete directory of all the mailing lists on the Internet. This is an experimental service which is not as comprehensive as it aims to be, but it offers a good starting point for anyone looking for a list devoted to a particular topic.

Web site announcement services

Submit It! at *www.submit-it.com* is one of the most popular site announcement services. When your pages are ready to be put on the Web, you can send the URL to this site and it will forward your details to the 20 most popular search engines for free. Commercial users can pay a small fee to have the URL copied to over a hundred search engines. Submit It! also includes the Link Exchange service, which offers free banner advertising for participating sites. This works in the same way as commercial web banner advertising, but no money is exchanged, and the banners display information and act as links to other sites in the scheme.

On-line information sources

Unsurprisingly, much Internet-related information is available on-line. The examples that follow are a very brief indication of the huge number of resources that can be used for free.

RFCs (Requests For Comment)

RFCs are the Internet's technical manuals and include full details of how the different parts of the Internet work. Each document is really a proposal, although some proposals have gone on to become Internet standards. The language and the ideas used in most RFCs are really quite impenetrable to outsiders. They are technical documents written by computer experts, for example, RFCs 1034 and 1035 include full technical definitions of the domain name system (see Appendix 3), including the theory and how it works in practice. However, a handful – such as RFC 1855, which is a guide to Netiquette (Internet etiquette) – are intended for a wider readership. Apart from being reference tools, RFCs are also a historical record. The numbers are sequential (lower-numbered RFCs are older than higher-numbered ones), and, taken together, RFCs provide the definitive documentary record of the Internet's development. The system is still being used: for example, RFC 1876 is a proposal for including latitude, longitude and altitude in domain names – an idea that may come into its own once satellite and mobile systems become more widely used.

The full set of RFCs is available in many places on the Internet, usually via FTP. Copying them to a computer takes a sizeable amount of filing space, so most people read them on-line instead. To find a local site that holds these documents try using a search engine to look for RFC, RFCs or RFC Index.

On-line dictionaries

WhatIs – *www.whatis.com* – offers a comprehensive dictionary of Internet and computing terms as well as short articles about writing HTML, how the Internet works, and so on.

FAQ finders

A list of literally thousands of FAQs is available at *ps.superb.net/FAQ* You can search for FAQs by keyword or by following a list of headings and subheadings.

Virus and virus hoax information

Department of Energy Computer Incident Advisory Capability
ciac.llnl.gov/ciac/CIACHoaxes.html

Computer Virus Myths page
www.kumite.com/myths

IBM's Hype Alert web site
www.av.ibm.com/BreakingNews/HypeAlert

Symantec Anti Virus Research Center
www.symantec.com/avcenter

McAfee Associates Virus Hoax List
www.mcafee.com/support/hoax.asp

Dr. Solomon's Hoax Page
www.drsolomon.com/vircen/vanalyse/va005.html

Datafellows Hoax Warnings
www.Europe.Datafellows.com/news/hoax.htm

Traditional media

Books and magazines can still be extremely useful when you are trying to master the Internet. The information available covers the full range of Internet facilities, from help for total beginners to reference materials for professionals.

Choosing books

Hundreds, if not thousands, of books have been written about the Internet. They fall into three categories:

- technical reference manuals
- web site and other resource directories
- beginners' guides.

As far as beginners are concerned, almost all reference manuals are pitched at a level somewhere between intimidating and incomprehensible. They are written for people who want to know about the nuts and bolts of the Internet, and the specialised information they offer requires much more sophisticated computer skills than most Internet users are likely to have or need. If you need to know how to write your own CGI scripts or how to get the best from Perl, then you may find them useful. Otherwise, they are best left on the shelf.

Directories and listings are the tour guides of the Internet. Some are sober and straightforward, while others – especially those that concentrate on the more controversial aspects of Internet life – are written in a jaunty and colourful journalistic style that often matches the culture of the Internet itself. These guides can be surprisingly useful but can also date quickly, because sites appear and disappear. Although the writing may be entertaining, it is often better to use the Web's own search facilities to find information on a given subject instead of relying on printed information – in fact, the information in most guides is collated by doing just this. On the other hand, these directories can point you in the direction of resources you might not have thought of looking for. And, of course, having a ready-made listing in print is often more convenient than having to do the searching yourself, even if one or two URLs no longer work.

Beginner's guides vary hugely in both usefulness and price, with no guaranteed correlation between the two. The majority of books are written for the US market, and many of these include trial offers for US ISPs. These are, of course, useless for UK readers, who would need to pay transatlantic telephone charges to take advantage of them. When choosing a guide, look out for the following:

- **Free software** Although copying software from the Internet is relatively straightforward, getting it free with a book in the form of a CD-ROM or floppy disk is even simpler. However, the software offered by some books falls into the category of 'shovelware' (it is not particularly outstanding and has been included only to fill up the CD-ROM), while others offer more useful products and packages. An ideal book/CD-ROM combination provides plenty of examples of all the different kinds of software you may need, including web browsers, and email newsreaders, FTP software and plenty of useful extras such as Telnet, Traceroute and Finger. Most books supply software on CD-ROMs now, instead of floppy disks, so your computer will need to have a CD-ROM drive fitted if you want to try out the software.

- **Free trials and special offers** Free trials for the UK (which are usually offered for on-line services, but occasionally for ISPs or combined services) are always worth having, although you should read the small print to see exactly how much of a saving a special offer really gives you. All free trials are given in the hope that you will continue to use the service as a matter of habit. Even if you sign up for one of these, it is still worth looking at the advertising in the various Internet magazines to see if another service can offer you a better deal in the longer term.

- **Computer specific advice** Many books are written for users of the Unix operating system because it is so popular on the Internet. Unix computers are completely unlike personal ones, and their software works in an entirely different way. You can spot a book that takes a Unix approach to introducing the Internet by checking if it concentrates on Unix-specific Internet software packages such as Pine and Elm. Unix software tends to require lots of cryptic typed messages, whereas personal computer software is much more visually oriented and easier to use.

Choosing magazines

There are far fewer Internet magazines than general computer ones, and this makes it much easier to find quality information. Most magazines are general-purpose titles that include newsgroups, software reviews and listings of interesting web sites. The best offer useful features to help beginners get started. Only one or two are aimed specifically at beginners.

Internet Access (Paragon Publishing)
A beginner-oriented monthly, which is more or less identical to *Practical Internet* but offers more straightforward examples of what you can do on-line, and step-by-step details of how to go about it. The cover CD often includes free trial offers from various on-line services and ISPs.
Web site: *binky.paragon.co.uk/iaccess*

Internet Advisor (Future Publishing)
An accessible but not overly simplified introduction to the Net for beginners. Combines general interest Net-related information with a small number of reviews and more technical hands-on tutorials.
Web site: *www.netadvisor.co.uk*

Internet Business (Internet Business Magazine Ltd)
Aimed squarely at business users, this title includes a variety of business-related features written for anyone who uses, or is thinking of using, the Internet in a business setting. The style is serious and professional, and the content includes useful business-related news stories and information that does not appear in any other title. Although it does not have any directories, business-oriented ISPs advertise heavily in it. It is perhaps best thought of as a monthly manager's Internet briefing: strong on business ideas and background, but lacking practical 'nuts and bolts' details.
Web site: *www.ibmag.co.uk*

Internet Magazine (Emap Business Communications)
Bulky and glossy, it successfully balances informative features, topical stories, news, reviews and listings. The writing style is sober and informative without being dull. Articles cover a wide range of topics with plenty to interest both beginners and more seasoned Internet users.

Also included in the magazine is a comprehensive list of UK ISPs, with objective consumer tests of the performance of the most widely used ones. Advertising is perhaps more comprehensive and informative than that in the other Internet magazines and includes products and services of interest to both home and business users.
Web site: *www.internet-magazine.com*

Internet Money (Expo Group)

Aimed at would-be on-line entrepreneurs and business owners. The design is garish and the magazine has an unusual style which can sometimes make it hard to distinguish between editorial content and advertising.

Web site: *www.internet-money.co.uk*

Internet Monthly (IT Publishing UK)

Offering a fairly standard mix of introductory topics, lists of strange sites to visit and things to do on-line, together with help and technical advice, *Internet Monthly* is an accessible and budget-priced introduction aimed at complete beginners.

Web site: *www.internet-monthly.co.uk*

Internet Works (Future Publishing)

A resolutely business-oriented monthly, *Internet Works* is aimed at the corporate or small business user who is interested primarily in using a robust and secure Internet service to make money. Typical subjects covered include site design tips, the costs of high-speed connections such as leased lines, web site security, reviews of professional Internet equipment such as routers and ISDN terminal adapters, and topical industry comment. More sober than the home-oriented titles, and with a slightly more technical slant than the other Internet business monthlies.

Web site: *www.iwks.com*

.net (Future Publishing)

.net is one of the oldest surviving Net magazines and is aimed at slightly more experienced Internet users. The style is frank and explicit and can be deliberately controversial. The breadth and depth of the content and the colourful style can leave newcomers feeling baffled. Two versions are available: one with a cover CD-ROM, which offers free trials and software, and a cheaper one without.

Web site: *www.netmag.co.uk*

NetGamer (Paragon Publishing)

For the dedicated Internet game player, *NetGamer* includes details of how to find and play the latest multi-player on-line games, and also information about game hardware, such as 3D graphics cards. Very little more general Internet content.

Web site: *www.netgamer.net*

NetWorks series (Take That Ltd)
An occasional series of magazine-like titles that cover one specific area of Internet use. Information is typically very specialised. Previous titles have included information about using search engines, using the Internet for business, and Internet details for golf enthusiasts.
Web site: *www.net-works.co.uk*

Practical Internet (Paragon Publishing)
This is another all-round magazine which specialises in product reviews, introductory 'how to' features and various topical background articles. The content is slightly pedestrian compared with some of the other magazines, but beginners should be able to derive some benefit from most of the features. Also included is a comparative table of ISPs, which includes prices and geographical coverage.
Web site: *binky.paragon.co.uk/pi*

the net (Haymarket Magazines)
With a slightly glossy approach that features better-than-average design and plenty of topical content, *the net* is perhaps best thought of as the on-line equivalent of a local listings magazine, with some extra computer and Internet technology features as background reading.
Web site: *www.thenetmag.co.uk*

Total Internet (Rapide Publishing)
This is a good all-round magazine aimed at slightly more experienced Net users and has an interesting range of news, product reviews and background articles. Most of each issue is devoted to a large web directory listing, which covers a huge range of topics which changes every month. Also included is a list of ISPs – although only their contact details and prices are provided – and cybercafés.
Web site: *www.rapide.co.uk/tinet.htm*

Web Pages (Paragon Publishing)
Largely a collection of how-to step-by-step tutorial features, explaining some aspect of web site design, creation and maintenance. The information is specific to the more expensive web design software.
Web site: *webpages.made-easy.co.uk*

Webspace (Forme Digital Media)
Another business-oriented monthly, which is a less technically minded alternative for business owners and entrepreneurs looking for

information about moving their business on-line. Includes practical information, case histories, relevant reviews, and industry comment. Web site: *www.forme.com*

What's Online (Paragon Publishing)
'An entertainment-orientated Web, Internet and online-service guide that's aimed at novices' according to the publicity. *What's Online* is a web-site listings magazine with plenty of jumping off points for future exploration, but not much in the way of help or more general background information for absolute beginners.
Web site: *binky.paragon.co.uk/whats*

Wired (Condé Nast)
An attempt to produce an Internet lifestyle magazine, this US publication tries to inspire a vision of what the Internet should be about. It has topical and futuristic stories about what may happen on the Net next, self-consciously historical Internet retrospectives and topical features about the most controversial issues of the moment, such as censorship, privacy, electronic cash, and so on. The design is garish, and the articles are aimed squarely at 'geeks', who either make a living from computers and the Internet or would very much like to. It does not have any 'how to' articles, and even the web listings are short and stylised. Beginners may find the style of this magazine heavy going, but some of the more forward-looking and topical articles can be thought-provoking.
Web site: *www.wired.com/wired*

On-line services

AOL	(0800) 2791234
CompuServe	(0990) 000200
MSN	(0345) 002000
Which? Online	(0645) 830240
Virgin Net	(0500) 558800

Information about Freeserve and screaming.net is available direct from Dixons/PC World and Tempo stores respectively.

Appendix 8

Some places to visit

Web pages come and go, and so a list like this one can never be static, and the links themselves cannot, unfortunately, be guaranteed to work. Nor can it pretend to be comprehensive. There are literally tens of millions of web pages, and the small number shown below is just a selection.

Many high-street names have web sites, and these have most often not been listed because they can often be guessed by adding 'http://www.' before the name, and either 'co.uk' or '.com' after it. Tesco's web site, for example, is *http://www.tesco.co.uk*

Note that the home shopping sites are not necessarily recommended as being outstanding in any way – they are simply listed as illustrations. When considering placing an order, shoppers should always do what they can to minimise any risks involved in shopping on-line (see page 167 for details).

News

news.bbc.co.uk
Possibly the best news coverage anywhere on the Web

www.telegraph.co.uk
One of the earliest electronic news sources, and still one of the most popular

www.mirror.co.uk
Everything you'd expect from the electronic version of this newspaper

www.reuters.com
International and financial news, from one of the world's premiere news agencies

www.economist.com
Financial news, information, and analysis

www.compulink.co.uk/~private-eye
Private Eye on-line, with summaries of current articles, and some old favourites

Weather

www.bbc.co.uk./weather
National weather listings

www.intellicast.com
Complete local weather listings – for almost anywhere in the world

www.meto.gov.uk/sec3/sec3.html
The Met Office's own UK forecast

www.sat.dundee.ac.uk
The very latest satellite pictures. Registration is required, but is completely free

Science and technology

terraserver.microsoft.com
Satellite photos of the earth's surface

oposite.stsci.edu
The home page of the Hubble Space telescope

www.media.mit.edu
Find out about the technology of the next decade from the MIT Media Lab

encke.jpl.nasa.gov
Information for comet watchers

www.newscientist.com
An excellent popular science site, with a huge archive of old articles

exn.ca
The Discovery Channel on-line magazine and news source

Computing

www.zdnet.com
Computer news and analysis from the USA

www.zdnet.co.uk
The same, but repackaged for UK readers

www.microsoft.com
Microsoft's almost impossibly huge web site

www.gamesdomain.co.uk
Information, tips, and reviews for computer gamers

www.technosphere.org.uk
Create your own electronic creature, then help it survive in a fractal environment

www.clock.co.uk/works
Ferret racing, Mornington Crescent and other entertainments from Camden Lock in London

www.tomshardware.com
News and information for those who like to know what's inside their PCs

www.apple.com
The Apple computer company web site

www.shareware.com
A good source of on-line shareware

www.tucows.com
Another popular source for shareware

www.winsite.com
Yet another popular source of shareware, this time for users of Microsoft Windows

www.geocities.com
Free space for web pages, approximately arranged by interest

Directories

www.yell.co.uk
Yellow Pages on–line. The film-finder is particularly useful

www.scoot.co.uk
An alternative to Yell, Scoot can even provide a local map when you're looking for a business or service

www.thomson-directories.co.uk
Thomson directories on–line

www.bt.com/phonenetuk
BT's directory enquiries on–line. Can seem slow, and searches are geographically limited

www.infobel.be/infobel
Slow, but interesting on–line people-finder. Includes an International section with a copy of the UK home ('white pages') and business phone directories

Consumer help

www.open.gov.uk/oft/ofthome.htm
Home pages of the Office of Fair Trading

www.xodesign.co.uk/tsnet
The Trading Standards Office, for the latest information on product recalls, legal issues, and related news

www.asa.org.uk
The Advertising Standards Authority. Find out how to complain about advertising here

Jobs

www.computerweekly.co.uk
One of the best sources of jobs for those working in information technology

www.jobsunlimited.co.uk
Part of the electronic *Guardian*, this site offers a huge range of jobs for professionals in many fields

www.uk.compurecruit.com
A free service for employees, who can create an electronic CV on-line, and for employers, who can advertise vacancies and check the CVs of potential recruits

www.jobx.com/homepage.html
Apparently 'the UK and Europe's most visited job-hunting site'. Concentrates on corporate jobs

Art and Entertainment

www.radiotimes.beeb.com
Includes features and background articles as well as comprehensive TV listings

www.ultimatetv.com
Astonishingly comprehensive collection of TV-related information and news

www.michelangelo.com/buonarroti.html
The life and work of the man who sculpted *David*, and painted the ceiling of the Sistine Chapel

www.tate.org.uk/home.htm
The Tate Gallery

www.stephenking.com
The home page of US horror author Stephen King

www.pemberley.com/janeinfo/janewrit.html
Detailed collection of information about the works of Jane Austen

www.imdb.com
Internet Movie Database – information and comments about almost every film ever made

www.ubl.com
The ultimate band listings – links to hundreds of band web sites

www.thedj.com
An Internet radio station. Requires the Spinner plug-in

Humour

www.theonion.com
Scathingly satirical weekly magazine. Not for under 18s.

www.unitedmedia.com/comics/dilbert
Home page of the IT world's favourite anti-hero

www.pooh.muscat.co.uk/pooh-sticks
Play pooh-sticks on-line

www.urbanlegends.com
Shaggy-dog stories that just grew

www.like.it/vertigo/cliches.html
The Complete Movie Cliché list

Sport

www.geocities.com/Colosseum/Field/7690/links.html
Links to many cricket sites, in the UK and elsewhere

www.fa-premier.com
Official site of the Carling Premier League

www.mclaren.co.uk
Home of the McClaren formula one racing team

Travel

www.emap.com/bargainholidays
Cheap flights abroad

www.expedia.msn.com
Another potential source of cheap flights

www.nationalexpress.com
Timetable and other travel information for National Express coaches

www.lonelyplanet.com
One of the best sites for low-budget travellers

www.railtrack.co.uk
Information about RailTrack, including the latest UK timetable

www.fco.gov.uk
The Foreign Office, with official advice for travellers, and information about what local consulates can be expected to do

For kids and parents

viking.no
All about the Vikings. For 10- to 14-year-olds

www.globalfriends.com/html/worldtour.htm
A world tour specially written for children

www.bham.ac.uk/webmaster/ukuwww.html
Links to all the UK's universities

www.encyclopedia.com
A free on-line encyclopedia

www.yucky.com
The yuckiest site on the Net

www.reedbooks.co.uk/docs/children/thomas/index.htm
Thomas the Tank Engine's home page

On-line shopping

www.amazon.co.uk
Books for the UK market. Replace '.co.uk' with '.com' for the US site

www.artstream.com
Artwork, and crafts, both tangible and digital

www.autotrader.com
Buy and sell your car on-line. Colour photos are included

www.bol.co.uk
Another UK bookshop

www.borders.com
Over 10 million books, CDs and videos

www.cdnow.com
Cheap CDs from the USA

www.dawson-and-son.com
Traditional non-electronic toys and games

www.groceries.org.uk
Buy groceries on-line

www.wallpaperstore.com
A wide range of wallpaper and fabrics

www.magazineshop.co.uk
Subscribe to all your favourite magazines

www.officeshopper.com
Perhaps the UK's largest office supplies store

www.propertyfind.co.uk
Buy and sell your property by auction

www.scifi-uk.com
All manner of products for science fiction enthusiasts

www.ticketmaster.co.uk
Ticket bookings for popular shows and concerts

www.uk-property.com
One of the larger UK property-selling sites

www.ukshops.co.uk
A very wide range of shops of all sorts

www.videoparadise.com
Many, many videos

www.watkinsbooks.com
A bookshop specialising in mind, body and spirit titles

shopping.uk.yahoo.com
Lots of links to secure UK shopping sites

Glossary

Words or phrases in italics have a separate entry in the Glossary

Acceptable Use Policy (AUP) A set of rules outlining what users can and cannot do on the Internet, and what the consequences are likely to be if they break these rules.

account A particular user's Internet connection, so called because it usually has to be paid for.

address The electronic equivalent of a postal address – a unique string of words, usually separated by dots, colons, slashes and other punctuation (but not spaces), that is used to send or retrieve information from a certain computer or email account.

America Online (AOL) One of the world's largest on-line service providers.

anonymous remailer A special *email* forwarding address on the Internet which can be used to make email messages and *newsgroup postings* anonymous.

ARCHIE ARCHIE exists to make it easier to find files using *FTP*. It searches for *keywords* in text files and in file descriptions.

ASCII (American Standard Code for Information Interchange) The coding standard used in the computer world to make sure that when a user types an 'A' in an *email* message and sends it to someone else, the recipient sees the letter 'A' and not a completely different letter, and so on.

ASCII art Art made of letters and other symbols.

attachment One or more binaries which are attached to an *email* using *Base64*, *BinHex*, *MIME* and *Uuencoding*

backbone An extremely fast connection on the Internet that acts as a trunk route between two major computer centres.

Base64 A system used to translate *binaries* into text so they can be sent over the Internet.

binaries Any information that is not text – for example, word-processor documents with formatting, sounds, images or video clips.

BinHex A system used to convert *binaries* to text so they can be sent over the Internet.

bookmark A feature of most web browsers, which marks a *web page* so that a user can go straight to it on another occasion.

bot (from robot) A computer that does something 'intelligent', such as holding a conversation on *IRC*.

bounce When *email* cannot be delivered, it is returned to the sender with a brief note. It is then said to have bounced.

browse The act of looking through pages on the *World Wide Web*, sometimes with a goal in mind, sometimes just to see where the *links* take you.

browser A piece of software that can be used for browsing the *World Wide Web*.

cache A place on your hard drive where your *browser* stores copies of the last few *web pages* you have visited.

CompuServe A very large international on-line service.

Deja News A popular archive of *newsgroup* postings at *www.dejanews.com* combined with an easy-to-use *search engine*.

DNS (Domain Name Server) See *name server*.

domain (also called domain name) The part of an Internet address that identifies one particular computer or Internet service.

down A computer that is not available is said to be down. See also *up*.

Dynamic HTML (DHTML) The latest version of the *HTML* standard.

Ecommerce Selling goods and services electronically using the Net.

email (electronic mail) The name given to messages in electronic form that are sent from computer to computer.

expire Used for *newsgroup* postings – these are deleted after a set period to make room for new postings. An expired posting is no longer available.

e-zine (electronic magazine) A web publication that is updated regularly but usually produced by amateurs for others with similar interests.

FAQ Frequently asked question list. A document that answers the most commonly asked questions on a particular subject. Most *newsgroups* have one.

file format A description of the kind of software needed to understand what is inside a file, for example, AVI – Microsoft Video for Windows video player; MOV – Apple Quicktime video player; JPEG – JPEG image file; GIF – GIF image file.

Finger An Internet tool used to get information about a remote computer system or a distant *email* account: for example, the location of a particular user's terminal or when he or she last *logged* on to a particular *server*.

firewall An Internet security system that protects an internal network.

flame A nasty message sent to someone who has been annoying.

flame war An endless round of flames.

forging It is possible to make an email message appear as if it has come from one person when really it has come from another. This is called header forging.

FTP (File Transfer Protocol) The system used on the Internet to copy information from one computer to another.

FTP site A computer that offers an FTP facility on the Internet.

gateway A computer on the Internet that links one part of the network, or one service, to another.

geek The stereotypical Internet user. Geeks are good with computers but are typically socially inept and tend to spend most of their time on-line to the exclusion of other interests.

geek code A collection of letters and other symbols added to some *sigs*, which give a shorthand account of the writer's personal and professional circumstances.

Gopher A primitive text-only precursor to the *WWW*.

groupware Software designed to work on a network, such as the Internet or an *intranet* which makes it easier for a group of people to work together.

header The section at the top of an *email* or *newsgroup* message that contains information about where the message has come from, when it was sent, and so on.

host An Internet computer that has been set up to offer a service to users.

HTML (Hypertext Mark-up Language) The computer language used to create *web pages*.

http:// The letters added at the beginning of a web address (or URL) that let the *browser* know it is supposed to be accessing a web server.

hypertext Text with *links* in it.

Internet service provider (ISP) An organisation that supplies a connection to the Internet, usually in return for a fee.

Internet Explorer A widely used web *browser* that works very closely with Windows 95 and appears as part of Windows 98.

intranet Internal computer network used within an organisation.

IRC (Internet Relay Chat) A system which connects thousands of people around the world. Unlike other Internet services, IRC happens 'live'.

Java Programming language which enhances web pages.

junk email The electronic equivalent of junk paper mail.

keyword Keyword searches look for occurrences of one or more words.

Kibo Nickname of James Parry, an Internet celebrity. Originally famous because he replied to every posting on *Usenet* that mentioned his name, Kibo now has his own religion ('kibology') and *newsgroup* and still appears regularly on Usenet.

killfile An invaluable feature of *email* and newsreading software which blacklists certain subjects or *postings*/messages from certain people so they no longer appear. A good way to deal with *flames* and *junk email*.

leased line A permanent, currently very expensive, Internet connection that does not require a modem or a telephone link.

link A word, phrase or address that appears on a *web page*, underlined or in a different colour, and links to a different related web page, email address or *newsgroup*.

log in (or log on) Connect to a computer.

mailing list A group of people with a shared interest who keep in touch by sharing *email* with each other through a central email address.

Microsoft One of the largest software companies in the world, and creators of *Internet Explorer*.

MIME (Multipurpose Internet Mail Extensions) A not-quite-standardised system used to send *binaries* within *email* messages.

mirror Some *FTP* sites have replicas in different locations. This is done to make it quicker to access the information locally and also to take the load off the main site.

modem A computer add-on that connects the computer to the Internet (or to another computer) over the telephone line.

MOO (Object Oriented MUD) A variation on the MUD idea.

MUD (Multi User Dimension, or Dungeon) An on-line game system in which players can explore a virtual world and interact with each other in various more or less violent ways. Often accessed via *Telnet*.

MUSH (Multi User Shared Hallucination) A more elaborate version of the *MUD* idea, in which players can help to build the environment they are in instead of simply exploring it.

name server Sometimes abbreviated to DNS, a name server is a computer that converts an Internet address into a string of numbers.

Netscape The company responsible for Navigator and the more recent Communicator, two very popular web *browsers*.

newsgroup International discussion areas. There are about 20,000, devoted to almost every topic imaginable.

news server A special computer that keeps an up-to-date copy of the thousands of daily *postings* made to *Usenet*.

off-line Not connected to the Internet. For example, it is possible to write an *email* off-line, then connect to the Internet to send it. This saves you money.

on-line Connected to the Internet, and – by implication – spending money through phone charges, connection charges or both.

on-line service provider Apart from providing the usual Internet services, an on-line service provider adds extra facilities such as software libraries and live chat.

packet The basic unit of information on the Internet.

PGP (Pretty Good Privacy) A system devised to secure *email* from prying eyes by converting it into an encrypted form.

Ping A short message that says 'Are you there?'. Used to check if a remote computer is switched on or accessible before a user attempts to use it.

plan A few lines of information that are sometimes returned by *Finger*.

point Used in the phrase 'point your browser at <a URL>. This means 'copy this URL to your browser and see what's on this page'.

POP3 (Post Office Protocol) An advanced system used to copy *email* between a home computer and the Internet.

portal A *search engine* which also offers *email* and other useful Internet facilities.

posting A message sent to a *newsgroup* or the act of sending a message to a *newsgroup*.

postmaster The individual at a computer site who looks after *email*. Sometimes, but not always, the same as the *Sys-admin*.

PPP (Point to Point Protocol) A system used to connect *modems* to the Internet. Much preferred to *SLIP*.

proxy A *web server* installed by an *ISP* that keeps copies of popular *web pages* from around the world.

pull Applied to Internet accounts – 'pulling an account' means removing it so that a user is denied access.

Push media Information that is offered to you, as opposed to that which you actively look for.

real life Life away from the Internet.

search engine Used for tracking down useful and interesting information from the mass of *links* and pages on the *WWW*.

server An Internet computer that provides a service.

shouting WRITING SOMETHING IN CAPITALS IS CONSIDERED SHOUTING, and very rude.

sig (signature file) A standard file that is often added to the end of *email* and *newsgroup postings* and contains a witty quote, a *web page* reference, etc.

sign-on Connect to the Internet and/or start using one of its facilities.

site A place on the Internet which offers information, for example, a *web site* offers *WWW* pages.

smileys Minimal examples of *ASCII art* used to add extra emotion to text-only conversations. For example :-) means smiling or happy.

SMTP (Simple Mail Transfer Protocol) one system used to copy waiting *email* between the computers. See also *POP3*.

snail-mail Mail sent the old-fashioned way with paper, ink and stamps.

spam Flooding *newsgroups* with copies of the same message – usually one advertising a service.

SLIP (Serial Line Internet Protocol) a system used to connect modems to the Internet. Point to Point Protocol (PPP) is a better system.

surf The act of looking through pages on the *WWW*. Identical to *browsing*.

Sys-admin The person responsible for maintaining a computer system.

T1 A type of leased line, providing a 1.5Mbs permanent connection to the Internet, approximately 45 times faster than that available with a typical *modem*.

T3 A faster type of leased line, providing a 45Mbs permanent Internet connection. Used by the larger ISPs for their permanent Internet link.

TCP/IP (Transmission Control Protocol/Internet Protocol) The system used on the Internet to move information between computers.

TCP/IP stack Part of the software which enables a PC to send or receive information using *TCP/IP*.

Telnet An Internet service which allows you to *log on* to a computer somewhere else, perhaps on another continent, via the Internet and use it as if you were sitting in front of it.

Traceroute The Internet equivalent of a homing missile. It lists all the Internet connections between a user's computer and a remote computer.

troll A newsgroup posting that looks serious but is really a practical joke intended to provoke an irate response. Often very cleverly disguised.

ukp 'UK pounds'.

Unix Whereas home computers use operating systems such as Windows 95, MacOS and Dos, many computers on the Internet (including those maintained by ISPs, large companies and universities) use a system called UNIX.

up A computer is said to be up when it is working properly.

URL (Uniform Resource Locator) The address of a *web page*.

Usenet The network of *newsgroups*.

user name (or user–id) The name you use to identify yourself to your *ISP*'s computer system.

Uuencoding A technique developed to make it possible to send *binaries* across the Internet.

Veronica An extension to the *Gopher* service that makes it easier to navigate through *keyword* searches.

WAIS (Wide Area Information Services) An extension to *Veronica*.

webmaster The person responsible for maintaining a *web site*.

web page A single page of information on the *WWW*.

web server A computer that stores *web pages* and passes them over the Internet whenever anyone looks at that site.

web site In the same way that a book or magazine is made up of printed pages, a web site consists of *web pages* which have a common theme.

Winsock A piece of software used by PCs running the Microsoft Windows operating system, which links the Internet connection to the rest of the software inside the PC.

World Wide Web (WWW) The most popular and most accessible way to use the Internet. The WWW is a collection of text, pictures, sounds, video clips, graphics and other information arranged in pages with links between them.

Codes in email addresses

International codes

.ac   an academic institution
.co   a company that trades in a single country
.com   a commercial organisation that trades internationally
.gov   a government department or other related facility
.nato   a NATO installation
.net   an organisation or company that provides Internet access
.org   a non-commercial organisation, such as a charity
.tm   a trade-marked business name

UK-specific codes
.ltd   a UK Limited Company
.mod   anything run by the UK Ministry of Defence
.nhs   anything run by the National Health Service
.plc   a UK Public Limited Company
.police for the police (not much used)
.sch   a school

US codes
.edu   a school or university
.k12   a school
.mil   a military base
.(state) a two-letter state abbreviation (always followed by .us)

At the time of writing there are plans to extend these codes to include:

.arts   related to arts and culture
.firm   a business
.info   an information service
.nom   a specific private or business name
.rec   related to recreation and hobbies
.store   a trading establishment
.web   related to the WWW

Domain country codes

ad	Andorra	bs	Bahamas	ee	Estonia
ae	United Arab Emirates	bt	Bhutan	eg	Egypt
		bv	Bouvet Is.	eh	Western Sahara
af	Afghanistan	bw	Botswana	er	Eritrea
ag	Antigua and Barbuda	by	Belarus	es	Spain
		bz	Belize	et	Ethiopia
ai	Anguilla	ca	Canada	fi	Finland
al	Albania	cc	Cocos (Keeling) Is.	fj	Fiji
am	Armenia	cf	Central African Republic	fk	Falkland Is.
an	Antilles			fm	Micronesia
ao	Angola	cg	Congo	fo	Faroe Is.
aq	Antarctica	ch	Switzerland	fr	France
ar	Argentina	ci	Ivory Coast (Côte d'Ivoire)	fx	France (European Terr.)
as	American Samoa				
at	Austria	ck	Cook Is.	ga	Gabon
au	Australia	cl	Chile	gd	Grenada
aw	Aruba	cm	Cameroon	ge	Georgia
az	Azerbaijan	cn	China	gf	French Guiana
ba	Bosnia and Herzegovina	co	Colombia	gh	Ghana
		cr	Costa Rica	gi	Gibraltar
bb	Barbados	cu	Cuba	gl	Greenland
bd	Bangladesh	cv	Cape Verde	gm	Gambia
be	Belgium	cx	Christmas Is.	gn	Guinea
bf	Burkina Faso	cy	Cyprus	gp	Guadeloupe
bg	Bulgaria	cz	Czech Republic	gq	Equatorial Guinea
bh	Bahrain	de	Germany	gr	Greece
bi	Burundi	dj	Djibouti	gs	S. Georgia & S. Sandwich Is.
bj	Benin	dk	Denmark		
bm	Bermuda	dm	Dominica	gt	Guatemala
bn	Brunei Darussalam	do	Dominican Republic	gu	Guam (USA)
				gw	Guinea Bissau
bo	Bolivia	dz	Algeria	gy	Guyana
br	Brazil	ec	Ecuador	hk	Hong Kong

hm	Heard and McDonald Is.	mg	Madagascar	py	Paraguay
hn	Honduras	mh	Marshall Is.	qa	Qatar
hr	Croatia	mk	Macedonia	re	Réunion
ht	Haiti	ml	Mali	ro	Romania
hu	Hungary	mm	Myanmar	ru	Russian Federation
id	Indonesia	mn	Mongolia		
ie	Ireland	mo	Macau	rw	Rwanda
il	Israel	mp	Northern Mariana Is.	sa	Saudi Arabia
in	India			sb	Solomon Is
int	International	mq	Martinique	sc	Seychelles
io	British Indian Ocean Terr.	mr	Mauritania	sd	Sudan
		ms	Montserrat	se	Sweden
iq	Iraq	mt	Malta	sg	Singapore
ir	Iran	mu	Mauritius	sh	St Helena
is	Iceland	mv	Maldives	si	Slovenia
it	Italy	mw	Malawi	sj	Svalbard & Jan Mayen Is.
jm	Jamaica	mx	Mexico		
jo	Jordan	my	Malaysia	sk	Slovak Republic
jp	Japan	mz	Mozambique	sl	Sierra Leone
ke	Kenya	na	Namibia	sm	San Marino
kg	Kyrgyzstan	nc	New Caledonia	sn	Senegal
kh	Cambodia	ne	Niger	so	Somalia
ki	Kiribati	nf	Norfolk Island	sr	Suriname
km	Comoros	ng	Nigeria	st	São Tomé & Príncipe
kn	Saint Kitts & Nevis	ni	Nicaragua		
		nl	Netherlands	sv	El Salvador
kp	North Korea	no	Norway	sy	Syria
kr	South Korea	np	Nepal	sz	Swaziland
kw	Kuwait	nr	Nauru	tc	Turks & Caicos Is.
ky	Cayman Is.	nu	Niue	td	Chad
kz	Kazakhstan	nz	New Zealand	tf	French Southern Territories
la	Laos	om	Oman		
lb	Lebanon	pa	Panama	tg	Togo
lc	Saint Lucia	pe	Peru	th	Thailand
li	Liechtenstein	pf	French Polynesia	tj	Tajikistan
lk	Sri Lanka	pg	Papua New Guinea	tk	Tokelau
lr	Liberia			tm	Turkmenistan
ls	Lesotho	ph	Philippines	tn	Tunisia
lt	Lithuania	pk	Pakistan	to	Tonga
lu	Luxembourg	pl	Poland	tp	East Timor
lv	Latvia	pm	Saint Pierre & Miquelon	tr	Turkey
ly	Libya			tt	Trinidad and Tobago
ma	Morocco	pn	Pitcairn		
mc	Monaco	pr	Puerto Rico	tv	Tuvalu
md	Moldova	pt	Portugal	tw	Taiwan
		pw	Palau	tz	Tanzania

ua	Ukraine	vc	Saint Vincent &	ye	Yemen
ug	Uganda		Grenadines	yt	Mayotte
uk	United Kingdom	ve	Venezuela	yu	Yugoslavia
um	USA Minor	vg	Virgin Is. (British)	za	South Africa
	Outlying Is.	vi	Virgin Is. (US)	zm	Zambia
us	United States	vn	Vietnam	zr	Zaire
uy	Uruguay	vu	Vanuatu	zw	Zimbabwe
uz	Uzbekistan	wf	Wallis & Futuna Is.		
va	Holy See (Vatican)	ws	Samoa		

Index

abbreviations 98–9
Acceptable Use Policy (AUP) 107, **278**
accessing the Internet 20–36
  see also Internet service providers; on-line services
acclimatisation 18
ActiveX 150, 230
address book facility 43–4
  addresses **278**
  address conversions 241–2
  anonymous addresses 146–7, 148
  customised 202–5
  DNS lookup 121–2
  email *see* email addresses
  false 107–8, 109, 246
  hiding 206
  ISPs 240
  typing 240
  'undesirable' 103
  see also Uniform Resource Locators
Adobe 223
ADSL systems 200–1
advertising 14, 52, 89
  ad tracking 162
  costs 16, 162
  detail, capacity for 163–4
  manipulative 159
  see also junk mail; spam

agents 68–9
aggressive attitudes and arguments 49, 50, 74–5, 88–9, 90–1, 94, 105, 106
Alcatol 188
alt. groups 83, 175
AltaVista 67, 68, 69, 86, 162, 217, 218, 219, 221, 261
America Online (AOL) 21, 22, 25, 26, 29, 57, 94, 108, 158, 165, 183, 223, 269, **278**
  addresses 242
  Buddy lists 122
  IM software 59
  locate facility 122
  on-line chat 57
  Profiles 122
  security 42, 141
anonymisers 152, 258
anonymity 146–7
anonymous remailers 146–7, 258, **278**
AOL *see* America Online
AOLPress 224
Apple Macintosh 124, 126, 129, 155, 173, 185, 190, 261
Archie 135–7, **278**
archive services 52, 85–6, 116, 148, 149, 242–3
art and entertainment web sites 274

ASCII **278**
ASCII transfers of information 134
attachments 42, 44–6, 52, 115, **278**
  compressing 46, 115
  message size 45
  size restriction 44
  split messages 44–5
auctions on-line 169
audio clips 46, 124–5, 128
AUP *see* Acceptable Use Policy
Autonomy 68–9
autoresponders 47, 118, 180

backbone 112, **278**
bandwidth 104, 112–13, 186, 187
banking, on-line 165–6
banner ads 110–11
Base64 127, **279**
BBSs *see* bulletin board services
beginners 25, 103, 264–5
Berners-Lee, Tim 13
BETA hoax 154
beta software 259
binaries 92–3, 104, 116, 134, **279**
  decoding 125–7
binaries groups 93
BinHex 126, **279**
bookmarks 159, **279**
books about the Internet 264–5
Boolean Operators 220
bot wars 55
bots 54, **279**
British Telecom 24, 33, 49, 189, 194, 195, 197, 253
browser windows 215–16
browsers *see* web browsers
Buddy lists 122
bulletin board services (BBSs) 30–1
business use 14–16, 59, 157, 160–4, 187, 202–11
business-package deals 207–9

cable modems 200–1
cable TV companies 194, 195
Cable and Wireless 24, 196, 253
cache system 117, 216, 226, **279**
Cancelbot 81
CD-ROM 34, 265
cellular modems (data cards) 193–4
CGI *see* Common Gateway Interface
chat rooms 56, 57, 58, 122, 158
children 157–9
  children's web sites 158, 159, 276
  Net babysitter software 157
  using the Internet 16–17
Church of Scientology 81, 147
civil liberties concerns 144, 146
ClariNet 84
clients 237–8
  email client 237
  thin client concept 22437–8
clock, internal 122
'clueless' 103
codes 142, 145–6
  keys 145
combined services 30
  trying out 34–5, 265
commercial verification 156
Common Gateway Interface (CGI) 231–2
Communicator 76, 130, 181, 216, 259
company networks 20, 31–2, 37–8
CompuServe 21, 22, 25, 26, 57, 94, 241, 269, **279**
computer games 17, 120, 170–2
  networked games 170, 171–2
  virtual worlds 170–1
computer security experts 151
computer specific advice 265
computer web sites 273

Microsoft 43, 45, 48, 59, 76, 84,
104, 129, 153, 154, 165, 181,
223, 230, 232, 259, **281**
Microsoft Network (MSN) 30
MIDI files 129, 228
Millennium Bug *see* year 2000
date-change problem
MIME *see* Multipurpose Internet
Mail Extensions
Mirabilis 59
mirror sites 71, 131–2, 261, **281**
mobile phones 188
modems 20, 189–94, **281**
BT approval 189
cable modems 200–1
cellular modems (data cards)
193–4
compatibility problems 179
data compression system 194
extras and special deals 192
fax facility 47, 192
'flash' modems 192
internal/external 190
modem to user ratio 179
portable modems 193
reliability 179
speed 177, 188, 190–2, 194
voicemail facility 192
Money 165
MOOs *see* Object Oriented MUDs
MPEG3 system (MP3) 124–5
MSN 269
MUDs *see* Multi User Dimensions
Multi User Dimensions (MUDs)
170, 171, 258, **281**
Multi User Shared Hallucinations
(MUSHs) 170, **282**
multimedia extras 128–9
multiple remailers 147
Multipurpose Internet Mail
Extensions (MIME) 44, 123–4,
281

MUSHs *see* Multi User Shared
Hallucinations

name-calling 50, 75, 94, 105
nameservers **282**
Navigator 130, 150, 181
.net 267
Net celebrities 75
Net culture 17, 28, 96, 103–6
aggressive attitudes 106
constant innovation 104–5
elitist 104
frank and vigorous debate 105
non-commercial ethic 95, 104
pranks and practical jokes 105
tolerance for unconventional
ideas 105–6
Netcom 81, 83
NetGamer 267
Netiquette 262
NetMeeting 59
Netscape 27, 76, 104, 130, 150,
181, 259, **282**
Network Computers (NCs) 185,
186–7, 238
networked games 170, 171–2
Networks series 268
New Scientist web site 64
news features
on-line services 28–9
World Wide Web 28–9
news management facilities 90
news servers 75, 173, 175, 237,
282
newsgroup 'wars' 105
newsgroups 9, 11–13, 16, 20,
73–95, **282**
advertising in 89
alt. groups 83, 175
archives 85–6
creating 170, 173–5
culture 17, 28, 74

WebPhones 60, 257
year 2000 date-change problem
253
spam 12, 27, 85, 91, 104, 108,
109, 110, 116, 246, **283**
special characters 124
speed
email 114–15, 178
FTP 132
ISPs 114, 177–9
modems 177, 188, 190–2, 194
newsgroups 115–16, 178
on-line services 114, 117
trials 178
the Web 116–17
spiders 70
sport web sites 275
SSL *see* Secure Sockets Layer
styled text 45
Submit It! 233, 262
supermarkets, Internet access in 33
support 179–81
surfing the Web 63, 65, **283**
survival tips 106–11

Talk 58
TCP/IP *see* Transmission Control
Protocol/Internet Protocol
technical consultancies 208–11
technical support 95, 181
telephone
bank holiday rates 114
charges 24
DACS box 193
Internet facilities 188
mobile phones 188
phone phreakers 139
second lines 192–3
video links 61
WebPhones 60–1, 145, 257
year 2000 date-change problem
253

see also Integrated Services
Digital Network; leased lines
Telnet 120, 137, 171, 265, **284**
terminating access to the Internet
106, 107, 110
the Web *see* World Wide Web
thin client concept 237–8
see also Network Computers
threads 77, 90
Time 122
time management 43
time-keeping 122
to-do lists 43
topic lists 66
Total Internet 268
Traceroute 120, 265, **284**
Transmission Control
Protocol/Internet Protocol
(TCP/IP) 236, **283**
travel web sites 275–6
Tripod 223
Trojan horses 155
trolls 90, **284**
troublemakers 90–1, 103
Tucows 71, 124, 260–1

ukp (UK pounds) 106, **284**
Unamailer 143
Uniform Resource Locators
(URLs) 63, 65, 68, 90, 238,
246–7, 262, **284**
capitalisation 6
in email 215
in newsgroups 215
typing in 212–13
universities and colleges 20, 84,
174–5, 243
Unix system 58, 265, **284**
URLs *see* Uniform Resource
Locators
Usenet 11, 12–13, 22, 73–95, 77,
125, 148, **284**